University of St. Francis

GEN 172.42 B775
Bourne, Randolph Silliman
War and the intellectuals

W9-AEP-498

1995

WAR AND THE INTELLECTUALS

Essays by Randolph S. Bourne, 1915–1919

AMERICAN PERSPECTIVES

EDITED BY BERNARD WISHY AND
WILLIAM E. LEUCHTENBURG

in preparation

WAR and the INTELLECTUALS

essays by

RANDOLPH S. BOURNE

1915-1919

Edited with an Introduction by
CARL RESEK

HARPER TORCHBOOKS
The University Library

HARPER & ROW, PUBLISHERS
NEW YORK, EVANSTON AND LONDON

College of St. Francis Library
Joliet, Illinois

FOR

TRUDE

WAR AND THE INTELLECTUALS

Introduction copyright © 1964 by Carl Resek

First HARPER TORCHBOOK edition published 1964

HARPER & ROW, PUBLISHERS, INCORPORATED
49 East 33rd Street
New York 16, N.Y.

172.42
B775

Contents

152,984

Introduction

by CARL RESEK

R andolph Bourne's life has had special fascination for a group of writers of his own generation who have alternately admired and denigrated him, interred and disinterred his writings, until it has become apparent, as John Dos Passos wrote, that if ever a man had a ghost it was Bourne:

> A tiny twisted unscared ghost in a black cloak
> hopping along the grimy old brick and brownstone
>   streets still left in downtown New York,
> crying out in a shrill soundless giggle:
> *War is the health of the state.*[1]

But Dos Passos' imagery, like that of most of Bourne's biographers, was colored too much by the trauma that World War I caused in many intellectuals. Their subsequent view of themselves as "shrill and soundless"—unable to make themselves heard—never was shared by Bourne. Had he lived he would not have repeated his famous chant endlessly because he had said about all he wanted to on the war and because out of context the phrase had little meaning. In its proper place it meant that mindless power thrived on war because war corrupted a nation's moral fabric and especially corrupted its intellectuals. Put that way it sounded less like a giggle than a heavy indictment.

Bourne was born in Bloomfield, New Jersey, in 1886 in the month of Chicago's Haymarket riot. In those days Bloomfield also witnessed its share of industrial unrest and of conflicts between its early settlers and new immigrants streaming in through the port of New York. Still other tensions were building up in the privacy of its households. To-

---

[1] Dos Passos, *1919* (N.Y.: Harcourt, Brace & Co., 1932), pp. 105–106.

wards the close of the century, the usual differences that exist between one generation and the next were growing into an extensive rebellion against Victorian standards. Bourne, eventually a spokesman for this movement, was born into a family that was, on his mother's side, relentlessly aristocratic. Proud of ancestors among the first generation of settlers in New England, they owned Bloomfield's finest real estate, married in their own social class and sent their sons to college and law school. They voted Republican and regularly attended the town's first Presbyterian Church. Randolph was raised on one Bible verse a day and, as he recalled later, on frequent entreaties to be a gentleman.

His father Charles was the first rebel in the family. The son of a church pastor, Charles was a handsome, dashing man who paid little attention to his several business ventures. None was successful or of the kind that met the family's standards of proper enterprise. Randolph was a small child when his mother moved back with her family and, at her brothers' bidding, Charles left the household. The incident was important in Bourne's intellectual development. In his numerous auto-biographical writings he scarcely ever mentioned his father. In conversation he spoke of him rarely but always with affection and some pity. It is probable that the father's experience was the source of many of Bourne's sharp barbs against the older generation and at least some of his fury against the Protestant ethic. "What suffering the family sometimes causes in the name of loyalty and self-sacrifice," he once wrote a friend and then added, "personally, I had none of this sort of suffering and was always allowed to do quite as I liked."

He was allowed considerable liberties because he was restricted physically. About the time his father left home, Bourne was stricken with a disease that left him with a double curvature of the spine and eventually retarded his growth. Together with a birth injury that had disfigured one side of his face this gave him a startling appearance. Some of his friends and biographers dwelled on their initial impressions of him. Theodore Dreiser, never reluctant to shame reality, could grow lyrical in describing Bourne's deformity and the night in Greenwich Village when he met "that frightening dwarf." Other writers, including John Dos Passos, also made considerable capital from Bourne's dramatic appearance. In fact, Bourne never allowed himself or his friends to linger on the subject and the deformity influenced his life much less than naturalistic writers assumed. He engaged in a variety of sports, especially such as gave his healthy legs exercise. He skated, climbed, played tennis and above all hiked. With his fiancée he once walked from New York to Provincetown.

His youth in Bloomfield, in spite of all, was touched with some of the idyllic qualities of small town life at the turn of the century. His home was surrounded by huge grounds that he later lovingly recalled as his "domain, a principality." Here all the children of the neighborhood seemed to have found a playground. Today, several of them, now Bloomfield's oldest citizens, recall the hospitality at the Bournes' home, and especially of Mrs. Bourne's kitchen, where a neighbor might always find some delicacy though never a recipe. It is tempting to find here a source for that perpetual open house that Bourne eventually ran in Greenwich Village where one could find, on almost any night of the week and on any Sunday afternoon, "a dozen or more persons sitting around a tenement kitchen listening to some young poet, perhaps Vachel Lindsay, reading from his most recent manuscript," and where, as the poet Babette Deutsch later recalled, ideas danced like colored balloons along the ceiling.

Bourne was a precocious and brilliant student. At two, the maid in the house noticed that he was reading the labels on groceries. By the time he started school he could read the Bible and what other books he was allowed from the family shelf. His teachers had little to contribute to his education, except, as it seemed to him, that they were the first great restraining influence in his life. From the first grade schoolmar'm who stood him in the corner because he refused to answer her questions simply, to the literature professors at Columbia—"mild-mannered men who knew their place and kept it"—he found few who had anything vital to say. His articles on the American schoolroom and his worship of John Dewey were imbued with feelings drawn from his own schooling.

In 1903 Bourne was admitted to Princeton but his uncles' resources suddenly ran out. For six years he held a variety of jobs that included playing the piano at minstrel and vaudeville shows and as accompaniment for silent movies. For some time he worked in factories. In one he punched out music rolls for player pianos and discovered in himself that sensitivity to human exploitation that was to be a marked trait of his literary career. In that world of intellectuals in which he later moved he was among the few who knew the prospects of a life that could be spent attending a machine.[2] He once remarked that "being a factory hand for so long and doing nothing except what I was told to do" threatened to break down all his initiative and to squeeze from him even the love of literature.

When at last he saved enough money to enter Columbia in 1909, he paid close attention to the University's employment policies. Among the several controversies he engaged in, the most bitter was his lone war in behalf of the University's underpaid and overworked scrub-women. When a school official answered him, in a public letter, that the University's "business is to dispense instruction to as large a number of students as possible," and not to engage in "wild-cat Utopian schemes in the treatment of its servants," Bourne decided that business indeed was the business of a university and thereafter judged the failures of higher education in that light.[3]

He judged its successes in similarly personal terms. John Dewey, James Harvey Robinson, and Franz Boas were among the great teachers whose classes he attended at Columbia and they inspired him to read deeply in the literature of the current vitalist and pragmatic revolt against rationalism. William James, Nietzsche and Henri Bergson were his favorite authors. They taught him "a dynamic, creative attitude towards life" and freed him from what he called, in an inspired passage, "the ethics of a parsimonious world."[4] In the new philosophies he obviously found, as did so many others of his generation, an absolution from ancestral dogma. "How well I know the silent sect-pressures, ceaselessly trying to mold you to the ways of thinking and acting!" he wrote a friend and then listed all the books by William James that must be read. "He has settled so many of my worries that I preach him as a prophet." Bourne's letters took on apocalyptic tones and he began to write those angry, slashing portraits of his home town and of the older generation that won him, through the pages of the *Atlantic Monthly*, a respectable following. Years later he called these pieces "very bold and very trivial" but they were better than most in the genre and started him, while still in college, on a literary career.

One other Columbia professor had a great influence on Bourne. From Charles Beard's lectures and from his books Bourne learned about economic interpretation of history, an idea that also fed his

[2] See "What is Exploitation?"
[3] See "The Idea of a University."
[4] See "Paul Elmer More."

skepticism. But Beard's prime impact was to turn Bourne's attention to politics and political theory and to provide him with the framework for many of the essays included in this collection. Beard's ideas clearly show through the historical passages in the essay on the state. They are also revealed in Bourne's criticism of our entry into World War I though Beard himself supported the war. It is as if the pupil anticipated the teacher, since so many of Bourne's charges of Woodrow Wilson's betrayal were to be echoed in Beard's later attacks on Franklin Roosevelt. That Beard had great respect for his pupil is evident from the fact that in 1914, shortly before its first issue went to press, he secured Bourne a position on the editorial staff of the *New Republic*. For that journal and for several others Bourne wrote about three hundred pieces during the next three years.

The present collection includes, in its first part, most of his writings on the war. It is a small body of prose, but it may well have made him, as one admirer later put it, "the intellectual hero of World War I." Bourne offered none of the usual simplistic interpretations of the conflict. He made no charges against munitions makers, bankers or imperialists and cared less about the causes of the war than about its moral consequences. With the exception of "The Collapse of American Strategy," none of the writings stands up as profound comment on policy. Their unifying theme lay in Bourne's determined refusal to invest the war, as some of his fellow intellectuals had, with a holy mission to make the world safer for democracy. A league of nations he regarded as only an alliance of all against each, a means of petrifying the *status quo*. He was certain that the war would impoverish domestic reform and that reformers and intellectuals, however large their wartime services, would have little to say about the post-war world. If the intellectuals were not strong enough to prevent war, they could not be strong enough to influence the peace. The power of Bourne's essays is surely derived from these prophetic passages.

There is special interest in Bourne's critique of John Dewey's acquiescence to the war. As a frequent contributor on educational subjects to the *New Republic*, Bourne won a nationwide reputation and attention in Europe as one of the ablest popular advocates of Dewey's educational theories. He regarded the progressive school as the best workshop of democracy and individual fulfillment. But the war essays were a dramatic rejection of Dewey's and Bourne's own, earlier, pragmatism. The assumptions the two shared are sometimes hidden behind Bourne's occasionally vague, deprecatory use of the term "intellectual." Bourne discovered that they had both been too concerned with the instrumental side of philosophy and had not paid sufficient attention to the underlying values on which instrumental philosophy must rest. Dewey had therefore been too ready to accept the war as an opportunity for achieving peace and justice. But the greater charge against him and other intellectuals was that they had slain the spirit of William James and had accepted as absolutes the state of war and the warring state.

Bourne perceived much of this problem subjectively. Absolutes of any sort implied the revival of small town orthodoxy. War meant the rule of the herd mind activated in patriotic parades and by Kiwanis Club resolutions. As Bourne explained in the autobiographical "Below the Battle," the war threatened him with a spiritual return to Bloomfield. The result was the intensely emotional essay on the state in which war as "the health of the state" is associated with the demise of the intellectual, the discipline of the factory, and the rule of the schoolmaster. And surely, one may add, the rule of Wilson, the schoolmaster president. It is suggestive that the essay was being written simultaneously with an autobiographical novel, also left unfinished.

The articles and reviews presented in the second part of this collection indicate Bourne's long-range and difficult search for a "transnational culture" that would become the source of a more democratic ethic than America had invoked during the war. He hoped to find and nurture those "underlying values" that instrumental philosophy had taken for granted and that the nation at war had ignored. Though most of the pieces in this section were written prior to "The State," they are best seen in the light of that essay because they are consequences of its political assumptions. That reversed order also expresses the direction of Bourne's changing interests. He never thought of art and politics as different entities. They could be separated only at each other's peril. But increasingly he saw himself in the role of cultural arbiter, in the first place as the nay-sayer who defended art against false idols, be they patriotism, the academy, the commercial spirit, or even the nay-sayers themselves. The precise nature of the relation between art and politics eluded him to the last as he probably wished, since the ambiguity insured the artist's creativity and freedom. In general, the artist educated. "I imagine people must be appealed to to desire certain things mightily, "Bourne wrote Van Wyck Brooks, describing the revolutionary function of the cultural leader. From Nietzsche he learned that desire could be transformed into a "will to power," and the shaping of desire therefore became a political as well as artistic duty. The great danger was to suppress it "by that reason which is so often a mere disguise of another and more acceptable desire." The essays on "The Puritan's Will to Power" and on H. L. Mencken and Paul Elmer More are probably the finest expression of this idea and they also mark Bourne's growth beyond his earlier Greenwich Village nihilism. The posthumous "History of a Literary Radical" spells out his synthesis of literary revolt and acquiescence which rested on the hopeful conclusion that the best in the past would yield the lineaments of the future.

Bourne died a few days after the Armistice, a victim of the flu epidemic of 1918. Almost the whole of his reputation thus rests on a career that coincided with the years of World War I. The war defined his image for succeeding generations of admirers. Not long after he died there was created a legend as tenacious and dramatic as any to come out of the war. At its heart lay the belief that Bourne died destitute, an outcast among former friends and hounded by the Government. "In that last winter of the war," one of his acquaintances wrote twenty years later, "he looked very worn . . . . His clothes were shabby, and, I suppose, (though none of his friends realized it at the time) he did not always have enough to eat." The tale is repeated in a dozen memoirs, several poems and at least two novels. That the Justice Department seized his manuscripts, that journals closed their doors to him or lost their sponsors,—this has been the stuff of his biographies.

There is little ground for most of these stories. *The Seven Arts* did lose its backers but it is not clear, as most of its editors later claimed, that Bourne's articles were solely responsible. There was "some fuss on *The Dial*," he wrote his mother, "but I am being paid just the same, and have to write only two articles a month. I am strong with a young man who says he gave his $25,000 largely on the strength of my contributions." From a notebook in which he kept a list of all the articles he sold and his earnings on each, it is certain that his income remained steady to the last, and for a largely free-lance writer of that day, respectable. The numerous memoirs that dwelled on his enforced destitution were especially painful to his immediate family to whom he left a substantial sum earmarked, as one would have expected, for the education of his nieces and nephews. And his manuscripts were not seized but lost, unfortunately, while in transit by railroad. He was once questioned by a naval intelligence officer but for the reason that his fiancée, an actress, had been seen dancing on a Provincetown beach and her movements were thought to be signals to a naval vessel lying offshore.

The Bourne "legend" is an essential part of the intellectual history of the nineteen-twenties. It had to do with the habit, so prevalent in that decade, of seeing the creative thinker or artist as an outcast, a victim, at best a martyr. It was a relationship to society that, in literature, was frequently represented as a spiritual and even physical wound. Hemingway's *The Sun Also Rises* contained one notable expression of the myth. And Bourne, with his bent back and twisted face, his death at the age of thirty-two, also seemed to express it. He played an international role. Bourne, Rupert Brooke and a few others, wrote Gilberto Freyre in 1930, "founded with their blood the country that today is the heritage of those of us between twenty and thirty. . . . Youth was for him a large and terrible night of Saint Joan which he spent . . . in bending over his personality as over a dark pool."

The legends of the twenties were surely related to the horrors of the war and to the loss of a just peace. In the wake of the disaster a sensitive man could well see himself as the victim of an absurd fate. But Bourne, in appearance the most fated of men, rarely allowed himself that image. "The young radical," he wrote, "is not asked to be a martyr, but he is asked to be a thinker, an intellectual leader." The war had not been made by men unable to withstand events, but by those unable to withstand the tension of opposing them and who indeed, "danced with reality." While Bourne raged against the war as it was happening, a few of his most ardent admirers either invested it with lofty purposes or abandoned politics for the arts. Van Wyck Brooks, for example, did both. "I could not see why a magazine of art should destroy itself by opposing the war," he wrote later, recalling the shutting down of *The Seven Arts,* "and, for the rest, I asked myself, what would have become of us if Germany had dominated Europe? If it had not been for wars, we should never have had a country."[5] The Bourne legend screened this distinction in his circle of

5 Brooks, *Fenollosa and His Circle* (N.Y.: E. P. Dutton & Co., 1962), p. 309.

friends and blurred the fact that his essays on the war were directed more against his fellow intellectuals than against official policy. That may be why the state never troubled to persecute him and why some intellectuals thought of him, as one of them put it, "precious to us because of what he was, rather than because of what he had actually written."[6]

Sarah Lawrence College
August 1, 1963

[6] Lewis Mumford, "The Image of Randolph Bourne," *New Republic,* LXIV (September 24, 1930), 151–2. Elsewhere, and paradoxically, Mumford held Bourne responsible for the withdrawal from politics and the romantic defeatism of the post-war generation. (Mumford, "The Aftermath of Utopianism," *Christianity and Crisis,* I (March 24, 1944), 2–7.

The War

1

The War and the Intellectuals[1]

To those of us who still retain an irreconcilable animus against war, it has been a bitter experience to see the unanimity with which the American intellectuals have thrown their support to the use of war-technique in the crisis in which America found herself. Socialists, college professors, publicists, new-republicans, practitioners of literature, have vied with each other in confirming with their intellectual faith the collapse of neutrality and the riveting of the war-mind on a hundred million more of the world's people. And the intellectuals are not content with confirming our belligerent gesture. They are now complacently asserting that it was they who effectively willed it, against the hesitation and dim perceptions of the American democratic masses. A war made deliberately by the intellectuals! A calm moral verdict, arrived at after a penetrating study of inexorable facts! Sluggish masses, too remote from the world-conflict to be stirred, too lacking in intellect to perceive their danger! An alert intellectual class, saving the people in spite of themselves, biding their time with Fabian strategy until the nation could be moved into war without serious resistance! An intellectual class, gently guiding a nation through sheer force of ideas into what the other nations entered only through predatory craft or popular hysteria or militarist madness! A war free from any taint of self-seeking, a war that will secure the triumph of democracy and internationalize the world! This is the picture which

[1] *The Seven Arts,* II (June 1917), 133–146.

the more self-conscious intellectuals have formed of themselves, and which they are slowly impressing upon a population which is being led no man knows whither by an indubitably intellectualized President. And they are right, in that the war certainly did not spring from either the ideals or the prejudices, from the national ambitions or hysterias, of the American people, however acquiescent the masses prove to be, and however clearly the intellectuals prove their putative intuition.

Those intellectuals who have felt themselves totally out of sympathy with this drag toward war will seek some explanation for this joyful leadership. They will want to understand this willingness of the American intellect to open the sluices and flood us with the sewage of the war spirit. We cannot forget the virtuous horror and stupefaction which filled our college professors when they read the famous manifesto of their ninety-three German colleagues in defence of their war.[2] To the American academic mind of 1914 defence of war was inconceivable. From Bernhardi[3] it recoiled as from a blasphemy, little dreaming that two years later would find it creating its own cleanly reasons for imposing military service on the country and for talking of the rough rude currents of health and regeneration that war would send through the American body politic. They would have thought anyone mad who talked of shipping American men by the hundreds of thousands—conscripts—to die on the fields of France. Such a spiritual change seems catastrophic when we shoot our minds back to those days when neutrality was a proud thing. But the intellectual progress has been so gradual that the country retains little sense of the irony. The war sentiment, begun so gradually but so perseveringly by the preparedness advocates who came from the ranks of big business, caught hold of one after another of the intellectual groups. With the aid of Roosevelt, the murmurs became a monotonous chant, and finally a chorus so mighty that to be out of it was at first to be disreputable and finally almost obscene. And slowly a strident rant was worked up against Germany which compared very creditably with the German fulminations against the greedy power of England. The nerve of the

[2] In October 1914 ninety-three German writers and teachers published an "Appeal to the Civilized World" in which they praised the military establishment and defended Germany's war effort.

[3] Friedrich von Bernhardi, German general and military historian. His book, *Germany and the Next War* (1912), advocated a war of conquest for Germany and was used by the allies for propaganda purposes.

war-feeling centred, of course, in the richer and older classes of the Atlantic seaboard, and was keenest where there were French or English business and particularly social connections. The sentiment then spread over the country as a class-phenomenon, touching everywhere those upper-class elements in each section who identified themselves with this Eastern ruling group. It must never be forgotten that in every community it was the least liberal and least democratic elements among whom the preparedness and later the war sentiment was found. The farmers were apathetic, the small business men and workingmen are still apathetic towards the war. The election was a vote of confidence of these latter classes in a President who would keep the faith of neutrality.[4] The intellectuals, in other words, have identified themselves with the least democratic forces in American life. They have assumed the leadership for war of those very classes whom the American democracy has been immemorially fighting. Only in a world where irony was dead could an intellectual class enter war at the head of such illiberal cohorts in the avowed cause of world-liberalism and world-democracy. No one is left to point out the undemocratic nature of this war-liberalism. In a time of faith, skepticism is the most intolerable of all insults.

Our intellectual class might have been occupied, during the last two years of war, in studying and clarifying the ideals and aspirations of the American democracy, in discovering a true Americanism which would not have been merely nebulous but might have federated the different ethnic groups and traditions. They might have spent the time in endeavoring to clear the public mind of the cant of war, to get rid of old mystical notions that clog our thinking. We might have used the time for a great wave of education, for setting our house in spiritual order. We could at least have set the problem before ourselves. If our intellectuals were going to lead the administration, they might conceivably have tried to find some way of securing peace by making neutrality effective. They might have turned their intellectual energy not to the problem of jockeying the nation into war, but to the problem of using our vast neutral power to attain democratic ends for the rest of the world and ourselves without the use of the malevolent technique of war. They might have failed. The point is that they scarcely tried. The time was spent not in clarification and education,

[4] In the 1916 campaign Woodrow Wilson pledged himself to non-intervention in the European war.

but in a mulling over of nebulous ideals of democracy and liberalism
and civilization which had never meant anything fruitful to those ruling classes who now so glibly used them, and in giving free rein to the
elementary instinct of self-defence. The whole era has been spiritually
wasted. The outstanding feature has been not its Americanism but its
intense colonialism. The offence of our intellectuals was not so much
that they were colonial—for what could we expect of a nation composed of so many national elements?—but that it was so one-sidedly
and partisanly colonial. The official, reputable expression of the intellectual class has been that of the English colonial. Certain portions of
it have been even more loyalist than the King, more British even than
Australia. Other colonial attitudes have been vulgar. The colonialism
of the other American stocks was denied a hearing from the start.
America might have been made a meeting-ground for the different
national attitudes. An intellectual class, cultural colonists of the different European nations, might have threshed out the issues here as they
could not be threshed out in Europe. Instead of this, the English
colonials in university and press took command at the start, and we
became an intellectual Hungary where thought was subject to an
effective process of Magyarization. The reputable opinion of the American intellectuals became more and more either what could be read
pleasantly in London, or what was written in an earnest effort to put
Englishmen straight on their war-aims and war-technique. This
Magyarization of thought produced as a counter-reaction a peculiarly
offensive and inept German apologetic, and the two partisans divided
the field between them. The great masses, the other ethnic groups,
were inarticulate. American public opinion was almost as little prepared for war in 1917 as it was in 1914.

The sterile results of such an intellectual policy are inevitable. During the war the American intellectual class has produced almost nothing in the way of original and illuminating interpretation. Veblen's
"Imperial Germany;" Patten's "Culture and War," and addresses;
Dewey's "German Philosophy and Politics;" a chapter or two in Weyl's
"American Foreign Policies;"—is there much else of creative value in
the intellectual repercussion of the war? It is true that the shock of war
put the American intellectual to an unusual strain. He had to sit idle
and think as spectator not as actor. There was no government to
which he could docilely and loyally tender his mind as did the Oxford
professors to justify England in her own eyes. The American's training

was such as to make the fact of war almost incredible. Both in his reading of history and in his lack of economic perspective he was badly prepared for it. He had to explain to himself something which was too colossal for the modern mind, which outran any language or terms which we had to interpret it in. He had to expand his sympathies to the breaking-point, while pulling the past and present into some sort of interpretative order. The intellectuals in the fighting countries had only to rationalize and justify what their country was already doing. Their task was easy. A neutral, however, had really to search out the truth. Perhaps perspective was too much to ask of any mind. Certainly the older colonials among our college professors let their prejudices at once dictate their thought. They have been comfortable ever since. The war has taught them nothing and will teach them nothing. And they have had the satisfaction, under the rigor of events, of seeing prejudice submerge the intellects of their younger colleagues. And they have lived to see almost their entire class, pacifists and democrats too, join them as apologists for the "gigantic irrelevance" of war.

We have had to watch, therefore, in this country the same process which so shocked us abroad,—the coalescence of the intellectual classes in support of the military programme. In this country, indeed, the socialist intellectuals did not even have the grace of their German brothers and wait for the declaration of war before they broke for cover. And when they declared for war they showed how thin was the intellectual veneer of their socialism. For they called us in terms that might have emanated from any bourgeois journal to defend democracy and civilization, just as if it was not exactly against those very bourgeois democracies and capitalist civilizations that socialists had been fighting for decades. But so subtle is the spiritual chemistry of the "inside" that all this intellectual cohesion—herd-instinct become herd-intellect— which seemed abroad so hysterical and so servile, comes to us here in highly rational terms. We go to war to save the world from subjugation! But the German intellectuals went to war to save their culture from barbarization! And the French went to war to save their beautiful France! And the English to save international honor! And Russia, most altruistic and self-sacrificing of all, to save a small State from destruction! Whence is our miraculous intuition of our moral spotlessness? Whence our confidence that history will not unravel huge economic and imperialist forces upon which our rationalizations float like bubbles? The Jew often marvels that his race alone should have been chosen as the true people of the cosmic God. Are not our intellectuals equally fatuous when they tell us that our war of all wars is stainless and thrillingly achieving for good?

An intellectual class that was wholly rational would have called insistently for peace and not for war. For months the crying need has been for a negotiated peace, in order to avoid the ruin of a deadlock. Would not the same amount of resolute statesmanship thrown into intervention have secured a peace that would have been a subjugation for neither side? Was the terrific bargaining power of a great neutral ever really used? Our war followed, as all wars follow, a monstrous failure of diplomacy. Shamefacedness should now be our intellectuals' attitude, because the American play for peace was made so little more than a polite play. The intellectuals have still to explain why, willing as they now are to use force to continue the war to absolute exhaustion, they were not willing to use force to coerce the world to a speedy peace.

Their forward vision is no more convincing than their past rationality. We go to war now to internationalize the world! But surely their League to Enforce Peace[5] is only a palpable apocalyptic myth, like the syndicalists' myth of the "general strike." It is not a rational programme so much as a glowing symbol for the purpose of focusing belief, of setting enthusiasm on fire for international order. As far as it does this it has pragmatic value, but as far as it provides a certain radiant mirage of idealism for this war and for a world-order founded on mutual fear, it is dangerous and obnoxious. Idealism should be kept for what is ideal. It is depressing to think that the prospect of a world so strong that none dare challenge it should be the immediate ideal of the American intellectual. If the League is only a makeshift, a coalition into which we enter to restore order, then it is only a description of existing fact, and the idea should be treated as such. But if it is an actually prospective outcome of the settlement, the keystone of American policy, it is neither realizable nor desirable. For the programme of such a League contains no provision for dynamic national growth or for international economic justice. In a world which requires recognition of economic internationalism far more than of political internationalism, an idea is reactionary which proposes to petrify

[5] Organized in 1915 as a non-partisan group, The League to Enforce Peace espoused a post-war league of nations that would use economic sanctions or military force against any member waging war.

and federate the nations as political and economic units. Such a scheme for international order is a dubious justification for American policy. And if American policy had been sincere in its belief that our participation would achieve international beatitude, would we not have made our entrance into the war conditional upon a solemn general agreement to respect in the final settlement these principles of international order? Could we have afforded, if our war was to end war by the establishment of a league of honor, to risk the defeat of our vision and our betrayal in the settlement? Yet we are in the war, and no such solemn agreement was made, nor has it even been suggested.[6]

The case of the intellectuals seems, therefore, only very speciously rational. They could have used their energy to force a just peace or at least to devise other means than war for carrying through American policy. They could have used their intellectual energy to ensure that our participation in the war meant the international order which they wish. Intellect was not so used. It was used to lead an apathetic nation into an irresponsible war, without guarantees from those belligerents whose cause we were saving. The American intellectual, therefore, has been rational neither in his hindsight nor his foresight. To explain him we must look beneath the intellectual reasons to the emotional disposition. It is not so much what they thought as how they felt that explains our intellectual class. Allowing for colonial sympathy, there was still the personal shock in a world-war which outraged all our preconceived notions of the way the world was tending. It reduced to rubbish most of the humanitarian internationalism and democratic nationalism which had been the emotional thread of our intellectuals' life. We had suddenly to make a new orientation. There were mental conflicts. Our latent colonialism strove with our longing for American unity. Our desire for peace strove with our desire for national responsibility in the world. That first lofty and remote and not altogether un-

---

[6] In an earlier, unpublished ms Bourne wrote, "In the first place, would not a League that provided for the armed enforcement of peace by the whole League upon any member who broke the peace before submitting the dispute to arbitration, be virtually an alliance of all against each, and would not the United States be compelled, under these terms, to enter a war in which we perhaps had no concern whatever? If the League is formed on the basis of the present Entente, with the addition of a sobered Germany, would such a League be essentially different from the armed truce which existed in Europe from 1871–1914? . . . Such a League under any circumstances, would be little more than a mutual guarantee of the status quo." ("Doubts About Enforcing Peace," Bourne MSS, Columbia University Libraries.)

sound feeling of our spiritual isolation from the conflict could not last. There was the itch to be in the great experience which the rest of the world was having. Numbers of intelligent people who had never been stirred by the horrors of capitalistic peace at home were shaken out of their slumber by the horrors of war in Belgium. Never having felt responsibility for labor wars and oppressed masses and excluded races at home, they had a large fund of idle emotional capital to invest in the oppressed nationalities and ravaged villages of Europe. Hearts that had felt only ugly contempt for democratic strivings at home beat in tune with the struggle for freedom abroad. All this was natural, but it tended to over-emphasize our responsibility. And it threw our thinking out of gear. The task of making our own country detailedly fit for peace was abandoned in favor of a feverish concern for the management of the war, advice to the fighting governments on all matters, military, social and political, and a gradual working up of the conviction that we were ordained as a nation to lead all erring brothers towards the light of liberty and democracy. The failure of the American intellectual class to erect a creative attitude toward the war can be explained by these sterile mental conflicts which the shock to our ideals sent raging through us.

Mental conflicts end either in a new and higher synthesis or adjustment, or else in a reversion to more primitive ideas which have been outgrown but to which we drop when jolted out of our attained position. The war caused in America a recrudescence of nebulous ideals which a younger generation was fast outgrowing because it had passed the wistful stage and was discovering concrete ways of getting them incarnated in actual institutions. The shock of the war threw us back from this pragmatic work into an emotional bath of these old ideals. There was even a somewhat rarefied revival of our primitive Yankee boastfulness, the reversion of senility to that republican childhood when we expected the whole world to copy our republican institutions. We amusingly ignored the fact that it was just that Imperial German regime, to whom we are to teach the art of self-government, which our own Federal structure, with its executive irresponsible in foreign policy and with its absence of parliamentary control, most resembles. And we are missing the exquisite irony of the unaffected homage paid by the American democratic intellectuals to the last and most detested of Britain's tory premiers as the representative of a "liberal" ally, as well as the irony of the selection of the best hated of America's bourbon "old guard" as the missionary of American democracy to Russia.[7]

The intellectual state that could produce such things is one where reversion has taken place to more primitive ways of thinking. Simple syllogisms are substituted for analysis, things are known by their labels, our heart's desire dictates what we shall see. The American intellectual class, having failed to make the higher syntheses, regresses to ideas that can issue in quick, simplified action. Thought becomes any easy rationalization of what is actually going on or what is to happen inevitably tomorrow. It is true that certain groups did rationalize their colonialism and attach the doctrine of the inviolability of British seapower to the doctrine of a League of Peace. But this agile resolution of the mental conflict did not become a higher synthesis, to be creatively developed. It gradually merged into a justification for our going to war. It petrified into a dogma to be propagated. Criticism flagged and emotional propaganda began. Most of the socialists, the college professors and the practitioners of literature, however, have not even reached this high-water mark of synthesis. Their mental conflicts have been resolved much more simply. War in the interests of democracy! This was almost the sum of their philosophy. The primitive idea to which they regressed became almost insensibly translated into a craving for action. War was seen as the crowning relief of their indecision. At last action, irresponsibility, the end of anxious and torturing attempts to reconcile peace-ideals with the drag of the world towards Hell. An end to the pain of trying to adjust the facts to what they ought to be! Let us consecrate the facts as ideal! Let us join the greased slide towards war! The momentum increased. Hesitations, ironies, consciences, considerations,—all were drowned in the elemental blare of doing something aggressive, colossal. The new-found Sabbath "peacefulness of being at war"! The thankfulness with which so many intellectuals lay down and floated with the current betrays the hesitation and suspense through which they had been. The American university is a brisk and happy place these days. Simple, unquestioning action has superseded the knots of thought. The thinker dances with reality.

With how many of the acceptors of war has it been mostly a dread

---

[7] The references are to Lord Balfour, British Foreign Secretary and former prime minister who headed the British war mission to the United States in April 1917, and to Elihu Root, appointed in the same month to head an American mission to revolutionary Russia.

of intellectual suspense? It is a mistake to suppose that intellectuality necessarily makes for suspended judgments. The intellect craves certitude. It takes effort to keep it supple and pliable. In a time of danger and disaster we jump desperately for some dogma to cling to. The time comes, if we try to hold out, when our nerves are sick with fatigue, and we seize in a great healing wave of release some doctrine that can be immediately translated into action. Neutrality meant suspense, and so it became the object of loathing to frayed nerves. The vital myth of the League of Peace provides a dogma to jump to. With war the world becomes motor again and speculation is brushed aside like cobwebs. The blessed emotion of self-defense intervenes too, which focused millions in Europe. A few keep up a critical pose after war is begun, but since they usually advise action which is in one-to-one correspondence with what the mass is already doing, their criticism is little more than a rationalization of the common emotional drive.

The results of war on the intellectual class are already apparent. Their thought becomes little more than a description and justification of what is going on. They turn upon any rash one who continues idly to speculate. Once the war is on, the conviction spreads that individual thought is helpless, that the only way one can count is as a cog in the great wheel. There is no good holding back. We are told to dry our unnoticed and ineffective tears and plunge into the great work. Not only is everyone forced into line, but the new certitude becomes idealized. It is a noble realism which opposes itself to futile obstruction and the cowardly refusal to face facts. This realistic boast is so loud and sonorous that one wonders whether realism is always a stern and intelligent grappling with realities. May it not be sometimes a mere surrender to the actual, an abdication of the ideal through a sheer fatigue from intellectual suspense? The pacifist is roundly scolded for refusing to face the facts, and for retiring into his own world of sentimental desire. But is the realist, who refuses to challenge or criticise facts, entitled to any more credit than that which comes from following the line of least resistance? The realist thinks he at least can control events by linking himself to the forces that are moving. Perhaps he can. But if it is a question of controlling war, it is difficult to see how the child on the back of a mad elephant is to be any more effective in stopping the beast than is the child who tries to stop him from the ground. The ex-humanitarian, turned realist, sneers at the snobbish neutrality, colossal conceit, crooked thinking, dazed sensibilities, of those who are still unable to find any balm of consolation for this war. We manufacture consolations here in America while there are probably not a dozen men fighting in Europe who did not long ago give up every reason for their being there except that nobody knew how to get them away.

But the intellectuals whom the crisis has crystallized into an acceptance of war have put themselves into a terrifyingly strategic position. It is only on the craft, in the stream, they say, that one has any chance of controlling the current forces for liberal purposes. If we obstruct, we surrender all power for influence. If we responsibly approve, we then retain our power for guiding. We will be listened to as responsible thinkers, while those who obstructed the coming of war have committed intellectual suicide and shall be cast into outer darkness. Criticism by the ruling powers will only be accepted from those intellectuals who are in sympathy with the general tendency of the war. Well, it is true that they may guide, but if their stream leads to disaster and the frustration of national life, is their guiding any more than a preference whether they shall go over the right-hand or the left-hand side of the precipice? Meanwhile, however, there is comfort on board. Be with us, they call, or be negligible, irrelevant. Dissenters are already excommunicated. Irreconcilable radicals, wringing their hands among the debris, become the most despicable and impotent of men. There seems no choice for the intellectual but to join the mass of acceptance. But again the terrible dilemma arises,—either support what is going on, in which case you count for nothing because you are swallowed in the mass and great incalculable forces bear you on; or remain aloof, passively resistant, in which case you count for nothing because you are outside the machinery of reality.

Is there no place left, then, for the intellectual who cannot yet crystallize, who does not dread suspense, and is not yet drugged with fatigue? The American intellectuals, in their preoccupation with reality, seem to have forgotten that the real enemy is War rather than imperial Germany. There is work to be done to prevent this war of ours from passing into popular mythology as a holy crusade. What shall we do with leaders who tell us that we go to war in moral spotlessness, or who make "democracy" synonymous with a republican form of government? There is work to be done in still shouting that all the revolutionary by-products will not justify the war, or make war anything else than the most noxious complex of all the evils that afflict men. There must be some to find no consolation whatever, and some to sneer at those who buy the cheap emotion of sacrifice. There must be some irreconcilables left who will not even accept the war with walrus tears. There must be some to call unceasingly for peace, and some to insist that the terms of settlement shall be not only liberal but democratic. There must be some intellectuals who are not willing to use the old discredited counters again and to support a peace which would leave all the old inflammable materials of armament lying about the world. There must still be opposition to any contemplated "liberal" world-order founded on military coalitions. The "irreconcilable" need not be disloyal. He need not even be "impossibilist." His apathy towards war should take the form of a heightened energy and enthusiasm for the education, the art, the interpretation that make for life in the midst of the world of death. The intellecual who retains his animus against war will push out more boldly than ever to make his case solid against it. The old ideals crumble; new ideals must be forged. His mind will continue to roam widely and ceaselessly. The thing he will fear most is premature crystallization. If the American intellectual class rivets itself to a "liberal" philosophy that perpetuates the old errors, there will then be need for "democrats" whose task will be to divide, confuse, disturb, keep the intellectual waters constantly in motion to prevent any such ice from ever forming.

2

Below the Battle[1]

He is one of those young men who, because his parents happened to mate during a certain ten years of the world's history, has had now to put his name on a wheel of fate, thereby submitting himself to be drawn into a brief sharp course of military training before being shipped across the sea to kill Germans or be killed by them. He does not like this fate that menaces him, and he dislikes it because he seems to find nothing in the programme marked out for him which touches remotely his aspirations, his impulses, or even his desires. My friend is not a happy young man, but even the unsatisfactory life he is living seems supplemented at no single point by the life of the drill-ground or the camp or the stinking trench. He visualizes the obscenity of the battlefield and turns away in nausea. He thinks of the weary regimentation of young men, and is filled with disgust. His mind has turned sour on war and all that it involves. He is poor material for the military proclamation and the drill-sergeant.

I want to understand this friend of mine, for he seems rather typical of a scattered race of young Americans of today. He does not fall easily into the categories of patriot and coward which the papers are making popular. He feels neither patriotism nor fear, only an apathy toward the war, faintly warmed into a smouldering resentment at the

[1] *The Seven Arts,* II (July 1917) 270–277. Intellectually and emotionally this piece is autobiographical. The circumstances were drawn from the lives of several of Bourne's friends. One of the models was the music critic Paul Rosenfeld.

men who have clamped down the war-pattern upon him and that vague mass of people and ideas and workaday living around him that he thinks of as his country. Now that resentment has knotted itself into a tortured tangle of what he should do, how he can best be true to his creative self? I should say that his apathy cannot be imputed to cowardly ease. My friend earns about fifteen hundred dollars a year as an architect's assistant, and he lives alone in a little room over a fruitshop. He worked his way through college, and he has never known even a leisurely month. There is nothing Phæacian about his life. It is scarcely to save his skin for riotous living that he is reluctant about war. Since he left college he has been trying to find his world. He is often seriously depressed and irritated with himself for not having hewed out a more glorious career for himself. His work is just interesting enough to save it from drudgery, and yet not nearly independent and exacting enough to give him a confident professional sense. Outside his work, life is deprived and limited rather than luxurious. He is fond of music and goes to cheap concerts. He likes radical meetings, but never could get in touch with the agitators. His friends are seeking souls just like himself. He likes midnight talks in cafés and studios, but he is not especially amenable to drink. His heart of course is hungry and turbid, but his two or three love-affairs have not clarified anything for him. He eats three rather poor restaurant meals a day. When he reads, it is philosophy—Nietzsche, James, Bergson—or the novels about youth—Rolland, Nexö, Cannan, Frenssen, Beresford. He has a rather constant mood of futility, though he is in unimpeachable health. There are moments when life seems quite without sense or purpose. He has enough friends, however, to be not quite lonely, and yet they are so various as to leave him always with an ache for some more cohesive, purposeful circle. His contacts with people irritate him without rendering him quite unhopeful. He is always expecting he doesn't know quite what, and always being frustrated of he doesn't quite know what would have pleased him. Perhaps he never had a moment of real external or internal ease in his life.

Obviously a creature of low vitality, with neither the broad vision to be stirred by the President's war message, nor the red blood to itch for the dummy bayonet-charge. Yet somehow he does not seem exactly weak, and there is a consistency about his attitude which intrigues me. Since he left college eight years ago, he has been through most of the intellectual and emotional fads of the day. He has always cursed himself for being so superficial and unrooted, and he has tried to write a little of the thoughts that stirred him. What he got down on paper was, of course, the usual large vague feeling of a new time that all of us feel. With the outbreak of the Great War, most of his socialist and pacifist theories were knocked flat. The world turned out to be an entirely different place from what he had thought it. Progress and uplift seemed to be indefinitely suspended, though it was a long time before he realized how much he had been corroded by the impact of news and the endless discussions he heard. I think he gradually worked himself into a truly neutral indifference. The reputable people and the comfortable classes who were having all the conventional emotions rather disgusted him. The neurotic fury about self-defence seemed to come from types and classes that he instinctively detested. He was not scared, and somehow he could not get enthusiastic about defending himself with "preparedness" unless he were badly scared. Things got worse. All that he valued seemed frozen until the horible mess came to a close. He had gone to an unusually intelligent American college, and he had gotten a feeling for a humane civilization that had not left him. The war, it is true, bit away piece by piece every ideal that made this feeling seem plausible. Most of the big men—intellectuals —whom he thought he respected had had so much of their idealism hacked away and got their nerves so frayed that they became at last, in their panic, willing and even eager to adopt the war-technique in aid of their government's notions of the way to impose democracy on the world.

My poor young friend can best be understood as too naive and too young to effect this metamorphosis. Older men might mix a marvellous intellectual brew of personal anger, fear, a sense of "dishonor," fervor for a League of Peace, and set going a machinery that crushed everything intelligent, humane and civilized. My friend was less flexible. War simply did not mix with anything that he had learned to feel was desirable. Something in his mind spewed it out whenever it was suggested as a cure for our grievous American neutrality. As I got all this from our talks, he did not seem weak. He merely had no notion of the patriotism that meant the springing of a nation to arms. He read conscientiously *The New Republic's* feast of eloquent idealism, with its appealing harbingers of a cosmically efficacious and well-bred war. He would often say, This is all perfectly convincing; why, then, are we not all convinced? He seemed to understand the argument for

American participation. We both stood in awe at the superb intellectual structure that was built up. But my friend is one of those unfortunate youths whose heart has to apprehend as well as his intellect, and it was his heart that inexorably balked. So he was in no mood to feel the worth of American participation, in spite of the infinite tact and Fabian strategy of the Executive and his intellectualist backers. He felt apart from it all. He had not the imagination to see a healed world-order built out of the rotten materials of armaments, diplomacy and "liberal" statesmanship. And he wasn't affected by the psychic complex of panic, hatred, rage, class-arrogance and patriotic swagger that was creating in newspaper editors and in the *"jeunesse dorée"* around us the authentic *élan* for war.

My friend is thus somehow in the nation but not of the nation. The war has as yet got no conceivable clutch on his soul. He knows that theoretically he is united with a hundred million in purpose, sentiment and deed for an idealistic war to defend democracy and civilization against predatory autocracy. Yet somehow, in spite of all the excitement, nobody has as yet been able to make this real to him. He is healthy, intelligent, idealistic. The irony is that the demand which his country now makes on him is one to which not one single cell or nerve of idealism or desire responds. The cheap and silly blare of martial life leaves him cold. The easy inflation of their will-to-power which is coming to so many people from their participation in volunteer or government service, or, better still, from their urging others to farm, enlist, invest, retrench, organize,—none of this allures him. His life is uninteresting and unadventurous, but it is not quite dull enough to make this activity or anything he knows about war seem a release into lustier expression. He has ideals but he cannot see their realization through a desperate struggle to the uttermost. He doubts the "saving" of an America which can only be achieved through world-suicide. He wants democracy, but he does not want the kind of democracy we will get by this war enough to pay the suicidal cost of getting it in the way we set about it.

Dulce et decorum est pro patria mori, sweet and becoming is it to die for one's country. This is the young man who is suddenly asked to die for his country. My friend was much concerned about registration. He felt coercive forces closing in upon him. He did not want to register for the purposes of being liable to conscription. It would be doing something positive when he felt only apathy. Furthermore, if he was to resist, was it not better to take a stand now than to wait to be drafted? On the other hand, was it not too much of a concession to rebel at a formality? He did not really wish to be a martyr. Going to prison for a year for merely refusing to register was rather a grotesque and futile gesture. He did not see himself as a hero, shedding inspiration by his example to his fellows. He did not care what others did. His objection to prison was not so much fear perhaps as contempt for a silly sacrifice. He could not keep up his pose of complete aliency from the war-enterprise, now that registration was upon him. Better submit stoically, he thought, to the physical pressure, mentally reserving his sense of spiritual aliency from the enterprise into which he was being remorselessly moulded. Yet my friend is no arrant prig. He does not pretend to be a "world-patriot," or a servant of some higher law than his country's. Nor does he feel blatantly patriotic. With his groping philosophy of life, patriotism has merely died as a concept of significance for him. It is to him merely the emotion that fills the herd when it imagines itself engaged in massed defence or massed attack. Having no such images, he has no feeling of patriotism. He still feels himself inextricably a part of this blundering, wistful, crass civilization we call America. All he asks is not to be identified with it for warlike ends. He does not feel pro-German. He tells me there is not a drop of any but British blood in his veins. He does not love the Kaiser. He is quite willing to believe that it is the German government and not the German people whom he is asked to fight, although it may be the latter whom he is obliged to kill. But he cannot forget that it is the American government rather than the American people who got up the animus to fight the German government. He does not forget that the American government, having through tragic failure slipped into the war-technique, is now trying to manipulate him into that war-technique. And my friend's idea of *patria* does not include the duty of warlike animus, even when the government decides such animus is necessary to carry out its theories of democracy and the future organization of the world. There are ways in which my friend would probably be willing to die for his country. If his death now meant the restoration of those ravaged lands and the bringing back of the dead, that would be a cause to die for. But he knows that dead cannot be brought back or the brotherly currents restored. The work of madness will not be undone. Only a desperate war will be prolonged. Everything seems to him so mad that there is nothing left worth dying for. *Pro patria mori,* to my friend, means something different from lying gaunt as a conscript on a foreign battlefield, fallen in the last desperate fling of an interminable world-war.

Does this mean that if he is drafted he will refuse to serve? I do not know. It will not be any plea of "conscientious objection" that keeps him back. That phrase to him has already an archaic flavor which implies a ruling norm, a stiff familiar whom he must obey in the matter. It implies that one would be delighted to work up one's blood-lust for the business, except that this unaccountable conscience, like a godly grandmother, absolutely forbids. In the case of my friend, it will not be any objective "conscience." It will be something that is woven into his whole modern philosophic feel for life. This is what paralyzes him against taking one step toward the war-machine. If he were merely afraid of death, he would seek some alternative service. But he does not. He remains passive and apathetic, waiting for the knife to fall. There is a growing cynicism in him about the brisk and inept bustle of war-organization. His attitude suggests that if he is worked into war-service, he will have to be coerced every step of the way.

Yet he may not even rebel. He may go silently into the ranks in a mood of cold contempt. His horror of useless sacrifice may make even the bludgeoning of himself seem futile. He may go in the mood of so many young men in the other countries, without enthusiasm, without idealism, without hope and without belief, victims of a tragically blind force behind them. No other government, however, has had to face from the very start quite this appalling skepticism of youth. My friend is significant because all the shafts of panic, patriotism and national honor have been discharged at him without avail. All the seductions of "liberal" idealism leave him cold. He is to be susceptible to nothing but the use of crude, rough, indefeasible violence. Nothing could be more awkward for a "democratic" President than to be faced with this cold, staring skepticism of youth, in the prosecution of his war. The attitude of my friend suggests that there is a personal and social idealism in America which is out of reach of the most skilful and ardent appeals of the older order, an idealism that cannot be hurt by the taunts of cowardice and slacking or kindled by the slogans of capitalistic democracy. This is the cardinal fact of our war—the non-mobilization of the younger intelligentsia.

What will they do to my friend? If the war goes on they will need him. Pressure will change skepticism into bitterness. That bitterness will well and grow. If the country submissively pours month after month its wealth of life and resources into the work of annihilation, that bitterness will spread out like a stain over the younger American generation. If the enterprise goes on endlessly, the work, so blithely undertaken for the defence of democracy, will have crushed out the only genuinely precious thing in a nation, the hope and ardent idealism of its youth.

3

The Collapse of American Strategy[1]

I

In the absorbing business of organizing American participation in the war, public opinion seems to be forgetting the logic of that participation. It was for the purpose of realizing certain definite international ideals that the American democracy consented to be led into war. The meeting of aggression seemed to provide the immediate pretext, but the sincere intellectual support of the war came from minds that hoped ardently for an international order that would prevent a recurrence of world-war. Our action they saw as efficacious toward that end. It was almost wholly upon this ground that they justified it and themselves. The strategy which they suggested was very carefully worked out to make our participation count heavily toward the realization of their ideals. Their justification and their strategy alike were inseparably bound up with those ideals. It was implicit in their position that any alteration in the ideals would affect the strategy and would cast suspicion upon their justification. Similarly any alteration in the strategy would make this liberal body of opinion suspicious of the devotion of the Government to those ideals, and would tend to deprive the American democracy of any confident morale it might have had in entering the war. The American case hung upon the continued perfect working partnership of ideals, strategy and morale.

[1] *The Seven Arts*, II (Aug. 1917), 409–424.

In the eyes of all but the most skeptical radicals, American entrance into the war seemed to be marked by a singularly perfect union of these three factors. The President's address to Congress on April 2, supported by the December Peace note and the principles of the famous Senate address, gave the Government and American "liberalism" an apparently unimpeachable case.[2] A nation which had resisted for so long a time the undertow of war, which had remained passive before so many provocations and incitements, needed the clearest assurance of unselfish purpose to carry it through the inevitable chaos and disillusionment of adopting a war-technique. That moment seemed to give this assurance. But it needed not only a clear, but a steady and unwavering assurance. It had to see day by day, in each move of war-policy which the Administration made, an unmistakable step toward the realization of the ideals for which the American people had consented to come into the war. American hesitation was overcome only by an apparently persuasive demonstration that priceless values of civilization were at stake. The American people could only be prevented from relapsing into their first hesitation, and so demoralizing the conduct of the war, by the sustained conviction that the Administration and the Allied governments were fighting single-mindedly for the conservation of those values. It is therefore pertinent to ask how this conviction has been sustained and how accurately American strategy has been held to the justifying of our participation in the war. It is pertinent to ask whether the prevailing apathy may not be due to the progressive weakening of the assurance that our war is being in any way decisive in the securing of the values for which we are presumably fighting.

It will not be forgotten that the original logic of American participation hung primarily upon the menace of Germany's renewed submarine campaign. The case for America's entrance became presumably irresistible only when the safety of the British Commonwealth and of the Allies and neutrals who use the Atlantic highway was at stake. American liberal opinion had long ago decided that the logic of our moral neutrality had passed. American isolation was discredited as it

[2] On December 18, 1916, Wilson asked the belligerents to define their objectives and the bases on which they would be willing to negotiate. On January 22, 1917, in an address to the Senate, he offered the people of the belligerent countries his own vision of a "peace without victory." A week later, the resumption of unrestricted submarine warfare by Germany produced the series of events that led to Wilson's War Message on April 2.

became increasingly evident how urgent was our duty to participate in the covenant of nations which it was hoped would come out of the settlement. We were bound to contribute our resources and our good-will to this enterprise. Our position made it certain that however we acted we should be the deciding factor. But up to February first, 1917, it was still an arguable question in the minds of "liberals" whether we could best make that contribution through throwing in our lot with the more pacific nations or by continuing a neutrality benevolent toward their better cause. For this benevolent neutrality, however strained, was still endurable, particularly when supplemented by the hope of mediation contained in the "peace without victory" manœuvres and the principles of the Senate speech.

This attempt to bring about a negotiated peace, while the United States was still nominally neutral, but able to bring its colossal resources against the side which refused to declare its terms, marked the highwater level of American strategy.

For a negotiated peace, achieved before either side had reached exhaustion and the moral disaster was not irremediable, would have been the most hopeful possible basis for the covenant of nations. And the United States, as the effective agent in such a negotiated peace and as the most powerful neutral, might have assumed undisputed leadership in such a covenant.

The strategy of "peace without victory" failed because of the refusal of Germany to state her terms. The war went on from sheer lack of a common basis upon which to work out a settlement. American strategy then involved the persistent pressure of mediation. The submarine menace, however, suddenly forced the issue. The safety of the seas, the whole Allied cause, seemed suddenly in deadly peril. In the emergency benevolent neutrality collapsed. Liberal opinion could find no other answer to the aggression than war. In the light of the sequel those radicals who advocated a policy of "armed neutrality" seem now to have a better case. For American action obtained momentum from the imminence of the peril. The need was for the immediate guarantee of food and ships to the menaced nations and for the destruction of the attacking submarines. "Armed neutrality" suggested a way of dealing promptly and effectively with the situation. The providing of loans, food, ships, convoys, could ostensibly have taken place without a declaration of war, and without developing the country's morale or creating a vast military establishment. It was generally believed that time was the decisive factor. The decision for war has therefore meant an inevitable and perhaps fatal course of delay. It was obvious that with our well-known unpreparedness of administrative technique, the lack of co-ordination in industry, and the unreadiness of the people and Congress for coercion, war meant the practical postponement of action for months. In such an emergency that threatened us, our only chance to serve was in concentrating our powers. Until the disorganization inherent in a pacific democracy was remedied, our only hope of effective aid would come from focussing the country's energies on a ship and food programme, supplemented by a naval programme devised realistically to the direct business at hand. The war could be most promptly ended by convincing the German government that the submarine had no chance of prevailing against the endless American succor which was beginning to raise the siege and clear the seas.

The decision, however, was for war, and for a "thorough" war. This meant the immediate throwing upon the national machinery of far more activity than it could handle. It meant attaching to a food and ship programme a military programme, a loan programme, a censorship programme. All these latter have involved a vast amount of advertising, of agitation, of discussion, and dissension. The country's energies and attention have been drained away from the simple exigencies of the situation and from the technique of countering the submarine menace and ending the war. Five months have passed since the beginning of unrestricted submarine warfare. We have done nothing to overcome the submarine. The food and ship programmes are still unconsolidated. The absorption of Congress and the country in the loan and the conscript army and the censorship has meant just so much less absorption in the vital and urgent technique to provide which we entered the war. The country has been put to work at a vast number of activities which are consonant to the abstract condition of war, but which may have little relation to the particular situation in which this country found itself and to the particular strategy required. The immediate task was to prevent German victory in order to restore the outlines of our strategy toward a negotiated peace. War has been impotent in that immediate task. Paradoxically, therefore, our very participation was a means of weakening our strategy. We have not overcome the submarine or freed the Atlantic world. Our entrance has apparently made not a dent in the morale of the German people. The effect of our entrance, it was anticipated by liberals, would be the

152,984

College of St. Francis Library
Joliet, Illinois

shortening of the war. Our entrance has rather tended to prolong it. Liberals were mistaken about the immediate collapse of the British Commonwealth. It continued to endure the submarine challenge without our material aid. We find ourselves, therefore, saddled with a war-technique which has compromised rather than furthered our strategy.

This war-technique compromises the outlines of American strategy because instead of making for a negotiated peace it has had the entirely unexpected result of encouraging those forces in the Allied countries who desire "la victoire intégrale," the "knockout blow." In the President's war-message the country was assured that the principles of the negotiated peace remained quite unimpaired. The strategy that underlay this, it will be remembered, was to appeal to the Teutonic peoples over the heads of their rulers with terms so liberal that the peoples would force their governments to make peace. The strategy of the American government was, while prosecuting the war, to announce its war-aims and to persuade the Allies to announce their war-aims in such terms as would split the peoples of the Central Powers from their governments, thus bringing more democratic regimes that would provide a fruitful basis for a covenant of nations. We entered the war with no grievances of our own. It was our peculiar role to continue the initiative for peace, both by unmistakably showing our own purpose for a just peace based on some kind of international organization and by wielding a steady pressure on the Entente governments to ratify our programme. If we lost this initiative for peace, or if we were unable or unwilling to press the Entente toward an unmistakable liberalism, our strategy broke down and our justification for entering the war became seriously impaired. For we could then be charged with merely aiding the Entente's ambiguous scheme of European reorganization.

The success of this strategy of peace depended on a stern disavowal of the illiberal programmes of groups within the Allied countries and a sympathetic attitude toward the most democratic programmes of groups within the enemy Powers. Anything which weakened either this disavowal or this sympathy would imperil our American case. As potential allies in this strategy the American government had within the enemies' gates the followers of Scheidemann[3] who said at the last

[3] Phillipp Scheidemann, leader of the German Social Democratic Party. He supported his country's war effort but called for a "peace without annexations or indemnities."

sitting of the Reichstag: "If the Entente Powers should renounce all claims for annexation and indemnity and if the Central Powers should insist on continuing the war, a revolution will certanly result in Germany." It is not inconceivable that the American government and the German socialists had at the back of their minds the same kind of a just peace. The fact that the German socialists were not opposing the German government did not mean that any peace move in which the former were interested was necessarily a sinister Hohenzollern intrigue. The bitterest enemies of Hollweg[4] were not the radicals but the Pan-Germans themselves. It is they who were said to be circulating manifestoes through the army threatening revolution unless their programme of wholesale annexations is carried out. Whatever liberal reservoir of power there is in Germany, therefore, remains in the socialist ranks. If there is any chance of liberal headway against the sinister Pan-German campaign it is through this nucleus of liberal power. American strategy, if it has to find a liberal leverage in Germany, will have to choose the socialist group as against the Pan-Germans. It is not absolutely necessary to assume that the support of the Chancellor by the socialist majority is permanent. It is unplausible that the Scheidemann group co-operates with the Government for peace merely to consolidate the Junker and military class in power after the war. It is quite conceivable that the socialist majority desires peace in order to have a safe basis for a liberal overturn. Revolution, impossible while the Fatherland is in danger, becomes a practicable issue as soon as war is ended. A policy of aiding the Government in its pressure toward peace, in order to be in a tactical position to control the Government when the war-peril was ended, would be an extremely astute piece of statesmanship. There is no evidence that the German socialists are incapable of such far-sighted strategy. Certainly the "German peace" of a Scheidemann is bound to be entirely different from the "German peace" of a Hindenburg.[5] This difference is one of the decisive factors of the American strategy. To ignore it is to run the risk of postponing and perhaps obstructing the settlement of the war.

It is these considerations that make the refusal of passports to the

[4] Theobald von Bethmann-Hollweg, German Chancellor who resigned in July 1917 after he lost support of the Reichstag. The peace parties had regarded him as too conservative, and the militarists toppled him for being a defeatist.

[5] Paul von Hindenburg, German Chief-of-Staff and supreme commander of all forces of the Central Powers. The virtual ruler of war-time Germany, he rejected all proposals for a negotiated peace.

American socialists seem a serious weakening of the American strategy.[6] A conference of responsible socialists from the different countries might have clarified the question how far a Russian peace or a Scheidemann peace differed from the structure of a Wilson peace. By denying American participation in the conference, the Administration apparently renounced the opportunity to make contact with liberal leverage in Germany. It refused to take that aggressive step in cleaving German opinion which was demanded by its own strategy. It tended to discourage liberal opinion in Germany and particularly it discouraged the Russian democracy which was enthusiastic for a socialist conference.

This incident was symptomatic of the lessened adjustment which the Administration has shown toward the changing situation. It was the hope of the American liberals who advocated American entrance into the war that this country would not lose thereby its initiative for peace. They believed that our entrance would make our mediating power actually stronger. That hope has been disappointed through the unexpected radicalism of the new Russian government. The initiative for peace was bound to lie with the people that most wanted peace and was willing to make the most peremptory demands upon the Allied governments that they state the war-aims that would bring it. This tactic was an integral part of the original American strategy. The American liberals trusted the President to use American participation as an instrument in liberalizing the war-aims of all the Allied governments. In the event, however, it has not been America that has wanted peace sufficiently to be peremptory about it. It has been Russia. The initiative for peace has passed from President Wilson into the hands of the Council of Workmen's and Soldiers' Deputies. It is the latter who have brought the pressure to declare democratic war-aims. It is their dissatisfaction with the original Allied statement that has brought these new, if scarcely more satisfactory, declarations. In this discussion between the Governments regarding the restatement of war-aims, it was not upon Russia's side that this country found itself. The President's note to Russia had all the tone of a rebuke. It sounded like

[6] In May 1917 the State Department refused passports to Morris Hillquit and others on their way to the International Socialist Conference in Stockholm, Sweden. Representatives of the Russian Revolutionary Council of Workmen's and Soldier's Deputies were to be present as was Phillipp Scheidemann. In refusing the passports, Secretary of State Robert Lansing invoked the "Logan Act" of 1799 which prohibits private citizens from dealing in diplomacy.

the reaction of a Government which—supposedly itself the leader in the campaign for a just peace—found itself uncomfortably challenged to state its own sincerity.[7] The key to our American strategy has been surrendered to Russia. The plain fact is that the President has lost that position of leader which a Russian candor would have retained for him.

What is more serious is that the note to Russia implied not only his loss of the initiative for a negotiated peace but even the desire for it. "The day has come when we must conquer or submit." This has a very strange ring coming from a President who in his very war-message still insisted that he had not altered in any way the principles of his "peace without victory" note. The note to Russia did not attempt to explain how "peace without victory" was to be reconciled with "conquer or submit," nor has any such explanation been forthcoming. The implication is that the entire strategy of the negotiated peace has passed out of American hands into those of Russia, and that this country is committed to the new strategy of the "knockout blow." If this is true, then we have the virtual collapse of the strategy, and with it the justification, of our entrance into the war.

Whether American strategy has changed or not, the effect upon opinion in the Allied countries seems to be as if it had. Each pronouncement of America's war-aims is received with disconcerting unanimity in England, France and Italy as ratifying their own aspirations and policies. Any hint that Allied policies disagree with ours is received with marked disfavor by our own loyal press. When we entered the war, the Allied aims stood as stated in their reply to the President's December note. This reply was then interpreted by American liberals as a diplomatic programme of maximum demands. They have therefore called repeatedly upon the President to secure from the Allied governments a resolution of the ambiguities and a revision of the more extreme terms, in order that we might make common cause with them toward a just peace. In this campaign the American liberals have put themselves squarely on the side of the new Russia, which has also clamored for a clear and liberal statement of what the war is being fought for. Unfortunately the Administration has been unable

[7] Under pressure from the militant, socialist, Councils of Workmen's and Soldiers' Deputies (the "soviets"), Kerensky's Provisional Government disassociated itself from all Czarist treaties. Wilson responded to this by a statement of America's hopes for a just peace, but he also referred to possible post-war readjustments of power that might be necessary to secure the peace.

or unwilling to secure from the Allies any such resolution or revision. The Russian pressure has elicited certain statements, which, however, proved little more satisfactory to the Russian radicals than the original statement. Our own war-aims have been stated in terms as ambiguous and unsatisfactory as those of the Allies. Illiberal opinion in the other countries has not been slow in seizing upon President Wilson's pronouncements as confirming all that their hearts could wish. Most significant has been the satisfaction of Italian imperialistic opinion, the most predatory and illiberal force in any Allied country. The President has done nothing to disabuse Italian minds of their belief. He has made no disavowal of the Allied reactionary ratification. The sharp divergence of interpretation between the Allied governments and the Russian radicals persists. In lieu of any clear statement to the contrary, opinion in the Allied countries has good ground for believing that the American government will back up whatever of their original programme can be carried through. Particularly is this true after the President's chiding of Russia. The animus behind the enthusiasm for Pershing in France is the conviction that American force will be the decisive factor in the winning back of Alsace-Lorraine. It is no mere sentimental pleasure at American alliance. It is an immense stiffening of the determination to hold out to the uttermost, to the "peace with victory" of which Ribot speaks.[8] Deluded France carries on the war to complete exhaustion on the strength of the American millions who are supposedly rushing to save her. The immediate effect of American participation in England and Italy as well has been an intense will to hold out not for the "peace without victory" but "pour la victoire intégrale," for the conquest so crushing that Germany will never be feared again.

Now the crux of American strategy was the liberalization of Allied policy in order that that peace might be obtained which was a hopeful basis for a League of Nations. American participation has evidently not gone one inch toward liberalizing the Allies. We are further from the negotiated peace than we were in December, though the only change in the military and political situation is the Russian revolution which immensely increased the plausibility of that peace. As Allied hope of victory grows, the covenant of nations fades into the back-

[8] Alexandre Ribot, French Premier and Minister for Foreign Affairs, March–September 1917.

ground. And it is Allied hope of victory that our participation has inflamed and augmented.

The President's Flag Day address marks without a doubt the collapse of American strategy.[9] That address, coupled with the hints of "effective readjustments" in the note to Russia, implies that America is ready to pour out endless blood and treasure, not to the end of a negotiated peace, but to the utter crushing of the Central Powers, to their dismemberment and political annihilation. The war is pictured in that address as a struggle to the death against the military empire of Mittel-Europa. The American role changes from that of mediator in the interest of international organization to that of formidable support to the breaking of this menace to the peace and liberty of Europe. It will be remembered that American liberals interpreted our entrance into the war as primarily defensive, an enterprise to prevent Germany's threatened victory on the sea. We came in, not to secure an Allied "peace with victory," but to prevent a German "peace with victory," and so restore the situation favorable to a negotiated peace. The strategy of the negotiated peace depended largely on the belief that a military decision was either impossible or was not worth the colossal sacrifice it demanded. But it is only as the result of a sweeping military decision that any assured destruction of Mittel-Europa could come. In basing his case on Mittel-Europa, therefore, the President has clearly swung from a strategy of "peace without victory" to a strategy of "war to exhaustion for the sake of a military decision." He implies that a country which came only after hesitation to the defense of the seas and the Atlantic world will contentedly pour out its indefinite blood and treasure for the sake of spoiling the coalition of Mittel-Europa and of making readjustments in the map of Europe effective against German influence on the Continent. Such an implication means the "end of American isolation" with a vengeance. No one can be blamed who sees in the Flag Day Address the almost unlimited countersigning of Allied designs and territorial schemes.

The change of American strategy to a will for a military decision would explain the creation of the vast American army which in the

---

[9] Made at the Monument Grounds in Washington, D.C., the speech contained one of Wilson's most emotional attacks on German militarism and on German ambition to establish control "across the very center of Europe and beyond the Mediterranean into the heart of Asia . . ."

original policy was required only "as a reserve and a precaution." It explains our close co-operation with the Allied governments following the visits of the Missions.[10] An American army of millions would undoubtedly be a decisive factor in the remaking of the map of Europe and the permanent garrisoning of strategic points bearing upon Germany. But this change of strategy does not explain itself. The continental military and political situation has not altered in any way which justifies so fundamental an alteration in American strategy. American liberals justified our entrance into the war as a response to a sudden exigency. But the menace of Mittel-Europa has existed ever since the entrance of Bulgaria in 1915. If it now challenges us and justifies our change of strategy, it challenged us and justified our assault a full two years ago. American shudders at its bogey are doubly curious because it is probably less of a menace now than it has ever been. President Wilson ignores the effect of a democratic Russia on the success of such a military coalition. Such heterogeneous states could be held together only through the pressure of a strong external fear. But the passing of predatory Russia removes that fear. Furthermore, Bulgaria, the most democratic of the Balkan States, would always be an uncertain partner in such a coalition. Bagdad has long been in British hands. There are strong democratic and federalistic forces at work in the Austro-Hungarian monarchy. The materials seem less ready than ever for the creation of any such predatory and subjugated Empire as the Flag Day Address describes. Whatever the outcome of the war, there is likely to result an economic union which could bring needed civilization to neglected and primitive lands. But such a union would be a blessing to Europe rather than a curse. It was such a union that England was on the point of granting to Germany when the war broke out. The Balkans and Asia Minor need German science, German organization, German industrial development. We can hardly be fighting to prevent such German influence in these lands. The irony of the President's words lies in the fact that the hopes of Mittel-Europa as a military coalition seem to grow dimmer rather than brighter. He must know that this "enslavement" of the peoples of which he speaks can only be destroyed by the peoples themselves and not at the imposition of a military conqueror. The will to resist this Prussian enslavement seems to have been generated in Austro-Hungary. The President's

[10] The reference is to the English and French missions to Washington following America's entry into the war.

perspective is belated. If our fighting to crush this amazing plot is justified now, it was more than justified as soon as Rumania was defeated. The President convicts himself of criminal negligence in not urging us into the war at that time. If our role was to aid in conquest, we could not have begun our work too soon.

The new strategy is announced by the President in no uncertain terms—"The day has come when we must conquer or submit." But the strategy of conquest implies the necessity of means for consolidating the conquest. If the world is to be made safe for democracy, democracy must to a certain extent be imposed on the world. There is little point in conquering unless you carry through the purposes for which you have conquered. The earlier American strategy sought to bring democracy to Germany by appealing directly to the democratic forces in Germany itself. We relied on a self-motivated regeneration on the part of our enemy. We believed that democracy could be imposed only from within. If the German people cannot effect their own political reorganization, nobody can do it for them. They would continue to prefer the native Hohenzollerns to the most liberal government imposed by their conquering enemies. A Germany forced to be democratic under the tutelage of a watchful and victorious Entente would indeed be a constant menace to the peace of Europe. Just so far then as our changed American strategy contributes toward a conquest over Germany, it will work against our desire to see that country spontaneously democratized. There is reason for hope that democracy will not have to be forced on Germany. From the present submission of the German people to the war-regime nothing can be deduced as to their subserviency after the war. Prodigious slaughter will effect profound social changes. There may be going on a progressive selection in favor of democratic elements. The Russian army was transformed into a democratic instrument by the wiping-out in battle of the upper-class officers. Men of democratic and revolutionary sympathies took their places. A similar process may happen in the German army. The end of the war may leave the German "army of the people" a genuine popular army intent upon securing control of the civil government. Furthermore, the continuance of Pan-German predatory imperialism depends on a younger generation of Junkers to replace the veterans now in control. The most daring of those aristocrats will almost certainly have been destroyed in battle. The mortality in upper-class leadership will certainly have proved far larger than the mortality in lower-class leadership. The maturing of these tendencies is the hope of German democracy. A speedy ending of the war, before the country is exhausted and the popular morale destroyed, is likely best to mature these tendencies. In this light it is almost immaterial what terms are made. Winning or losing, Germany cannot replace her younger generation of the ruling class. And without a ruling class to continue the imperial tradition, democracy could scarcely be delayed. An enfeebled ruling class could neither hold a vast world military Empire together nor resist the revolutionary elements at home. The prolongation of the war delays democracy in Germany by convincing the German people that they are fighting for their very existence and thereby forcing them to cling even more desperately to their military leaders. In announcing an American strategy of "conquer or submit," the President virtually urges the German people to prolong the war. And not only are the German people, at the apparent price of their existence, tacitly urged to continue the fight to the uttermost, but the Allied governments are tacitly urged to wield the "knockout blow." All those reactionary elements in England, France and Italy, whose spirits drooped at the President's original bid for a negotiated peace, now take heart again at this apparent countersigning of their most extreme programmes.

American liberals who urged the nation to war are therefore suffering the humiliation of seeing their liberal strategy for peace transformed into a strategy for prolonged war. This government was to announce such war-aims as should persuade the peoples of the Central Powers to make an irresistible demand for a democratic peace. Our initiative with the Allied governments was to make this peace the basis of an international covenant, "the creation of a community of limited independencies," of which Norman Angell speaks. Those Americans who opposed our entrance into the war believed that this object could best be worked for by a strategy of continued neutrality and the constant pressure of mediation. They believed that war would defeat the strategy for a liberal peace. The liberal intellectuals who supported the President felt that only by active participation on an independent basis could their purposes be achieved. The event has signally betrayed them. We have not ended the submarine menace. We have lost all power for mediation. We have not even retained the democratic leadership among the Allied nations. We have surrendered the initiative for peace. We have involved ourselves in a moral obligation to send large armies to Europe to secure a military decision for the Allies.

We have prolonged the war. We have encouraged the reactionary elements in every Allied country to hold out for extreme demands. We have discouraged the German democratic forces. Our strategy has gradually become indistinguishable from that of the Allies. With the arrival of the British Mission our "independent basis" became a polite fiction. The President's Flag Day Address merely registers the collapse of American strategy. All this the realistic pacifists foresaw when they held out so bitterly and unaccountably against our entering the war. The liberals felt a naive faith in the sagacity of the President to make their strategy prevail. They looked to him single-handedly to liberalize the liberal nations. They trusted him to use a war-technique which should consist of an olive-branch in one hand and a sword in the other. They have had to see their strategy collapse under the very weight of that war-technique. Guarding neutrality, we might have counted toward a speedy and democratic peace. In the war, we are a rudderless nation, to be exploited as the Allies wish, politically and materially, and towed, to their aggrandizement, in any direction which they may desire.

4

A War Diary[1]

I

Time brings a better adjustment to the war. There had been so many times when, to those who had energetically resisted its coming, it seemed the last intolerable outrage. In one's wilder moments one expected revolt against the impressment of unwilling men and the suppression of unorthodox opinion. One conceived the war as breaking down through a kind of intellectual sabotage diffused through the country. But as one talks to people outside the cities and away from ruling currents of opinion, one finds the prevailing apathy shot everywhere with acquiescence. The war is a bad business, which somehow got fastened on us. They don't want to go, but they've got to go. One decides that nothing generally obstructive is going to happen and that it would make little difference if it did. The kind of war which we are conducting is an enterprise which the American government does not have to carry on with the hearty co-operation of the American people but only with their acquiescence. And that acquiescence seems sufficient to float an indefinitely protracted war for vague or even largely uncomprehended and unaccepted purposes. Our resources in men and materials are vast enough to organize the war-technique without enlisting more than a fraction of the people's conscious energy. Many men will not like being sucked into the actual fighting organism, but as the war goes on they will be sucked in as individuals and they

[1] *The Seven Arts,* II (Sept. 1917), 535–547.

will yield. There is likely to be no element in the country with the effective will to help them resist. They are not likely to resist of themselves concertedly. They will be licked grudgingly into military shape, and their lack of enthusiasm will in no way unfit them for use in the hecatombs necessary for the military decision upon which Allied political wisdom still apparently insists. It is unlikely that enough men will be taken from the potentially revolting classes seriously to embitter their spirit. Losses in the well-to-do classes will be sustained by a sense of duty and of reputable sacrifice. From the point of view of the worker, it will make little difference whether his work contributes to annihilation overseas or to construction at home. Temporarily, his condition is better if it contributes to the former. We of the middle classes will be progressively poorer than we should otherwise have been. Our lives will be slowly drained by clumsily levied taxes and the robberies of imperfectly controlled private enterprises. But this will not cause us to revolt. There are not likely to be enough hungry stomachs to make a revolution. The materials seem generally absent from the country, and as long as a government wants to use the war-technique in its realization of great ideas, it can count serenely on the human resources of the country, regardless of popular mandate or understanding.

II

If human resources are fairly malleable into the war-technique, our material resources will prove to be even more so, quite regardless of the individual patriotism of their owners or workers. It is almost purely a problem of diversion. Factories and mines and farms will continue to turn out the same products and at an intensified rate, but the government will be working to use their activity and concentrate it as contributory to the war. The process which the piping times of benevolent neutrality began will be pursued to its extreme end. All this will be successful, however, precisely as it is made a matter of centralized governmental organization and not of individual offerings of goodwill and enterprise. It will be coercion from above that will do the trick rather than patriotism from below. Democratic contentment may be shed over the land for a time through the appeal to individual thoughtfulness in saving and in relinquishing profits. But all that is really needed is the co-operation with government of the men who direct the large financial and industrial enterprises. If their interests is enlisted in diverting the mechanism of production into war-channels, it makes not the least difference whether you or I want our activity to count in aid of the war. Whatever we do will contribute toward its successful organization, and toward the riveting of a semi-military State-socialism on the country. As long as the effective managers, the "big men" in the staple industries remained loyal, nobody need care what the millions of little human cogs who had to earn their living felt or thought. This is why the technical organization for this American war goes on so much more rapidly than any corresponding popular sentiment for its aims and purposes. Our war is teaching us that patriotism is really a superfluous quality in war. The government of a modern organized plutocracy does not have to ask whether the people want to fight or understand what they are fighting for, but only whether they will tolerate fighting. America does not co-operate with the President's designs. She rather feebly acquiesces. But that feeble acquiescence is the all-important factor. We are learning that war doesn't need enthusiasm, doesn't need conviction, doesn't need hope, to sustain it. Once manœuvred, it takes care of itself, provided only that our industrial rulers see that the end of the war will leave American capital in a strategic position for world-enterprise. The American people might be much more indifferent to the war even than they are and yet the results would not be materially different. A majority of them might even be feebly or at least unconcertedly hostile to the war, and yet it would go gaily on. That is why a popular referendum seems so supremely irrelevant to people who are willing to use war as an instrument in the working-out of national policy.[2] And that is why this war, with apathy rampant, is probably going to act just as if every person in the country were filled with patriotic ardor, and furnished with a completely assimilated map of the League to Enforce Peace. If it doesn't, the cause will not be the lack of popular ardor, but the clumsiness of the government officials in organizing the technique of the war. Our country in war, given efficiency at the top, can do very well without our patriotism. The non-patriotic man need feel no pangs of conscience about not helping the war. Patriotism fades into the merest trivial sentimentality when it becomes, as so obviously in a

[2] In March 1917 Bourne, along with Max Eastman, Amos Pinchot, and others, called for a popular referendum on America's entry into the war.

situation like this, so pragmatically impotent. As long as one has to earn one's living or buy tax-ridden goods, one is making one's contribution to war in a thousand indirect ways. The war, since it does not need it, cannot fairly demand also the sacrifice of one's spiritual integrity.

III

The "liberals" who claim a realistic and pragmatic attitude in politics have disappointed us in setting up and then clinging wistfully to the belief that our war could get itself justified for an idealistic flavor, or at least for a world-renovating social purpose, that they had more or less denied to the other belligerents. If these realists had had time in the hurry and scuffle of events to turn their philosophy on themselves, they might have seen how thinly disguised a rationalization this was of their emotional undertow. They wanted a League of Nations. They had an unanalyzable feeling that this was a war in which we had to be, and be in it we would. What more natural than to join the two ideas and conceive our war as the decisive factor in the attainment of the desired end! This gave them a good conscience for willing American participation, although as good men they must have loathed war and everything connected with it. The realist cannot deny facts. Moreover, he must not only acknowledge them but he must use them. Good or bad, they must be turned by his intelligence to some constructive end. Working along with the materials which events give him, he must get where and what he can, and bring something brighter and better out of the chaos.

Now war is such an indefeasible and unescapable Real that the good realist must accept it rather comprehensively. To keep out of it is pure quietism, an acute moral failure to adjust. At the same time, there is an inexorability about war. It is a little unbridled for the realist's rather nice sense of purposive social control. And nothing is so disagreeable to the pragmatic mind as any kind of an absolute. The realistic pragmatist could not recognize war as inexorable—though to the common mind it would seem as near an absolute, coercive social situation as it is possible to fall into. For the inexorable abolishes choices, and it is the essence of the realist's creed to have, in every situation, alternatives before him. He gets out of his scrape in this way: Let the inexorable roll in upon me, since it must. But then, keeping firm my sense of control, I will somehow tame it and turn it to my own creative purposes. Thus realism is justified of her children, and the "liberal" is saved from the limbo of the wailing and irreconcilable pacifists who could not make so easy an adjustment.

Thus the "liberals" who made our war their own preserved their pragmatism. But events have shown how fearfully they imperilled their intuition and how untameable an inexorable really is. For those of us who knew a real inexorable when we saw one, and had learned from watching war what follows the loosing of a war-technique, foresaw how quickly aims and purposes would be forgotten, and how flimsy would be any liberal control of events. It is only we now who can appreciate "The New Republic"—the organ of applied pragmatic realism—when it complains that the League of Peace (which we entered the war to guarantee) is more remote than it was eight months ago; or that our State Department has no diplomatic policy (though it was to realize the high aims of the President's speeches that the intellectuals willed American participation); or that we are subordinating the political management of the war to real or supposed military advantages, (though militarism in the liberal mind had no justification except as a tool for advanced social ends). If, after all the idealism and creative intelligence that were shed upon America's taking up of arms, our State Department has no policy, we are like brave passengers who have set out for the Isles of the Blest only to find that the first mate has gone insane and jumped overboard, the rudder has come loose and dropped to the bottom of the sea, and the captain and pilot are lying dead drunk under the wheel. The stokers and engineers, however, are still merrily forcing the speed up to twenty knots an hour and the passengers are presumably getting the pleasure of the ride.

IV

The penalty the realist pays for accepting war is to see disappear one by one the justifications for accepting it. He must either become a genuine Realpolitiker and brazen it through, or else he must feel sorry for his intuition and be regretful that he willed the war. But so easy is forgetting and so slow the change of events that he is more likely to ignore the collapse of his case. If he finds that his government is relinquishing the crucial moves of that strategy for which he was willing to use the technique of war, he is likely to move easily to the ground that it will all come out in the end the same anyway. He soon becomes satisfied with tacitly ratifying whatever happens, or at least straining to find the grain of unplausible hope that may be latent in the situation.

But what then is there really to choose between the realist who accepts evil in order to manipulate it to a great end, but who somehow unaccountably finds events turn sour on him, and the Utopian pacifist who cannot stomach the evil and will have none of it? Both are helpless, both are coerced. The Utopian, however, knows that he is ineffective and that he is coerced, while the realist, evading disillusionment, moves in a twilight zone of half-hearted criticism, and hopings for the best, where he does not become a tacit fatalist. The latter would be the manlier position, but then where would be his realistic philosophy of intelligence and choice? Professor Dewey has become impatient at the merely good and merely conscientious objectors to war who do not attach their conscience and intelligence to forces moving in another direction. But in wartime there are literally no valid forces moving in another direction. War determines its own end,—victory, and government crushes out automatically all forces that deflect, or threaten to deflect, energy from the path of organization to that end. All governments will act in this way, the most democratic as well as the most autocratic. It is only "liberal" naïveté that is shocked at arbitrary coercion and suppression. Willing war means willing all the evils that are organically bound up with it. A good many people still seem to believe in a peculiar kind of democratic and antiseptic war. The pacifists opposed the war because they knew this was an illusion, and because of the myriad hurts they knew war would do the promise of democracy at home. For once the babes and sucklings seem to have been wiser than the children of light.

V

If it is true that the war will go on anyway whether it is popular or not or whether its purposes are clear, and if it is true that in wartime constructive realism is an illusion, then the aloof man, the man who will not obstruct the war but who cannot spiritually accept it, has a clear case for himself. Our war presents no more extraordinary phenomenon than the number of the more creative minds of the younger generation who are still irreconcilable toward the great national enterprise which the government has undertaken. The country is still dotted with young men and women, in full possession of their minds, faculties and virtue, who feel themselves profoundly alien to the work which is going on around them. They must not be confused with the disloyal or the pro-German. They have no grudge against the country, but their patriotism has broken down in the emergency. They want to see the carnage stopped and Europe decently constructed again. They want a democratic peace. If the swift crushing of Germany will bring that peace, they want to see Germany crushed. If the embargo on neutrals will prove the decisive coup, they are willing to see the neutrals taken ruthlessly by the throat. But they do not really believe that peace will come by any of these means, or by any use of our war-technique whatever. They are genuine pragmatists and they fear any kind of an absolute, even when bearing gifts. They know that the longer a war lasts the harder it is to make peace. They know that the peace of exhaustion is a dastardly peace, leaving enfeebled the morale of the defeated, and leaving invincible for years all the most greedy and soulless elements in the conquerors. They feel that the greatest obstacle to peace now is the lack of the powerful mediating neutral which we might have been. They see that war has lost for us both the mediation and the leadership, and is blackening us ever deeper with the responsibility for having prolonged the dreadful tangle. They are skeptical not only of the technique of war, but also of its professed aims. The President's idealism stops just short of the pitch that would arouse their own. There is a middle-aged and belated taint about the best ideals which publicist liberalism has been able to express. The appeals to propagate political democracy leave these people cold in a world which has become so disillusioned of democracy in the face of universal economic servitude. Their ideals outshoot the government's. To them the real arena lies in the international class-struggle, rather than in the competition of artificial national units. They are watching to see what the Russian socialists are going to do for the world, not what the timorous capitalistic American democracy may be planning. They can feel no enthusiasm for a League of Nations, which should solidify the old units and continue in disguise the old theories of international relations. Indispensable, perhaps? But not inspiring; not something to give one's spiritual allegiance to. And yet the best advice that American wisdom can offer to those who are out of sympathy with the war is to turn one's influence toward securing that our war contribute toward this end. But why would not this League turn out to be little more than a well-oiled machine for the use of that enlightened imperialism toward which liberal American finance is already whetting its tongue? And what is enlightened imperialism as an international ideal as against the anarchistic communism of the nations which the new Russia suggests in renouncing imperialist intentions?

VI

Skeptical of the means and skeptical of the aims, this element of the younger generation stands outside the war, and looks upon the conscript army and all the other war-activities as troublesome interruptions on its thought and idealism, interruptions which do not touch anywhere a fibre of its soul. Some have been much more disturbed than others, because of the determined challenge of both patriots and realists to break in with the war-obsession which has filled for them their sky. Patriots and realists can both be answered. They must not be allowed to shake one's inflexible determination not to be spiritually implicated in the war. It is foolish to hope. Since the 30th of July, 1914, nothing has happened in the arena of war-policy and war-technique except for the complete and unmitigated worst. We are tired of continued disillusionment, and of the betrayal of generous anticipations. It is saner not to waste energy in hope within the system of war-enterprise. One may accept dispassionately whatever changes for good may happen from the war, but one will not allow one's imagination to connect them organically with war. It is better to resist cheap consolations, and remain skeptical about any of the good things so confidently promised us either through victory or the social reorganization demanded by the war-technique. One keeps healthy in wartime not by a series of religious and political consolations that something good is coming out of it all, but by a vigorous assertion of values in which war has no part. Our skepticism can be made a shelter behind which is built up a wider consciousness of the personal and social and artistic ideals which American civilization needs to lead the good life.

We can be skeptical constructively, if, thrown back on our inner resources from the world of war which is taken as the overmastering
reality, we search much more actively to clarify our attitudes and express a richer significance in the American scene. We do not feel the
war to be very real, and we sense a singular air of falsity about the
emotions of the upper-classes toward everything connected with war.
This ostentatious shame, this grovelling before illusory Allied heroisms
and nobilities, has shocked us. Minor novelists and minor poets and
minor publicists are still coming back from driving ambulances in
France to write books that nag us into an appreciation of the "real
meaning." No one can object to the generous emotions of service in
a great cause or to the horror and pity at colossal devastation and
agony. But too many of these prophets are men who have lived rather
briskly among the cruelties and thinnesses of American civilization and
have shown no obvious horror and pity at the exploitations and the
arid quality of the life lived here around us. Their moral sense had
been deeply stirred by what they saw in France and Belgium, but it
was a moral sense relatively unpractised by deep concern and reflection
over the inadequacies of American democracy. Few of them had used
their vision to create literature impelling us toward a more radiant
American future. And that is why, in spite of their vivid stirrings, they
seem so unconvincing. Their idealism is too new and bright to affect
us, for it comes from men who never cared very particularly about
great creative American ideas. So these writers come to us less like
ardent youth, pouring its energy into the great causes, than like youthful mouthpieces of their strident and belligerent elders. They did not
convert us, but rather drove us farther back into the rightness of
American isolation.

VII

There was something incredibly mean and plebeian about that
abasement into which the war-partisans tried to throw us all. When
we were urged to squander our emotion on a bedevilled Europe, our
intuition told us how much all rich and generous emotions were needed
at home to leaven American civilization. If we refused to export them
it was because we wanted to see them at work here. It is true that
great reaches of American prosperous life were not using generous

emotions for any purpose whatever. But the real antithesis was not between being concerned about luxurious automobiles and being concerned about the saving of France. America's "benevolent neutrality" had been saving the Allies for three years through the ordinary channels of industry and trade. We could afford to export material goods and credit far more than we could afford to export emotional capital. The real antithesis was between interest in expensively exploiting American material life and interest in creatively enhancing American personal and artistic life. The fat and earthy American could be blamed not for not palpitating more richly about France, but for not palpitating more richly about America and her spiritual drouths. The war will leave the country spiritually impoverished, because of the draining away of sentiment into the channels of war. Creative and constructive enterprises will suffer not only through the appalling waste of financial capital in the work of annihilation, but also in the loss of emotional capital in the conviction that war overshadows all other realities. This is the poison of war that disturbs even creative minds. Writers tell us that, after contact with the war, literature seems an idle pastime, if not an offense, in a world of great deeds. Perhaps literature that can be paled by war will not be missed. We may feel vastly relieved at our salvation from so many feeble novels and graceful verses that khaki-clad authors might have given us. But this nobly-sounding sense of the futility of art in a world of war may easily infect conscientious minds. And it is against this infection that we must fight.

VIII

The conservation of American promise is the present task for this generation of malcontents and aloof men and women. If America has lost its political isolation, it is all the more obligated to retain its spiritual integrity. This does not mean any smug retreat from the world, with a belief that the truth is in us and can only be contaminated by contact. It means that the promise of American life is not yet achieved, perhaps not even seen, and that, until it is, there is nothing for us but stern and intensive cultivation of our garden. Our insulation will not be against any great creative ideas or forms that Europe brings. It will be a turning within in order that we may have something to give without. The old American ideas which are still expected to bring life to the world seem stale and archaic. It is grotesque to try to carry democracy to Russia. It is absurd to try to contribute to the world's store of great moving ideas until we have a culture to give. It is absurd for us to think of ourselves as blessing the world with anything unless we hold it much more self-consciously and significantly than we hold anything now. Mere negative freedom will not do as a twentieth-century principle. American ideas must be dynamic or we are presumptuous in offering them to the world.

IX

The war—or American promise: one must choose. One cannot be interested in both. For the effect of the war will be to impoverish American promise. It cannot advance it, however liberals may choose to identify American promise with a league of nations to enforce peace. Americans who desire to cultivate the promises of American life need not lift a finger to obstruct the war, but they cannot conscientiously accept it. However intimately a part of their country they may feel in its creative enterprises toward a better life, they cannot feel themselves a part of it in its futile and self-mutilating enterprise of war. We can be apathetic with a good conscience, for we have other values and ideals for America. Our country will not suffer for our lack of patriotism as long as it has that of our industrial masters. Meanwhile, those who have turned their thinking into war-channels have abdicated their leadership for this younger generation. They have put themselves in a limbo of interests that are not the concerns which worry us about American life and make us feverish and discontented.

Let us compel the war to break in on us, if it must, not go hospitably to meet it. Let us force it perceptibly to batter in our spiritual walls. This attitude need not be a fatuous hiding in the sand, denying realities. When we are broken in on, we can yield to the inexorable. Those who are conscripted will have been broken in on. If they do not want to be martyrs, they will have to be victims. They are entitled to whatever alleviations are possible in an inexorable world. But the others can certainly resist the attitude that blackens the whole conscious sky with war. They can resist the poison which makes art and all the desires for more impassioned living seem idle and even shameful. For many of us, resentment against the war has meant a vivider consciousness of what we are seeking in American life.

This search has been threatened by two classes who have wanted to deflect idealism to the war,—the patriots and the realists. The patriots have challenged us by identifying apathy with disloyalty. The reply is that war-technique in this situation is a matter of national mechanics rather than national ardor. The realists have challenged us by insisting that the war is an instrument in the working-out of beneficent national policy. Our skepticism points out to them how soon their "mastery" becomes "drift," tangled in the fatal drive toward victory as its own end, how soon they become mere agents and expositors of forces as they are. Patriots and realists disposed of, we can pursue creative skepticism with honesty, and at least a hope that in the recoil from war we may find the treasures we are looking for.

5

American Use For German Ideals[1]

In all the intensity of feeling aroused by the war, we have somehow let escape us the consideration that the German ideals are the only broad and seizing ones that have lived in the world in our generation. Mad and barbarous as they may seem to minds accustomed to much thinner and nicer fare, one must have withdrawn far within a provincial Anglo-Saxon shell not to feel the thrill of their sheer heroic power. We have heard so much of the German industrialism and militarism that we have overlooked the reservoir bursting with spiritual energy that twentieth-century Germany has become. The bubbling intellectual and economic energy of present-day Italy is German; Nietzsche has raged through Italian thought, and when it was not Nietzsche it was Hegel. British political thought for forty years has come straight from German sources. What is the new social politics of liberalism but a German collectivism, half-heartedly grafted on a raw stock of individualist "liberty"? Our own progressivism has been a filter through the British strain, diluted with evangelical Christianity. Our educational framework has been German, though unintelligently so. Architecture and art-forms in England and Scandinavia are strikingly German. Town-planning methods and ideals have been lifted bodily. The French seem to have been driven by repulsion into sadly spiteful degenerations of taste in architecture and art-forms. Scarcely a country has been untouched by the German influence. No other country, except Russia,

[1] *The New Republic,* IV (Sept. 4, 1915), 117–119.

has been so flooding its influence over the twentieth-century world.

Surely the final test of a vital and fecund civilization, a civilization that has arrived, is the creation of novel and indigenous art-forms, that express with creative fidelity the spirit of the time. And mainly in Germany has there flowered in these first years of the century an original art—that shown in public buildings and domestic architecture of clean, massive and soaring lines, sculpture of militaristic solidity like the Leipzig and Bismarck monuments, endless variety of decorative and graphic art, printing and household design, civic art as embodied in the laying-out of cities and squares and parks. All this development has been of social art. Music and painting, the private cultivations, have been relatively feeble. Into social, public, reproducible forms has gone this burst of the daring German genius. And everywhere, as in the great ages of creative art, the styles are those in which form grows out of function, so that the work of factories and water-towers and railroad bridges suggests the motives of design. Steel and cement set the lines for wholly novel forms. The world sneers at this art. The world would. But the surge of German art-spirit, with its creation of novel forms, means one thing—that German ideals have a sure spiritual fecundity.

Our American mind has missed the significance of these social forms. We are not used to thinking in terms of the impersonal. The cosmic heroisms of the German ideal fall, too, strangely on our ears. We are not accustomed to gloat over history. It comes to us as a shock to find a people who believe in national spirits which are heroic, and through the German spirit, in a world-spirit; for "the world-spirit," says one of their professor-warriors, "speaks to-day through Germany." We have no analogy for the fact that "the ideal of organization, the thought of a tremendously valuable whole, uniting its free members for effective work, labors in the subconsciousness of millions of Germans, labors even where it does not come to the light of philosophic discussion."

Yet it is scarcely strange that the Germans should expect that a pioneer people like ourselves, of vast and restless energy, should sympathize with a pulsating ideal of organized energy which sinned through excess rather than defect, a true pioneer of twentieth-century civilization, which strove, as a great German has put it, "not for world-dominion, but for a rational organization of the world on the basis of voluntary coöperation, through the welding of a federal union of nations akin in interests and civilization."

The outstanding fact is that native American opinion did not take the side of the German ideal. When we were challenged we went with hearty unanimity against this ideal, the most fertile and potent before our eyes. Whether because we relapsed atavistically to our British roots, or because the incalculable energies of the German ideal really daunted us, we preferred to range our sympathy with the nations that were living on their funded nineteenth-century spiritual capital, rather than breaking new paths and creating new forms for a new time. Believing the German to be in error, we did not even feel a weakness for the tragic and heroic error as against the safe and fuddling plausibility.

I do not say that we did wrong in repudiating the German ideals, I only want to know what our repudiation means. It seemed intuitive rather than deliberate. It seemed to mean that we sensed in the German ideals tastes and endeavors profoundly alien to our own. And although it becomes more and more evident that, whatever the outcome of the war, all the opposing countries will be forced to adopt German organization, German collectivism, and have indeed shattered already most of the threads of their old easy individualism, we have taken the occasion rather to repudiate that modest collectivism which was raising its head here in the shape of the progressive movement in national politics.

We must not let ourselves forget that such an attitude implies a rejection of the most overwhelming and fecund group of ideas and forms in the modern world, ideas which draw all nations after them in imitation, while the nations pour out their lifeblood to crush the generator. Such a renunciation imposes upon us huge responsibility. We cannot seriously think merely of spewing everything German out of our mouths. To refuse the patient German science, the collectivist art, the valor of the German ideals, would be simply to expatriate ourselves from the modern world. They will not halt for any paltry distaste of ours. By taking sides against Germany we have committed ourselves to the arduous task of setting up ideals more worthy than hers to win the allegiance of our generation and time.

In this severe enterprise we shall get little help from the Allies whose cause we find to be that of "civilization." Both England and France are fighting to conserve, rather than to create. Our ideal we can only find in our still pioneer, still struggling American spirit. It will not be found in any purported defence of present "democracy," "civilization," "humanity." The horrors of peace in industrial plutocracies will always make such terms very nebulous. It will have to be in terms of values which secure all the vital fruits of the German ideals, without the tragic costs. It must be just as daring, just as modern, just as realistic. It must set the same social ends, the realization of the individual through the beloved community. It must replace a negative ideal of freedom as the mere removal of barriers by a freedom of expansion which consists, to quote the German, "in making the outward social forms adequate to the measure of the fullness of the national spirit."

Our ideal must be just as creative, just as social as the German, but pragmatically truer and juster. For we find in the German ideal, rousing and heroic as it is, the fatal flaw that has shattered the world's sympathies. The German "does his best in creating a highly organized community for the purpose of furthering in society the historic development of eternal values." Here is the vitiating touch—not in the ideals, but in their direction and animus. For if your enterprise is to be the working out of ideas, your success clearly depends upon living in a world where such ideas can be worked out. If they are set for you and the impulsion is all from behind, you take the truly colossal risk of assuming the perfect congeniality of the universe with your historic ideas. Let there be the smallest perversity in your world, the smallest kink on your historic path, and your ideal becomes a gigantic engine that has broken loose and lies threshing about in endless havoc. To work out a rigid ideal, the resistance you meet must be of the kind that transfigures both you and the resister. Belgium was not transfigured. If resistance is tough, your march becomes like the ruthless hewing-through of might.

It has been the tragedy of the German spirit that it has had to dwell in a perverse universe, so that what from within looked always like the most beneficent working-out of a world-idea seemed from without like the very running-amuck of voracious power. German ideals have, in fact, been floated on the stream of a great will, which has been no more a part of their detailed embodiments than the current is a part of the river craft. The German ideals, embodied in the German forms, are those of a peace-state. They can be conceived of as existing perfectly and indefinitely without this war. The German has confused the current with the rich and precious freight it was bearing. He often suggests a wistful desire to be tolerant. His ideals are tolerant. But, with his will, he is tragically unable to secure mutual understanding. His idea, with its terrific historic momentum, goes on grinding itself out, heedless of the world-situations in which it finds itself.

Our American contribution will then be not to crush the craft but to change the direction of the current. For the will, to substitute a great desire! Our ideals will not be pushes, but goals. For the expression of eternal values we will have the realizing of social ends' through intelligent experimentation. To envisage the good life that we desire for our community and society, and to work towards it with all the intelligence and skill and resources we have—this must be our ideal. Whatever the German has that is life-enhancing—and a nation that lives so habitually at a maximum of energy must have more than we —that we must have, but it must come as the fruit of our intense desire and our intelligence in adapting means to ends, not as an imposed historic value. Our future must be the most intense focussing of our aesthetic and scientific possibilities. In the pragmatism of Dewey and James and the social philosophy of Royce, we have the intellectual tools for such an enterprise, ethical, social, political. We already see this spirit, barred from politics, making its way in educational and civic movements and in the thought of a younger generation. To set up such an American ideal would be to meet in overflowing measure the responsibility we put ourselves under in rejecting the German. To work out a democratic socialized life by deliberately applying intelligence and taste to the command of human and natural resources would be to set before the world an ideal far more fecund than that with which the Germans have challenged us. It would be beneficent and healing. Its power would really be to unite the world.

6

Twilight of Idols[1]

I

Where are the seeds of American promise? Man cannot live by politics alone, and it is small cheer that our best intellects are caught in the political current and see only the hope that America will find her soul in the remaking of the world. If William James were alive would he be accepting the war-situation so easily and complacently? Would he be chiding the over-stimulated intelligence of peace-loving idealists, and excommunicating from the ranks of liberal progress the pitiful remnant of those who struggle "above the battle?" I like to think that his gallant spirit would have called for a war to be gallantly played, with insistent care for democratic values at home, and unequivocal alliance with democratic elements abroad for a peace that should promise more than a mere union of benevolent imperialisms. I think of James now because the recent articles of John Dewey's on the war suggest a slackening in his thought for our guidance and stir, and the inadequacy of his pragmatism as a philosophy of life in this emergency. Whether James would have given us just that note of spiritual adventure which would make the national enterprise seem creative for an American future,—this we can never know. But surely that philosophy of Dewey's which we had been following so uncritically for so long, breaks down almost noisily when it is used to grind out

[1] *The Seven Arts,* II (Oct. 1917), 688–702.

interpretation for the present crisis. These articles on "Conscience and Compulsion," "The Future of Pacifism," "What America Will Fight For," "Conscription of Thought," which *The New Republic* has been printing, seem to me to be a little off-color. A philosopher who senses so little the sinister forces of war, who is so much more concerned over the excesses of the pacifists than over the excesses of military policy, who can feel only amusement at the idea that any one should try to conscript thought, who assumes that the war-technique can be used without trailing along with it the mob-fanaticisms, the injustices and hatreds, that are organically bound up with it, is speaking to another element of the younger intelligentsia than that to which I belong. Evidently the attitudes which war calls out are fiercer and more incalculable than Professor Dewey is accustomed to take into his hopeful and intelligent imagination, and the pragmatist mind, in trying to adjust itself to them, gives the air of grappling, like the pioneer who challenges the arid plains, with a power too big for it. It is not an arena of creative intelligence our country's mind is now, but of mob-psychology. The soldiers who tried to lynch Max Eastman showed that current patriotism is not a product of the will to remake the world. The luxuriant releases of explosive hatred for which peace apparently gives far too little scope cannot be wooed by sweet reasonableness, nor can they be the raw material for the creation of rare liberal political structures. All that can be done is to try to keep your country out of situations where such expressive releases occur. If you have willed the situation, however, or accepted it as inevitable, it is fatuous to protest against the gay debauch of hatred and fear and swagger that must mount and mount, until the heady and virulent poison of war shall have created its own anti-toxin of ruin and disillusionment. To talk as if war were anything else than such a poison is to show that your philosophy has never been confronted with the pathless and the inexorable, and that, only dimly feeling the change, it goes ahead acting as if it had not got out of its depth. Only a lack of practice with a world of human nature so raw-nerved, irrational, uncreative, as an America at war was bound to show itself to be, can account for the singular unsatisfactoriness of these later utterances of Dewey. He did have one moment of hesitation just before the war began, when the war and its external purposes and unifying power seemed the small thing beside that internal adventure which should find our American promise. But that perspective has now disappeared, and one finds Dewey now untainted by skepticism as to our being about a business to which all our idealism should rally. That failure to get guaranties that this country's efforts would obligate the Allies to a democratic world-order Dewey blames on the defection of the pacifists, and then somehow manages to get himself into a "we" who "romantically," as he says, forewent this crucial link of our strategy. Does this easy identification of himself with undemocratically-controlled foreign policy mean that a country is democratic when it accepts what its government does, or that war has a narcotic effect on the pragmatic mind? For Dewey somehow retains his sense of being in the controlling class, and ignores those anxious questions of democrats who have been his disciples but are now resenters of the war.

What I come to is a sense of suddenly being left in the lurch, of suddenly finding that a philosophy upon which I had relied to carry us through no longer works. I find the contrast between the idea that creative intelligence has free functioning in wartime, and the facts of the inexorable situation, too glaring. The contrast between what liberals ought to be doing and saying if democratic values are to be conserved, and what the real forces are imposing upon them, strikes too sternly on my intellectual senses. I should prefer some philosophy of War as the grim and terrible cleanser to this optimism-haunted mood that continues unweariedly to suggest that all can yet be made to work for good in a mad and half-destroyed world. I wonder if James, in the face of such disaster, would not have abandoned his "moral equivalent of war" for an "immoral equivalent" which, in swift and periodic saturnalia, would have acted as vaccination against the sure pestilence of war.

II

Dewey's philosophy is inspiring enough for a society at peace, prosperous and with a fund of progressive good-will. It is a philosophy of hope, of clear-sighted comprehension of materials and means. Where institutions are at all malleable, it is the only clue for improvement. It is scientific method applied to "uplift." But this careful adaptation of means to desired ends, this experimental working out of control over brute forces and dead matter in the interests of communal life, depends on a store of rationality, and is effective only where there is strong desire for progress. It is precisely the school, the institution to which Dewey's philosophy was first applied, that is of all our institutions the most malleable. And it is the will to educate that has seemed, in these days, among all our social attitudes the most rationally motivated. It was education, and almost education alone, that seemed susceptible to the steady pressure of an "instrumental" philosophy. Intelligence really seemed about to come into conscious control of an institution, and that one the most potent in moulding the attitudes needed for a civilized society and the aptitudes needed for the happiness of the individual.

For both our revolutionary conceptions of what education means, and for the intellectual strategy of its approach, this country is immeasurably indebted to the influence of Professor Dewey's philosophy. With these ideas sincerely felt, a rational nation would have chosen education as its national enterprise. Into this it would have thrown its energy though the heavens fell and the earth rocked around it. But the nation did not use its isolation from the conflict to educate itself. It fretted for three years and then let war, not education, be chosen, at the almost unanimous behest of our intellectual class, from motives alien to our cultural needs, and for political ends alien to the happiness of the individual. But nations, of course, are not rational entities, and they act within their most irrational rights when they accept war as the most important thing the nation can do in the face of metaphysical menaces of imperial prestige. What concerns us here is the relative ease with which the pragmatist intellectuals, with Professor Dewey at the head, have moved out their philosophy, bag and baggage, from education to war. So abrupt a change in the direction of the national enterprise, one would have expected to cause more emotion, to demand more apologetics. His optimism may have told Professor Dewey that war would not materially demoralize our growth —would, perhaps, after all, be but an incident in the nation's life— but it is not easy to see how, as we skate toward the bankruptcy of war-billions, there will be resources available for educational enterprise that does not contribute directly to the war-technique. Neither is any passion for growth, for creative mastery, going to flourish among the host of militaristic values and new tastes for power that are springing up like poisonous mushrooms on every hand.

How could the pragmatist mind accept war without more violent protest, without a greater wrench? Either Professor Dewey and his friends felt that the forces were too strong for them, that the war had to be, and it was better to take it up intelligently than to drift blindly in; or else they really expected a gallant war, conducted with jealous regard for democratic values at home and a captivating vision of international democracy as the end of all the toil and pain. If their motive was the first, they would seem to have reduced the scope of possible control of events to the vanishing point. If the war is too strong for you to prevent, how is it going to be weak enough for you to control and mould to your liberal purposes? And if their motive was to shape the war firmly for good, they seem to have seriously miscalculated the fierce urgencies of it. Are they to be content, as the materialization of their hopes, with a doubtful League of Nations and the suppression of the I. W. W.? Yet the numbing power of the war-situation seems to have kept them from realizing what has happened to their philosophy. The betrayal of their first hopes has certainly not discouraged them. But neither has it roused them to a more energetic expression of the forces through which they intend to realize them. I search Professor Dewey's articles in vain for clues as to the specific working-out of our democratic desires, either nationally or internationally, either in the present or in the reconstruction after the war. No programme is suggested, nor is there feeling for present vague popular movements and revolts. Rather are the latter chided, for their own vagueness and impracticalities. Similarly, with the other prophets of instrumentalism who accompany Dewey into the war, democracy remains an unanalyzed term, useful as a call to battle, but not an intellectual tool, turning up fresh sod for the changing future. Is it the political democracy of a plutocratic America that we are fighting for, or is it the social democracy of the new Russia? Which do our rulers really fear more, the menace of Imperial Germany, or the liberating influence of a socialist Russia? In the application of their philosophy to politics, our pragmatists are sliding over this crucial question of ends. Dewey says our ends must be intelligently international rather than chauvinistic. But this gets us little distance along our way.

In this difficult time the light that has been in liberals and radicals has become darkness. If radicals spend their time holding conventions to attest their loyalty and stamp out the "enemies within," they do not spend it in breaking intellectual paths, or giving us shining ideas to which we can attach our faith and conscience. The spiritual apathy from which the more naive of us suffer, and which the others are so busy fighting, arises largely from sheer default of a clear vision that would melt it away. Let the motley crew of ex-socialists, and labor radicals, and liberals, and pragmatist philosophers, who have united for the prosecution of the war, present a coherent and convincing democratic programme, and they will no longer be confronted with the skepticism of the conscientious and the impossibilist. But when the emphasis is on technical organization, rather than organization of ideas, on strategy rather than desires, one begins to suspect that no programme is presented because they have none to present. This burrowing into war-technique hides the void where a democratic philosophy should be. Our intellectuals consort with war-boards in order to keep their minds off the question what the slow masses of the people are really desiring, or toward what the best hope of the country really drives. Similarly the blaze of patriotism on the part of the radicals serves the purpose of concealing the feebleness of their intellectual light.

Is the answer that clear formulation of democratic ends must be postponed until victory in the war is attained? But to make this answer is to surrender the entire case. For the support of the war by radicals, realists, pragmatists, is due—or so they say—to the fact that the war is not only saving the cause of democracy, but is immensely accelerating its progress. Well, what are those gains? How are they to be conserved? What do they lead to? How can we further them? Into what large idea of society do they group? To ignore these questions, and think only of the war-technique and its accompanying devotions, is to undermine the foundations of these people's own faith.

A policy of "win the war first" must be, for the radical, a policy of intellectual suicide. Their support of the war throws upon them the responsibility of showing inch by inch the democratic gains, and of laying out a charter of specific hopes. Otherwise they confess that they are impotent and that the war is submerging their expectations, or that they are not genuinely imaginative and offer little promise for future leadership.

III

It may seem unfair to group Professor Dewey with Mr. Spargo and Mr. Gompers, Mr. A. M. Simons,[1] and the Vigilantes. I do so only because in their acceptance of the war, they are all living out that

[1] John Spargo, author of *The Bitter Cry of Children* (1905) and *Applied*

popular American "instrumental" philosophy which Professor Dewey has formulated in such convincing and fascinating terms. On an infinitely more intelligent plane, he is yet one with them in his confidence that the war is motivated by democratic ends and is being made to serve them. A high mood of confidence and self-righteousness moves them all, a keen sense of control over events that makes them eligible to discipleship under Professor Dewey's philosophy. They are all hostile to impossibilism, to apathy, to any attitude that is not a cheerful and brisk setting to work to use the emergency to consolidate the gains of democracy. Not, Is it being used? but, Let us make a flutter about using it! This unanimity of mood puts the resenter of war out of the arena. But he can still seek to explain why this philosophy which has no place for the inexorable should have adjusted itself so easily to the inexorable of war, and why, although a philosophy of the creative intelligence in using means toward ends, it should show itself so singularly impoverished in its present supply of democratic values.

What is the matter with the philosophy? One has a sense of having come to a sudden, short stop at the end of an intellectual era. In the crisis, this philosophy of intelligent control just does not measure up to our needs. What is the root of this inadequacy that is felt so keenly by our restless minds? Van Wyck Brooks has pointed out searchingly the lack of poetic vision in our pragmatist "awakeners." Is there something in these realistic attitudes that works actually against poetic vision, against concern for the quality of life as above machinery of life? Apparently there is. The war has revealed a younger intelligentsia, trained up in the pragmatic dispensation, immensely ready for the executive ordering of events, pitifully unprepared for the intellectual interpretation or the idealistic focussing of ends. The young men in Belgium, the officers' training corps, the young men being sucked into the councils at Washington and into war-organization everywhere, have among them a definite element, upon whom Dewey, as veteran philosopher, might well bestow a papal blessing. They have absorbed the secret of scientific method as applied to political administration. They are liberal, enlightened, aware. They are touched with creative intelligence toward the solution of political and industrial problems.

Socialism (1912), who in 1917 resigned from the Socialist Party because of its criticism of Wilson's war policy; Samuel Gompers, since 1886 president of the American Federation of Labor; Algie M. Simons, socialist historian, author of *Social Forces in American History* (1911).

They are a wholly new force in American life, the product of the swing in the colleges from a training that emphasized classical studies to one that emphasized political and economic values. Practically all this element, one would say, is lined up in service of the war-technique. There seems to have been a peculiar congeniality between the war and these men. It is as if the war and they had been waiting for each other. One wonders what scope they would have had for their intelligence without it. Probably most of them would have gone into industry and devoted themselves to sane reorganization schemes. What is significant is that it is the technical side of the war that appeals to them, not the interpretative or political side. The formulation of values and ideals, the production of articulate and suggestive thinking, had not, in their education, kept pace, to any extent whatever, with their technical aptitude. The result is that the field of intellecual formulation is very poorly manned by this younger intelligentsia. While they organize the war, formulation of opinion is left largely in the hands of professional patriots, sensational editors, archaic radicals. The intellectual work of this younger intelligentsia is done by the sedition-hunting Vigilantes, and by the saving remnant of older liberals. It is true, Dewey calls for a more attentive formulation of war-purposes and ideas, but he calls largely to deaf ears. His disciples have learned all too literally the instrumental attitude toward life, and, being immensely intelligent and energetic, they are making themselves efficient instruments of the war-technique, accepting with little question the ends as announced from above. That those ends are largely negative does not concern them, because they have never learned not to subordinate idea to technique. Their education has not given them a coherent system of large ideas, or a feeling for democratic goals. They have, in short, no clear philosophy of life except that of intelligent service, the admirable adaptation of means to ends. They are vague as to what kind of a society they want, or what kind of society America needs, but they are equipped with all the administrative attitudes and talents necessary to attain it.

To those of us who have taken Dewey's philosophy almost as our American religion, it never occurred that values could be subordinated to technique. We were instrumentalists, but we had our private utopias so clearly before our minds that the means fell always into its place as contributory. And Dewey, of course, always meant his philosophy, when taken as a philosophy of life, to start with values. But there was always that unhappy ambiguity in his doctrine as to just how values were created, and it became easier and easier to assume that just any growth was justified and almost any activity valuable so long as it achieved ends. The American, in living out this philosophy, has habitually confused results with product, and been content with getting somewhere without asking too closely whether it was the desirable place to get. It is now becoming plain that unless you start with the vividest kind of poetic vision, your instrumentalism is likely to land you just where it has landed this younger intelligentsia which is so happily and busily engaged in the national enterprise of war. You must have your vision and you must have your technique. The practical effect of Dewey's philosophy has evidently been to develop the sense of the latter at the expense of the former. Though he himself would develop them together, even in him there seems to be a flagging of values, under the influence of war. *The New Republic* honorably clamors for the Allies to subordinate military strategy to political ends, technique to democratic values. But war always undermines values. It is the outstanding lesson of the whole war that statesmen cannot be trusted to get this perspective right, that their only motto is, first to win and then grab what they can. The struggle against this statesman-like animus must be a losing one as long as we have not very clear and very determined and very revolutionary democratic ideas and programmes to challenge them with. The trouble with our situation is not only that values have been generally ignored in favor of technique, but that those who have struggled to keep values foremost, have been too bloodless and too near-sighted in their vision. The defect of any philosophy of "adaptation" or "adjustment," even when it means adjustment to changing, living experience, is that there is no provision for thought or experience getting beyond itself. If your ideal is to be adjustment to your situation, in radiant co-operation with reality, then your success is likely to be just that and no more. You never transcend anything. You grow, but your spirit never jumps out of your skin to go on wild adventures. If your policy as a publicist reformer is to take what you can get, you are likely to find that you get something less than you should be willing to take. Italy in the settlement is said to be demanding one hundred in order to get twenty, and this machiavellian principle might well be adopted by the radical. Vision must constantly outshoot technique, opportunist efforts usually achieve less even than what seemed obviously possible. An impossibilist élan that appeals to desire will often carry further. A philosophy of adjustment will not even make for adjustment. If you try merely to "meet" situations as they come, you will not even meet them. Instead you will only pile up behind you deficits and arrears that will some day bankrupt you.

We are in the war because an American Government practised a philosophy of adjustment, and an instrumentalism for minor ends, instead of creating new values and setting at once a large standard to which the nations might repair. An intellectual attitude of mere adjustment, of mere use of the creative intelligence to make your progress, must end in caution, regression, and a virtual failure to effect even that change which you so clear-sightedly and desirously see. This is the root of our dissatisfaction with much of the current political and social realism that is preached to us. It has everything good and wise except the obstreperous vision that would drive and draw all men into it.

IV

The working-out of this American philosophy in our intellectual life then has meant an exaggerated emphasis on the mechanics of life at the expense of the quality of living. We suffer from a real shortage of spiritual values. A philosophy that worked when we were trying to get that material foundation for American life in which more impassioned living could flourish no longer works when we are faced with inexorable disaster and the hysterias of the mob. The note of complacency which we detect in the current expressions of this philosophy has a bad taste. The congruous note for the situation would seem to be, on the contrary, that of robust desperation,—a desperation that shall rage and struggle until new values come out of the travail, and we see some glimmering of our democratic way. In the creation of these new values, we may expect the old philosophy, the old radicalism, to be helpless. It has found a perfectly definite level, and there is no reason to think that it will not remain there. Its flowering appears in the technical organization of the war by an earnest group of young liberals, who direct their course by an opportunist programme of State-socialism at home and a league of benevolently-imperialistic nations abroad. At their best they can give us a government by prudent, enlightened college men instead of by politicians. At their best, they can abolish war by making everybody a partner in the booty of exploitation. That is all, and it is technically admirable. Only there is nothing in the outlook that touches in any way the happiness of the individual, the vivifying of the personality, the comprehension of social forces, the flair of art,—in other words, the quality of life. Our intellectuals have failed us as value-creators, even as value-emphasizers. The allure of the martial in war has passed only to be succeeded by the allure of the technical. The allure of fresh and true ideas, of free speculation, of artistic vigor, of cultural styles, of intelligence suffused by feeling, and feeling given fibre and outline by intelligence, has not come, and can hardly come, we see now, while our reigning philosophy is an instrumental one.

Whence can come this allure? Only from those who are thorough malcontents. Irritation at things as they are, disgust at the continual frustrations and aridities of American life, deep dissatisfaction with self and with the groups that give themselves forth as hopeful—out of such moods there might be hammered new values. The malcontents would be men and women who could not stomach the war, or the reactionary idealism that has followed in its train. They are quite through with the professional critics and classicists who have let cultural values die through their own personal ineptitude. Yet these malcontents have no intention of being cultural vandals, only to slay. They are not barbarians, but seek the vital and the sincere everywhere. All they want is a new orientation of the spirit that shall be modern, an orientation to accompany that technical orientation which is fast coming, and which the war accelerates. They will be harsh and often bad-tempered, and they will feel that the break-up of things is no time for mellowness. They will have a taste for spiritual adventure, and for sinister imaginative excursions. It will not be Puritanism so much as complacency that they will fight. A tang, a bitterness, an intellectual fibre, a verve, they will look for in literature, and their most virulent enemies will be those unaccountable radicals who are still morally servile, and are now trying to suppress all free speculation in the interests of nationalism. Something more mocking, more irreverent, they will constantly want. They will take institutions very lightly, indeed will never fail to be surprised at the seriousness with which good radicals take the stated offices and systems. Their own contempt will be scarcely veiled, and they will be glad if they can tease, provoke, irritate thought on any subject. These malcontents will be more or less of the American tribe of talent who used either to go immediately to Europe, or starved submissively at home. But these people will neither go to Europe, nor starve submissively. They are too much entangled emotionally in the possibilities of American life to leave it, and they have no desire whatever to starve. So they are likely to go ahead beating their heads at the wall until they are either bloody or light appears. They will give offense to their elders who cannot see what all the concern is about, and they will hurt the more middle-aged sense of adventure upon which the better integrated minds of the younger generation will have compromised. Optimism is often compensatory, and the optimistic mood in American thought may mean merely that American life is too terrible to face. A more skeptical, malicious, desperate, ironical mood may actually be the sign of more vivid and more stirring life fermenting in America today. It may be a sign of hope. That thirst for more of the intellectual "war and laughter" that we find Nietzsche calling us to may bring us satisfactions that optimism-haunted philosophies could never bring. Malcontentedness may be the beginning of promise. That is why I evoked the spirit of William James, with its gay passion for ideas, and its freedom of speculation, when I felt the slightly pedestrian gait into which the war had brought pragmatism. It is the creative desire more than the creative intelligence that we shall need if we are ever to fly.

7

The State[1]

I

To most of the Americans of the classes which consider themselves significant the war brought a sense of the sanctity of the State, which, if they had had time to think about it, would have seemed a sudden and surprising alteration in their habits of thought. In times of peace, we usually ignore the State in favor of partisan political controversies, or personal struggles for office, or the pursuit of party policies. It is the Government rather than the State with which the politically minded are concerned. The State is reduced to a shadowy emblem which comes to consciousness only on occasions of patriotic holiday.

Government is obviously composed of common and unsanctified men, and is thus a legitimate object of criticism and even contempt. If your own party is in power, things may be assumed to be moving safely enough; but if the opposition is in, then clearly all safety and honor have fled the State. Yet you do not put it to yourself in quite that way. What you think is only that there are rascals to be turned out of a very practical machinery of offices and functions which you take for granted. When we say that Americans are lawless, we usually mean that they are less conscious than other peoples of the august

[1] Bourne died while composing the first draft of this essay. Left unfinished and unpaginated, it was published, in incorrect sequences, in James Oppenheim, ed., *Untimely Papers* (New York: B. W. Huebsch, 1919). It is now in the Bourne MSS, Columbia University Libraries.

majesty of the institution of the State as it stands behind the objective government of men and laws which we see. In a republic the men who hold office are indistinguishable from the mass. Very few of them possess the slightest personal dignity with which they could endow their political rôle; even if they ever thought of such a thing. And they have no class distinction to give them glamor. In a Republic the Government is obeyed grumblingly, because it has no bedazzlements or sanctities to gild it. If you are a good old-fashioned democrat, you rejoice at this fact, you glory in the plainness of a system where every citizen has become a king. If you are more sophisticated you bemoan the passing of dignity and honor from affairs of State. But in practice, the democrat does not in the least treat his elected citizen with the respect due to a king, nor does the sophisticated citizen pay tribute to the dignity even when he finds it. The republican state has almost no trappings to appeal to the common man's emotions. What it has are of military origin, and in an unmilitary era such as we have passed through since the Civil War, even military trappings have been scarcely seen. In such an era the sense of the State almost fades out of the consciousness of men.

With the shock of war, however, the State comes into its own again. The Government, with no mandate from the people, without consultation of the people, conducts all the negotiations, the backing and filling, the menaces and explanations, which slowly bring it into collision with some other Government, and gently and irresistibly slides the country into war. For the benefit of proud and haughty citizens, it is fortified with a list of the intolerable insults which have been hurled towards us by the other nations; for the benefit of the liberal and beneficent, it has a convincing set of moral purposes which our going to war will achieve; for the ambitious and aggressive classes, it can gently whisper of a bigger rôle in the destiny of the world. The result is that, even in those countries where the business of declaring war is theoretically in the hands of representatives of the people, no legislature has ever been known to decline the request of an Executive, which has conducted all foreign affairs in utter privacy and irresponsibility, that it order the nation into battle. Good democrats are wont to feel the crucial difference between a State in which the popular Parliament or Congress declares war, and the State in which an absolute monarch or ruling class declares war. But, put to the stern pragmatic test, the difference is not striking. In the freest of republics as well as in the

most tyrannical of Empires, all foreign policy, the diplomatic negotiations which produce or forestall war, are equally the private property
of the Executive part of the Government, and are equally exposed to
no check whatever from popular bodies, or the people voting as a mass
themselves.

The moment war is declared, however, the mass of the people,
through some spiritual alchemy, become convinced that they have
willed and executed the deed themselves. They then with the exception
of a few malcontents, proceed to allow themselves to be regimented,
coerced, deranged in all the environments of their lives, and turned
into a solid manufactory of destruction toward whatever other people
may have, in the appointed scheme of things, come within the range
of the Government's disapprobation. The citizen throws off his contempt and indifference to Government, identifies himself with its purposes, revives all his military memories and symbols, and the State
once more walks, an august presence, through the imaginations of
men. Patriotism becomes the dominant feeling, and produces immediately that intense and hopeless confusion between the relations which
the individual bears and should bear towards the society of which he
is a part.

The patriot loses all sense of the distinction between State, nation
and government. In our quieter moments, the Nation or Country
forms the basic idea of society. We think vaguely of a loose population
spreading over a certain geographical portion of the earth's surface,
speaking a common language, and living in a homogeneous civilization.
Our idea of Country concerns itself with the non-political aspects of
a people, its ways of living, its personal traits, its literature and art,
its characteristic attitudes towards life. We are Americans because we
live in a certain bounded territory, because our ancestors have carried
on a great enterprise of pioneering and colonization, because we live
in certain kinds of communities which have a certain look and express
their aspirations in certain ways. We can see that our civilization is
different from contiguous civilizations like the Indian and Mexican.
The institutions of our country form a certain network which affects
us vitally and intrigues our thoughts in a way that these other civilizations do not. We are a part of country, for better or for worse. We
have arrived in it through the operation of physiological laws, and
not in any way through our own choice. By the time we have reached
what are called years of discretion, its influences have molded our

habits, our values, our ways of thinking, so that however aware we may become, we never really lose the stamp of our civilization, or could be mistaken for the child of any other country. Our feeling for our fellow-countrymen is one of similarity or of mere acquaintance. We may be intensely proud of and congenial to our particular network of civilization, or we may detest most of its qualities and rage at its defects. This does not alter the fact that we are inextricably bound up in it. The Country, as an inescapable group into which we are born, and which makes us its particular kind of a citizen of the world, seems to be a fundamental fact of our consciousness, an irreducible minimum of social feeling.

Now this feeling for country is essentially noncompetitive; we think of our own people merely as living on the earth's surface along with other groups, pleasant or objectionable as they may be, but fundamentally as sharing the earth with them. In our simple conception of country there is no more feeling of rivalry with other peoples than there is in our feeling for our family. Our interest turns within rather than without, is intensive and not belligerent. We grow up and our imaginations gradually stake out the world we live in, they need no greater conscious satisfaction for their gregarious impulses than this sense of a great mass of people to whom we are more or less attuned, and in whose institutions we are functioning. The feeling for country would be an uninflatable maximum were it not for the ideas of State and Government which are associated with it. Country is a concept of peace, of tolerance, of living and letting live. But State is essentially a concept of power, of competition; it signifies a group in its aggressive aspects. And we have the misfortune of being born not only into a country but into a State, and as we grow up we learn to mingle the two feelings into a hopeless confusion.

The State is the country acting as a political unit, it is the group acting as a repository of force, determiner of law, arbiter of justice. International politics is a "power politics" because it is a relation of States and that is what States infallibly and calamitously are, huge aggregations of human and industrial force that may be hurled against each other in war. When a country acts as a whole in relation to another country, or in imposing laws on its own inhabitants, or in coercing or punishing individuals or minorities, it is acting as a State. The history of America as a country is quite different from that of America as a State. In one case it is the drama of the pioneering conquest of the land, of the growth of wealth and the ways in which it was used, of the enterprise of education, and the carrying out of spiritual ideals, of the struggle of economic classes. But as a State, its history is that of playing a part in the world, making war, obstructing international trade, preventing itself from being split to pieces, punishing those citizens whom society agrees are offensive, and collecting money to pay for all.

Government, on the other hand, is synonymous with neither State nor Nation. It is the machinery by which the nation, organized as a State, carries out its State functions. Government is a framework of the administration of laws, and the carrying out of the public force. Government is the idea of the State put into practical operation in the hands of definite, concrete, fallible men. It is the visible sign of the invisible grace. It is the word made flesh. And it has necessarily the limitations inherent in all practicality. Government is the only form in which we can envisage the State, but it is by no means identical with it. That the State is a mystical conception is something that must never be forgotten. Its glamor and its significance linger behind the framework of Government and direct its activities.

Wartime brings the ideal of the State out into very clear relief, and reveals attitudes and tendencies that were hidden. In times of peace the sense of the State flags in a republic that is not militarized. For war is essentially the health of the State. The ideal of the State is that within its territory its power and influence should be universal. As the Church is the medium for the spiritual salvation of men, so the State is thought of as the medium for his political salvation. Its idealism is a rich blood flowing to all the members of the body politic. And it is precisely in war that the urgency for union seems greatest, and the necessity for universality seems most unquestioned. The State is the organization of the herd to act offensively or defensively against another herd similarly organized. The more terrifying the occasion for defense, the closer will become the organization and the more coercive the influence upon each member of the herd. War sends the current of purpose and activity flowing down to the lowest level of the herd, and to its most remote branches. All the activities of society are linked together as fast as possible to this central purpose of making a military offensive or a military defense, and the State becomes what in peace-times it has vainly struggled to become—the inexorable arbiter and determinant of men's businesses and attitudes and opinions. The slack is taken up, the cross-currents fade out, and the nation moves lumber-ingly and slowly, but with ever accelerated speed and integration, to-wards the great end, towards that "peacefulness of being at war," of which L. P. Jacks has so unforgettably spoken.[2]

The classes which are able to play an active and not merely a passive rôle in the organization for war get a tremendous liberation of activity and energy. Individuals are jolted out of their old routine, many of them are given new positions of responsibility, new techniques must be learnt. Wearing home ties are broken and women who would have remained attached with infantile bonds are liberated for service overseas. A vast sense of rejuvenescence pervades the significant classes, a sense of new importance in the world. Old national ideals are taken out, re-adapted to the purpose and used as universal touchstones, or molds into which all thought is poured. Every individual citizen who in peacetimes had no function to perform by which he could imagine himself an expression or living fragment of the State becomes an active amateur agent of the Government in reporting spies and dis-loyalists, in raising Government funds, or in propagating such meas-ures as are considered necessary by officialdom. Minority opinion, which in times of peace, was only irritating and could not be dealt with by law unless it was conjoined with actual crime, becomes, with the outbreak of war, a case for outlawry. Criticism of the State, objec-tions to war, luke-warm opinions concerning the necessity or the beauty of conscription, are made subject to ferocious penalties, far exceeding in severity those affixed to actual pragmatic crimes. Public opinion, as expressed in the newspapers, and the pulpits and the schools, becomes one solid block. "Loyalty," or rather war orthodoxy, becomes the sole test for all professions, techniques, occupations. Particularly is this true in the sphere of the intellectual life. There the smallest taint is held to spread over the whole soul, so that a professor of physics is *ipso facto* disqualified to teach physics or to hold honorable place in a university—the republic of learning—if he is at all unsound on the war. Even mere association with persons thus tainted is considered to disqualify a teacher. Anything pertaining to the enemy becomes taboo. His books are suppressed wherever possible, his language is forbidden. His artistic products are considered to convey in the subtlest spiritual way taints of vast poison to the soul that permits itself to enjoy them. So enemy music is suppressed, and energetic measures of opprobrium

[2] Lawrence Pearsall Jacks, Oxford philosopher and Unitarian clergyman.

taken against those whose artistic consciences are not ready to perform such an act of self-sacrifice. The rage for loyal conformity works impartially, and often in diametric opposition to other orthodoxies and traditional conformities, or even ideals. The triumphant orthodoxy of the State is shown at its apex perhaps when Christian preachers lose their pulpits for taking more or less in literal terms the Sermon on the Mount, and Christian zealots are sent to prison for twenty years for distributing tracts which argue that war is unscriptural.

War is the health of the State. It automatically sets in motion throughout society those irresistible forces for uniformity, for passionate cooperation with the Government in coercing into obedience the minority groups and individuals which lack the larger herd sense. The machinery of government sets and enforces the drastic penalties, the minorities are either intimidated into silence, or brought slowly around by a subtle process of persuasion which may seem to them really to be converting them. Of course the ideal of perfect loyalty, perfect uniformity is never really attained. The classes upon whom the amateur work of coercion falls are unwearied in their zeal, but often their agitation, instead of converting, merely serves to stiffen their resistance. Minorities are rendered sullen, and some intellectual opinion bitter and satirical. But in general, the nation in war-time attains a uniformity of feeling, a hierarchy of values culminating at the undisputed apex of the State ideal, which could not possibly be produced through any other agency than war. Other values such as artistic creation, knowledge, reason, beauty, the enhancement of life, are instantly and almost unanimously sacrificed, and the significant classes who have constituted themselves the amateur agents of the State are engaged not only in sacrificing these values for themselves but in coercing all other persons into sacrificing them.

War—or at least modern war waged by a democratic republic against a powerful enemy—seems to achieve for a nation almost all that the most inflamed political idealist could desire. Citizens are no longer indifferent to their Government, but each cell of the body politic is brimming with life and activity. We are at last on the way to full realization of that collective community in which each individual somehow contains the virtue of the whole. In a nation at war, every citizen identifies himself with the whole, and feels immensely strengthened in that identification. The purpose and desire of the collective community live in each person who throws himself wholeheartedly into the cause of war. The impeding distinction between society and the individual is almost blotted out. At war, the individual becomes almost identical with his society. He achieves a superb self-assurance, an intuition of the rightness of all his ideas and emotions, so that in the suppression of opponents or heretics he is invincibly strong; he feels behind him all the power of the collective community. The individual as social being in war seems to have achieved almost his apotheosis. Not for any religious impulse could the American nation have been expected to show such devotion *en masse,* such sacrifice and labor. Certainly not for any secular good, such as universal education or the subjugation of nature, would it have poured forth its treasure and its life, or would it have permitted such stern coercive measures to be taken against it, such as conscripting its money and its men. But for the sake of a war of offensive self-defense, undertaken to support a difficult cause to the slogan of "democracy," it would reach the highest level ever known of collective effort.

For these secular goods, connected with the enhancement of life, the education of man and the use of the intelligence to realize reason and beauty in the nation's communal living, are alien to our traditional ideal of the State. The State is intimately connected with war, for it is the organization of the collective community when it acts in a political manner, and to act in a political manner towards a rival group has meant, throughout all history—war.

There is nothing invidious in the use of the term, "herd," in connection with the State. It is merely an attempt to reduce closer to first principles the nature of this institution in the shadow of which we all live, move and have our being. Ethnologists are generally agreed that human society made its first appearance as the human pack and not as a collection of individuals or of couples. The herd is in fact the original unit, and only as it was differentiated did personal individuality develop. All the most primitive surviving tribes of men are shown to live in a very complex but very rigid social organization where opportunity for individuation is scarcely given. These tribes remain strictly organized herds, and the difference between them and the modern State is one of degree of sophistication and variety of organization, and not of kind.

Psychologists recognize the gregarious impulse as one of the strongest primitive pulls which keeps together the herds of the different species of higher animals. Mankind is no exception. Our pugnacious evolutionary history has prevented the impulse from ever dying out. This gregarious impulse is the tendency to imitate, to conform, to coalesce together, and is most powerful when the herd believes itself threatened with attack. Animals crowd together for protection, and men become most conscious of their collectivity at the threat of war. Consciousness of collectivity brings confidence and a feeling of massed strength, which in turn arouses pugnacity and the battle is on. In civilized man, the gregarious impulse acts not only to produce concerted action for defense, but also to produce identity of opinion. Since thought is a form of behavior, the gregarious impulse floods up into its realms and demands that sense of uniform thought which wartime produces so successfully. And it is in this flooding of the conscious life of society that gregariousness works its havoc.

For just as in modern societies the sex-instinct is enormously over-supplied for the requirements of human propagation, so the gregarious impulse is enormously over-supplied for the work of protection which it is called upon to perform. It would be quite enough if we were gregarious enough to enjoy the companionship of others, to be able to coöperate with them, and to feel a slight malaise at solitude. Unfortunately, however, this impulse is not content with these reasonable and healthful demands, but insists that like-mindedness shall prevail everywhere, in all departments of life. So that all human progress, all novelty, and non-conformity, must be carried against the resistance of this tyrannical herd-instinct which drives the individual into obedience and conformity with the majority. Even in the most modern and enlightened societies this impulse shows little sign of abating. As it is driven by inexorable economic demand out of the sphere of utility, it seems to fasten itself ever more fiercely in the realm of feeling and opinion, so that conformity comes to be a thing aggressively desired and demanded.

The gregarious impulse keeps its hold all the more virulently because when the group is in motion or is taking any positive action, this feeling of being with and supported by the collective herd very greatly feeds that will to power, the nourishment of which the individual organism so constantly demands. You feel powerful by conforming, and you feel forlorn and helpless if you are out of the crowd. While even if you do not get any access of power by thinking and feeling just as everybody else in your group does, you get at least the warm feeling of obedience, the soothing irresponsibility of protection.

Joining as it does to these very vigorous tendencies of the individual —the pleasure in power and the pleasure in obedience—this gregarious impulse becomes irresistible in society. War stimulates it to the highest possible degree, sending the influences of its mysterious herd-current with its inflations of power and obedience to the farthest reaches of the society, to every individual and little group that can possibly be affected. And it is these impulses which the State—the organization of the entire herd, the entire collectivity—is founded on and makes use of.

There is, of course, in the feeling towards the State a large element of pure filial mysticism. The sense of insecurity, the desire for protection, sends one's desire back to the father and mother, with whom is associated the earliest feeling of protection. It is not for nothing that one's State is still thought of as Father or Motherland, that one's relation towards it is conceived in terms of family affection. The war has shown that nowhere under the shock of danger have these primitive childlike attitudes failed to assert themselves again, as much in this country as anywhere. If we have not the intense Father-sense of the German who worships his Vaterland, at least in Uncle Sam we have a symbol of protecting, kindly authority, and in the many Mother-posters of the Red Cross, we see how easily in the more tender functions of war service, the ruling organization is conceived in family terms. A people at war have become in the most literal sense obedient, respectful, trustful children again, full of that naïve faith in the all-wisdom and all-power of the adult who takes care of them, imposes his mild but necessary rule upon them and in whom they lose their responsibility and anxieties. In this recrudescence of the child, there is great comfort, and a certain influx of power. On most people the strain of being an independent adult weighs heavily, and upon none more than those members of the significant classes who have had bequeathed to them or have assumed the responsibilities of governing. The State provides the convenientest of symbols under which these classes can retain all the actual pragmatic satisfaction of governing, but can rid themselves of the psychic burden of adulthood. They continue to direct industry and government and all the institutions of society pretty much as before, but in their own conscious eyes and in the eyes of the general public, they are turned from their selfish and predatory ways, and have become loyal servants of society, or something greater than they—the State. The man who moves from the direction of a large business in New York to a post in the war management industrial service in Washington does not apparently alter very much his power or his administrative technique. But psychically, what a transfiguration has occurred! His is now not only the power but the glory! And his sense of satisfaction is directly proportional not to the genuine amount of personal sacrifice that may be involved in the change but to the extent to which he retains his industrial prerogatives and sense of command.

From members of this class a certain insuperable indignation arises if the change from private enterprise to State service involves any real loss of power and personal privilege. If there is to be pragmatic sacrifice, let it be, they feel, on the field of honor, in the traditionally acclaimed deaths by battle, in that detour to suicide, as Nietzsche calls war. The State in wartime supplies satisfaction for this very real craving, but its chief value is the opportunity it gives for this regression to infantile attitudes. In your reaction to an imagined attack on your country or an insult to its government, you draw closer to the herd for protection, you conform in word and deed, and you insist vehemently that everybody else shall think, speak and act together. And you fix your adoring gaze upon the State, with a truly filial look, as upon the Father of the flock, the quasi-personal symbol of the strength of the herd, and the leader and determinant of your definite action and ideas.

The members of the working-classes, that portion at least which does not identify itself with the significant classes and seek to imitate it and rise to it, are notoriously less affected by the symbolism of the State, or, in other words, are less patriotic than the significant classes. For theirs is neither the power nor the glory. The State in wartime does not offer them the opportunity to regress, for, never having acquired social adulthood, they cannot lose it. If they have been drilled and regimented, as by the industrial régime of the last.century, they go out docilely enough to do battle for their State, but they are almost entirely without that filial sense and even without that herd-intellect sense which operates so powerfully among their "betters." They live habitually in an industrial serfdom, by which though nominally free, they are in practice as a class bound to a system of machine-production the implements of which they do not own, and in the distribution of whose product they have not the slightest voice, except what they can occasionally exert by a veiled intimidation which draws slightly more of the product in their direction. From such serfdom, military conscription is not so great a change. But into the military enterprise they go, not with those hurrahs of the significant classes whose instincts war so powerfully feeds, but with the same apathy with which they enter and continue in the industrial enterprise.

From this point of view, war can be called almost an upper-class sport. The novel interests and excitements it provides, the inflations of power, the satisfaction it gives to those very tenacious human impulses—gregariousness and parent-regression—endow it with all the qualities of a luxurious collective game which is felt intensely just in proportion to the sense of significant rule the person has in the class-division of his society. A country at war—particularly our own country at war—does not act as a purely homogeneous herd. The significant classes have all the herd-feeling in all its primitive intensity, but there are barriers, or at least differentials of intensity, so that this feeling does not flow freely without impediment throughout the entire nation. A modern country represents a long historical and social process of disaggregation of the herd. The nation at peace is not a group, it is a network of myriads of groups representing the coöperation and similar feeling of men on all sorts of planes and in all sorts of human interests and enterprises. In every modern industrial country, there are parallel planes of economic classes with divergent attitudes and institutions and interests—bourgeois and proletariat, with their many subdivisions according to power and function, and even their interweaving, such as those more highly skilled workers who habitually identify themselves with the owning and the significant classes and strive to raise themselves to the bourgeois level, imitating their cultural standards and manners. Then there are religious groups with a certain definite, though weakening sense of kinship, and there are the powerful ethnic groups which behave almost as cultural colonies in the New World, clinging tenaciously to language and historical tradition, though their herdishness is usually founded on cultural rather than State symbols. There are even certain vague sectional groupings. All these small sects, political parties, classes, levels, interests, may act as foci for herd-feelings. They intersect and interweave, and the same person may be a member of several different groups lying at different planes. Different occasions will set off his herd-feeling in one direction or another. In a religious crisis he will be intensely conscious of the necessity that his sect (or sub-herd) may prevail; in a political campaign, that his party shåll triumph.

To the spread of herd-feeling, therefore, all these smaller herds offer resistance. To the spread of that herd-feeling which arises from the threat of war, and which would normally involve the entire nation, the only groups which make serious resistance are those, of course, which continue to identify themselves with the other nation from which they or their parents have come. In times of peace they are for all practical purposes citizens of their new country. They keep alive their ethnic traditions more as a luxury than anything. Indeed these traditions tend rapidly to die out except where they connect with some still unresolved nationalistic cause abroad, with some struggle for freedom, or some irredentism. If they are consciously opposed by a too invidious policy of Americanism, they tend to be strengthened. And in time of war, these ethnic elements which have any traditional connection with the enemy, even though most of the individuals may have little real sympathy with the enemy's cause, are naturally lukewarm to the herd-feeling of the nation which goes back to State traditions in which they have no share. But to the natives imbued with State-feeling, any such resistance or apathy is intolerable. This herd-feeling, this newly awakened consciousness of the State, demands universality. The leaders of the significant classes, who feel most intensely this State-compulsion, demand a one hundred per cent. Americanism, among one hundred per cent. of the population. The State is a jealous God and will brook no rivals. Its sovereignty must pervade every one, and all feeling must be run into the stereotyped forms of romantic patriotic militarism which is the traditional expression of the State herd-feeling.

Thus arises conflict within the State. War becomes almost a sport between the hunters and the hunted. The pursuit of enemies within outweighs in psychic attractiveness the assault on the enemy without. The whole terrific force of the State is brought to bear against the heretics. The nation boils with a slow insistent fever. A white terrorism is carried on by the Government against pacifists, Socialists, enemy aliens, and a milder unofficial persecution against all persons or movements that can be imagined as connected with the enemy. War, which should be the health of the State, unifies all the bourgeois elements and the common people, and outlaws the rest. The revolutionary proletariat shows more resistance to this unification, is, as we have seen, psychically out of the current. Its vanguard, as the I. W. W., is remorselessly pursued, in spite of the proof that it is a symptom, not a cause, and its prosecution increases the disaffection of labor and intensifies the friction instead of lessening it.

But the emotions that play around the defense of the State do not take into consideration the pragmatic results. A nation at war, led by its significant classes, is engaged in liberating certain of its impulses which have had all too little exercise in the past. It is getting certain satisfactions and the actual conduct of the war or the condition of the country are really incidental to the enjoyment of new forms of virtue and power and aggressiveness. If it could be shown conclusively that the persecution of slightly disaffected elements actually increased enormously the difficulties of production and the organization of the war technique, it would be found that public policy would scarcely change. The significant classes must have their pleasure in hunting down and chastizing everything that they feel instinctively to be not imbued with the current State-enthusiasm, though the State itself be actually impeded in its efforts to carry out those objects for which they are passionately contending. The best proof of this is that with a pursuit of plotters that has continued with ceaseless vigilance ever since the beginning of the war in Europe, the concrete crimes unearthed and punished have been fewer than those prosecutions for the mere crime of opinion or the expression of sentiments critical of the State or the national policy. The punishment for opinion has been far more ferocious and unintermittent than the punishment of pragmatic crime. Unimpeachable Anglo-Saxon Americans who were freer of pacifist or socialist utterance than the State-obsessed ruling public opinion, received heavier penalties and even greater opprobrium, in many instances, than the definitely hostile German plotter. A public opinion which, almost without protest, accepts as just, adequate, beautiful, deserved and in fitting harmony with ideals of liberty and freedom of speech, a sentence of twenty years in prison for mere utterances, no matter what they may be, shows itself to be suffering from a kind of social derangement of values, a sort of social neurosis, that deserves analysis and comprehension.

On our entrance into the war, there were many persons who predicted exactly this derangement of values, who feared lest democracy suffer more at home from an America at war than could be gained for democracy abroad. That fear has been amply justified. The question whether the American nation would act like an enlightened democracy going to war for the sake of high ideals, or like a State-obsessed herd, has been decisively answered. The record is written and cannot be erased. History will decide whether the terrorization of opinion, and the regimentation of life was justified under the most idealistic of democratic administrations. It will see that when the American nation had ostensibly a chance to conduct a gallant war, with scrupulous regard to the safety of democratic values at home, it chose rather to adopt all the most obnoxious and coercive techniques of the enemy and of the other countries at war, and to rival in intimidation and ferocity of punishment the worst governmental systems of the age. For its former unconsciousness and disrespect of the State ideal, the nation apparently paid the penalty in a violent swing to the other extreme. It acted so exactly like a herd in its irrational coercion of minorities that there is no artificiality in interpreting the progress of the war in terms of the herd psychology. It unwittingly brought out into the strongest relief the true characteristics of the State and its intimate alliance with war. It provided for the enemies of war and the critics of the State the most telling arguments possible. The new passion for the State ideal unwittingly set in motion and encouraged forces that threaten very materially to reform the State. It has shown those who are really determined to end war that the problem is not the mere simple one of finishing a war that will end war.

For war is a complicated way in which a nation acts, and it acts so out of a spiritual compulsion which pushes it on, perhaps against all its interests, all its real desires, and all its real sense of values. It is States that make wars and not nations, and the very thought and almost necessity of war is bound up with the ideal of the State. Not for centuries have nations made war; in fact the only historical example of nations making war is the great barbarian invasions into southern Europe, the invasions of Russia from the East, and perhaps the sweep of Islam through Northern Africa into Europe after Mohammed's death. And the motivations for such wars were either the restless expansion of migratory tribes or the flame of religious fanaticism. Perhaps these great movements could scarcely be called wars at all, for war implies an organized people drilled and led; in fact, it necessitates the State. Ever since Europe has had any such organization, such huge conflicts between nations—nations, that is, as cultural groups—have been unthinkable. It is preposterous to assume that for centuries in Europe there would have been any possibility of a people *en masse,* (with their own leaders, and not with the leaders of their duly constituted State), rising up and overflowing their borders in a war raid upon a neighboring people. The wars of the Revolutionary armies of France were clearly in defense of an imperiled freedom, and, moreover, they were clearly directed not against other peoples, but against the autocratic governments that were combining to crush the Revolution. There is no instance in history of a genuinely national war. There are instances of national defenses, among primitive civilizations such as the Balkan peoples, against intolerable invasion by neighboring despots or oppression. But war, as such, cannot occur except in a system of competing States, which have relations with each other through the channels of diplomacy.

War is a function of this system of States, and could not occur except in such a system. Nations organized for internal administration, nations organized as a federation of free communities, nations organized in any way except that of a political centralization of a dynasty, or the reformed descendant of a dynasty, could not possibly make war upon each other. They would not only have no motive for conflict, but they would be unable to muster the concentrated force to make war effective. There might be all sorts of amateur marauding, there might be guerilla expeditions of group against group, but there could not be that terrible war *en masse* of the national State, that exploitation of the nation in the interests of the State, that abuse of the national life and resource in the frenzied mutual suicide, which is modern war.

It cannot be too firmly realized that war is a function of States and not of nations, indeed that it is the chief function of States. War is a very artificial thing. It is not the naïve spontaneous outburst of herd pugnacity; it is no more primary than is formal religion. War cannot exist without a military establishment, and a military establishment cannot exist without a State organization. War has an immemorial tradition and heredity only because the State has a long tradition and heredity. But they are inseparably and functionally joined. We cannot crusade against war without crusading implicitly against the State. And we cannot expect, or take measures to ensure, that this war is a war to end war, unless at the same time we take measures to end the State in its traditional form. The State is not the nation, and the State can be modified and even abolished in its present form, without harming the nation. On the contrary, with the passing of the dominance of the State, the genuine life-enhancing forces of the nation will be liberated. If the State's chief function is war, then the State must suck out of the nation a large part of its energy for its purely sterile purposes of defense and aggression. It devotes to waste or to actual destruction as much as it can of the vitality of the nation. No one will deny that war is a vast complex of life-destroying and life-crippling forces. If the State's chief function is war, then it is chiefly concerned with coördinating and developing the powers and techniques which make for destruction. And this means not only the actual and potential destruction of the enemy, but of the nation at home as well. For the very existence of a State in a system of States means that the nation lies always under a risk of war and invasion, and the calling away of energy into military pursuits means a crippling of the productive and life-enhancing processes of the national life.

All this organizing of death-dealing energy and technique is not a natural but a very sophisticated process. Particularly in modern nations, but also all through the course of modern European history, it could never exist without the State. For it meets the demands of no other institution, it follows the desires of no religious, industrial, political group. If the demand for military organization and a military establishment seems to come not from the officers of the State but from the public, it is only that it comes from the State-obsessed portion of the public, those groups which feel most keenly the State ideal. And in this country we have had evidence all too indubitable how powerless the pacifically minded officers of State may be in the face of a State-obsession of the significant classes. If a powerful section of the significant classes feels more intensely the attitudes of the State, then they will most infallibly mold the Government in time to their wishes, bring it back to act as the embodiment of the State which it pretends to be. In every country we have seen groups that were more loyal than the king—more patriotic than the Government—the Ulsterites in Great Britain, the Junkers in Prussia, l'Action Française in France, our patrioteers in America. These groups exist to keep the steering wheel of the State straight, and they prevent the nation from ever veering very far from the State ideal.

Militarism expresses the desires and satisfies the major impulse only of this class. The other classes, left to themselves, have too many necessities and interests and ambitions, to concern themselves with so expensive and destructive a game. But the State-obsessed group is either able to get control of the machinery of the State or to intimidate those in control, so that it is able through use of the collective force to regiment the other grudging and reluctant classes into a military programme. State idealism percolates down through the strata of society; capturing groups and individuals just in proportion to the prestige of this dominant class. So that we have the herd actually strung along between two extremes, the militaristic patriots at one end, who are scarcely distinguishable in attitude and animus from the most reactionary Bourbons of an Empire, and unskilled labor groups, which entirely lack the State sense. But the State acts as a whole, and the class that controls governmental machinery can swing the effective action of the herd as a whole. The herd is not actually a whole, emotionally. But by an ingenious mixture of cajolery, agitation, intimidation, the herd is licked into shape, into an effective mechanical unity, if not into a spiritual whole. Men are told simultaneously that they will enter the military establishment of their own volition, as their splendid sacrifice for their country's welfare, and that if they do not enter they will be hunted down and punished with the most horrid penalties; and under a most indescribable confusion of democratic pride and personal fear they submit to the destruction of their livelihood if not their lives, in a way that would formerly have seemed to them so obnoxious as to be incredible.

In this great herd-machinery, dissent is like sand in the bearings. The State ideal is primarily a sort of blind animal push towards military unity. Any interference with that unity turns the whole vast impulse towards crushing it. Dissent is speedily outlawed, and the Government, backed by the significant classes and those who in every locality, however small, identify themselves with them, proceeds against the outlaws, regardless of their value to the other institutions of the nation, or to the effect their persecution may have on public opinion. The herd becomes divided into the hunters and the hunted, and war-enterprise becomes not only a technical game but a sport as well.

It must never be forgotten that nations do not declare war on each other, nor in the strictest sense is it nations that fight each other. Much has been said to the effect that modern wars are wars of whole peoples and not of dynasties. Because the entire nation is regimented and the whole resources of the country are levied on for war, this does not mean that it is the country *qua* country which is fighting. It is the country organized as a State that is fighting, and only as a State would it possibly fight. So, literally, it is States which make war on each other and not peoples. Governments are the agents of States, and it is Governments which declare war on each other, acting truest to form in the interests of the great State ideal they represent. There is no case known in modern times of the people being consulted in the initiation of a war. The present demand for democratic control of foreign policy indicates how completely, even in the most democratic of modern nations, foreign policy has been the secret private possession of the executive branch of the Government.

However representative of the people Parliaments and Congresses may be in all that corcerns the internal administration of a country's political affairs, in international relations it has never been possible to maintain that the popular body acted except as a wholly mechanical ratifier of the Executive's will. The formality by which Parliaments and Congresses declare war is the merest technicality. Before such a declaration can take place, the country will have been brought to the very brink of war by the foreign policy of the Executive. A long series of steps on the downward path, each one more fatally committing the unsuspecting country to a warlike course of action will have been taken without either the people or its representatives being consulted or expressing its feeling. When the declaration of war is finally demanded by the Executive, the Parliament or Congress could not refuse it without reversing the course of history, without repudiating what has been representing itself in the eyes of the other States as the symbol and interpreter of the nation's will and animus. To repudiate an Executive at that time would be to publish to the entire world the evidence that the country had been grossly deceived by its own Government, that the country with an almost criminal carelessness had allowed its Government to commit it to gigantic national enterprises in which it had no heart. In such a crisis, even a Parliament which in the most democratic States represents the common man and not the significant classes who most strongly cherish the State ideal, will cheerfully sustain the foreign policy which it understands even less that it would care for if it understood, and will vote almost unanimously for an incalculable war, in which the nation may be brought well nigh to ruin. That is why the referendum which was advocated by some people as a test of American sentiment in entering the war was considered even by thoughtful democrats to be something subtly improper. The die had been cast. Popular whim could only derange and bungle monstrously the majestic march of State policy in its new crusade for the peace of the world. The irresistible State ideal got hold of the bowels of men. Whereas up to this time, it had been irreproachable to be neutral in word and deed, for the foreign policy of the State had so decided it, henceforth it became the most arrant crime to remain neutral. The Middle West, which had been soddenly pacifistic in our days of neutrality, became in a few months just as soddenly bellicose, and in its zeal for witch-burnings and its scent for enemies within gave precedence to no section of the country. The herd-mind followed faithfully the State-mind and, the agitation for a referendum being soon forgotten, the country fell into the universal conclusion that, since its Congress had formally declared the war, the nation itself had in the most solemn and universal way devised and brought on the entire affair. Oppression of minorities became justified on the plea that the latter were perversely resisting the rationally constructed and solemnly declared will of a majority of the nation. The herd-coalescence of opinion which became inevitable the moment the State had set flowing the war-attitudes became interpreted as a pre-war popular decision, and disinclination to bow to the herd was treated as a monstrously anti-social act. So that the State, which had vigorously resisted the idea of a referendum and clung tenaciously and, of course, with entire success to its autocratic and absolute control of foreign policy, had the pleasure of seeing the country, within a few months, given over to the retrospective impression that a genuine referendum had taken place. When once a country has lapped up these State attitudes, its memory fades; it conceives itself not as merely accepting, but of having itself willed the whole policy and technique of war. The significant classes with their trailing satellites, identify themselves with the State, so that what the State, through the agency of the Government, has willed, this majority conceives itself to have willed.

All of which goes to show that the State represents all the autocratic, arbitrary, coercive, belligerent forces within a social group, it is a sort of complexus of everything most distasteful to the modern free creative spirit, the feeling for life, liberty and the pursuit of happiness. War is the health of the State. Only when the State is at war does the modern society function with that unity of sentiment, simple uncritical patriotic devotion, coöperation of services, which have al-

ways been the ideal of the State lover. With the ravages of democratic ideas, however, the modern republic cannot go to war under
the old conceptions of autocracy and death-dealing belligerency. If a
successful animus for war requires a renaissance of State ideals, they
can only come back under democratic forms, under this retrospective
conviction of democratic control of foreign policy, democratic desire
for war, and particularly of this identification of the democracy with
the State. How unregenerate the ancient State may be, however, is
indicated by the laws against sedition, and by the Government's un-
reformed attitude on foreign policy. One of the first demands of the
more far-seeing democrats in the democracies of the Alliance was that
secret diplomacy must go. The war was seen to have been made possible by a web of secret agreements between States, alliances that were
made by Governments without the shadow of popular support or even
popular knowledge, and vague, half-understood commitments that
scarcely reached the stage of a treaty or agreement, but which proved
binding in the event. Certainly, said these democratic thinkers, war
can scarcely be avoided unless this poisonous underground system of
secret diplomacy is destroyed, this system by which a nation's power,
wealth and manhood may be signed away like a blank check to an
allied nation to be cashed in at some future crisis. Agreements which
are to affect the lives of whole peoples must be made between peoples
and not by Governments, or at least by their representatives in the
full glare of publicity and criticism.

Such a demand for "democratic control of foreign policy" seemed
axiomatic. Even if the country had been swung into war by steps
taken secretly and announced to the public only after they had been
consummated, it was felt that that attitude of the American State towards foreign policy was only a relic of the bad old days and must be
superseded in the new order. The American President himself, the
liberal hope of the world, had demanded, in the eyes of the world,
open diplomacy, agreements freely and openly arrived at. Did this
mean a genuine transference of power in this most crucial of State
functions from Government to people? Not at all. When the question
recently came to a challenge in Congress, and the implications of
open discussion were somewhat specifically discussed, and the desira-
bilities frankly commended, the President let his disapproval be known
in no uncertain way. No one ever accused Mr. Wilson of not being a
State idealist, and whenever democratic aspirations swung ideals too

far out of the State orbit, he could be counted on to react vigorously. Here was a clear case of conflict between democratic idealism and the very crux of the concept of the State. However unthinkingly he might have been led on to encourage open diplomacy in his liberalizing programme, when its implication was made vivid to him, he betrayed how mere a tool the idea had been in his mind to accentuate America's redeeming rôle. Not in any sense as a serious pragmatic technique had he thought of a genuinely open diplomacy. And how could he? For the last stronghold of State power is foreign policy. It is in foreign policy that the State acts most concentratedly as the organized herd, acts with fullest sense of aggressive power, acts with freest arbitrariness. In foreign policy, the State is most itself. States, with reference to each other, may be said to be in a continual state of latent war. The "armed truce," a phrase so familiar before 1914, was an accurate description of the normal relation of States when they are not at war. Indeed, it is not too much to say that the normal relation of States is war. Diplomacy is a disguised war, in which States seek to gain by barter and intrigue, by the cleverness of wits, the objectives which they would have to gain more clumsily by means of war. Diplomacy is used while the States are recuperating from conflicts in which they have exhausted themselves. It is the wheedling and the bargaining of the worn-out bullies as they rise from the ground and slowly restore their strength to begin fighting again. If diplomacy had been a moral equivalent for war, a higher stage in human progress, an inestimable means of making words prevail instead of blows, militarism would have broken down and given place to it. But since it is a mere temporary substitute, a mere appearance of war's energy under another form, a surrogate effect is almost exactly proportioned to the armed force behind it. When it fails, the recourse is immediate to the military technique whose thinly veiled arm it has been. A diplomacy that was the agency of popular democratic forces in their non-State manifestations would be no diplomacy at all. It would be no better than the Railway or Education Commissions that are sent from one country to another with rational constructive-purpose. The State, acting as a diplomatic-military ideal, is eternally at war. Just as it must act arbitrarily and autocratically in time of war, it must act in time of peace in this particular rôle where it acts as a unit. Unified control is necessarily autocratic control. Democratic control of foreign policy is therefore a contradiction in terms. Open discussion destroys swiftness and certainty of action. The giant State is paralyzed. Mr. Wilson retains his full ideal of the State at the same time that he desires to eliminate war. He wishes to make the world safe for democracy as well as safe for diplomacy. When the two are in conflict, his clear political insight, his idealism of the State, tells him that it is the naïver democratic values that must be sacrificed. The world must primarily be made safe for diplomacy. The State must not be diminished.

What is the State essentially? The more closely we examine it, the more mystical and personal it becomes. On the Nation we can put our hand as a definite social group, with attitudes and qualities exact enough to mean something. On the Government we can put our hand as a certain organization of ruling functions, the machinery of law-making and law-enforcing. The Administration is a recognizable group of political functionaries, temporarily in charge of the government. But the State stands as an idea behind them all, eternal, sanctified, and from it Government and Administration conceive themselves to have the breath of life. Even the nation, especially in times of war—or at least, its significant classes—considers that it derives its authority, and its purpose from the idea of the State. Nation and State are scarcely differentiated, and the concrete, practical, apparent facts are sunk in the symbol. We reverence not our country but the flag. We may criticize ever so severely our country, but we are disrespectful to the flag at our peril. It is the flag and the uniform that make men's hearts beat high and fill them with noble emotions, not the thought of and pious hopes for America as a free and enlightened nation.

It cannot be said that the object of emotion is the same, because the flag is the symbol of the nation, so that in reverencing the American flag we are reverencing the nation. For the flag is not a symbol of the country as a cultural group, following certain ideals of life, but solely a symbol of the political State, inseparable from its prestige and expansion. The flag is most intimately connected with military achievement, military memory. It represents the country not in its intensive life, but in its far-flung challenge to the world. The flag is primarily the banner of war; it is allied with patriotic anthem and holiday. It recalls old martial memories. A nation's patriotic history is solely the history of its wars, that is, of the State in its health and glorious functioning. So in responding to the appeal of the flag, we are responding to the appeal of the State, to the symbol of the herd organized as an offensive and defensive body, conscious of its prowess and its mystical herd-strength.

Even those authorities in the present Administration, to whom has been granted autocratic control over opinion, feel, though they are scarcely able to philosophize over, this distinction. It has been authoritatively declared that the horrid penalties against seditious opinion must not be construed as inhibiting legitimate, that is, partisan criticism of the Administration. A distinction is made between the Administration and the Government. It is quite accurately suggested by this attitude that the Administration is a temporary band of partisan politicians in charge of the machinery of Government, carrying out the mystical policies of State. The manner in which they operate this machinery may be freely discussed and objected to by their political opponents. The Governmental machinery may also be legitimately altered, in case of necessity. What may not be discussed or criticized is the mystical policy itself or the motives of the State in inaugurating such a policy. The President, it is true, has made certain partisan distinctions between candidates for office on the ground of support or non-support of the Administration, but what he meant was really support or non-support of the State policy as faithfully carried out by the Administration. Certain of the Administration measures were devised directly to increase the health of the State, such as the Conscription and the Espionage laws. Others were concerned merely with the machinery. To oppose the first was to oppose the State and was therefore not tolerable. To oppose the second was to oppose fallible human judgment, and was therefore, though to be deprecated, not to be wholly interpreted as political suicide.

The distinction between Government and State, however, has not been so carefully observed. In time of war it is natural that Government as the seat of authority should be confused with the State or the mystic source of authority. You cannot very well injure a mystical idea which is the State, but you can very well interfere with the processes of Government. So that the two become identified in the public mind, and any contempt for or opposition to the workings of the machinery of Government is considered equivalent to contempt for the sacred State. The State, it is felt, is being injured in its faithful surrogate, and public emotion rallies passionately to defend it. It even makes any criticism of the form of Government a crime.

The inextricable union of militarism and the State is beautifully shown by those laws which emphasize interference with the Army and Navy as the most culpable of seditious crimes. Pragmatically, a case of capitalistic sabotage, or a strike in war industry would seem to be far more dangerous to the successful prosecution of the war than the isolated and ineffectual efforts of an individual to prevent recruiting. But in the tradition of the State ideal, such industrial interference with national policy is not identified as a crime against the State. It may be grumbled against; it may be seen quite rationally as an impediment of the utmost gravity. But it is not *felt* in those obscure seats of the herd-mind which dictate the identity of crime and fix their proportional punishments. Army and Navy, however, are the very arms of the State; in them flows its most precious life-blood. To paralyze them is to touch the very State itself. And the majesty of the State is so sacred that even to attempt such a paralysis is a crime equal to a successful stroke. The will is deemed sufficient. Even though the individual in his effort to impede recruiting should utterly and lamentably fail, he shall be in no wise spared. Let the wrath of the State descend upon him for his impiety! Even if he does not try any overt action, but merely utters sentiments that may incidentally in the most indirect way cause some one to refrain from enlisting, he is guilty. The guardians of the State do not ask whether any pragmatic effect flowed out of this evil will or desire. It is enough that the will is present. Fifteen or twenty years in prison is not deemed too much for such sacrilege.

Such attitudes and such laws, which affront every principle of human reason, are no accident, nor are they the result of hysteria caused by the war. They are considered just, proper, beautiful by all the classes which have the State ideal, and they express only an extreme of health and vigor in the reaction of the State to its non-friends.

Such attitudes are inevitable as arising from the devotees of the State. For the State is a personal as well as a mystical symbol, and it can only be understood by tracing its historical origin. The modern State is not the national and intelligent product of modern men desiring to live harmoniously together with security of life, property and opinion. It is not an organization which has been devised as pragmatic means to a desired social end. All the idealism with which we have been instructed to endow the State is the fruit of our retrospective imaginations. What it does for us in the way of security and benefit of life, it does incidentally as a by-product and development of its original functions, and not because at any time men or classes in the full possession of their insight and intelligence have desired that it be so. It is very important that we should occasionally lift the incorrigible veil of that *ex post facto* idealism by which we throw a glamor of rationalization over what is, and pretend in the ecstasies of social conceit that we have personally invented and set up for the glory of God and man the hoary institutions which we see around us. Things are what they are, and come down to us with all their thick encrustations of error and malevolence. Political philosophy can delight us with fantasy and convince us who need illusion to live that the actual is a fair and approximate copy—full of failings, of course, but approximately sound and sincere—of that ideal society which we can imagine ourselves as creating. From this it is a step to the tacit assumption that we have somehow had a hand in its creation and are responsible for its maintenance and sanctity.

Nothing is more obvious, however, than that every one of us comes into society as into something in whose creation we had not the slightest hand. We have not even the advantage of consciousness before we take up our careers on earth. By the time we find ourselves here we are caught in a network of customs and attitudes, the major directions of our desires and interests have been stamped on our minds, and by the time we have emerged from tutelage and reached the years of discretion when we might conceivably throw our influence to the reshaping of social institutions, most of us have been so molded into the society and class we live in that we are scarcely aware of any distinction between ourselves as judging, desiring individuals and our social environment. We have been kneaded so successfully that we approve of what our society approves, desire what our society desires, and add to the group our own passional inertia against change, against the effort of reason, and the adventure of beauty.

Every one of us, without exception, is born into a society that is given, just as the fauna and flora of our environment are given. Society and its institutions are, to the individual who enters it, as much naturalistic phenomena as is the weather itself. There is therefore, no natural sanctity in the State any more than there is in the weather. We may bow down before it, just as our ancestors bowed before the sun and moon, but it is only because something in us unregenerate finds satisfaction in such an attitude, not because there is anything inherently reverential in the institution worshipped. Once the State has begun to function, and a large class finds its interest and its expression of power in maintaining the State, this ruling class may compel obedience from any uninterested minority. The State thus becomes an instrument by which the power of the whole herd is wielded for the benefit of a class. The rulers soon learn to capitalize the reverence which the State produces in the majority, and turn it into a general resistance towards a lessening of their privileges. The sanctity of the State becomes identified with the sanctity of the ruling class and the latter are permitted to remain in power under the impression that in obeying and serving them, we are obeying and serving society, the nation, the great collectivity of all of us.[2]

II

An analysis of the State would take us back to the beginnings of society, to the complex of religious and personal and herd-impulses which has found expression in so many forms. What we are interested in is the American State as it behaves and as Americans behave towards it in this twentieth century, and to understand that, we have to go no further back than the early English monarchy of which our American republic is the direct descendant. How straight and true is that line of descent almost nobody realizes. Those persons who believe in the sharpest distinction between democracy and monarchy can scarcely appreciate how a political institution may go through so many transformations and yet remain the same. Yet a swift glance must show us that in all the evolution of the English monarchy, with all its broadenings and its revolutions, and even with its jump across the sea into a colony which became an independent nation and then a powerful State, the same State functions and attitudes have been preserved essentially unchanged. The changes have been changes of form and not of inner spirit, and the boasted extension of democracy has been not a process by which the State was essentially altered to meet the shifting of classes, the extension of knowledge, the needs of social organization, but a mere elastic expansion by which the old spirit of the State easily absorbed the new and adjusted itself successfully to its exigencies. Never once has it been seriously shaken. Only

[2] There is no break in the ms but part one obviously ends here. The following section probably was intended to form a separate chapter.

once or twice has it been seriously challenged, and each time it has speedily recovered its equilibrium and proceeded with all its attitudes and faiths reënforced by the disturbance.

The modern democratic State, in this light, is therefore no bright and rational creation of a new day, the political form under which great peoples are to live healthfully and freely in a modern world, but the last decrepit scion of an ancient and hoary stock, which has become so exhausted that it scarcely recognizes its own ancestor, does, in fact repudiate him while it clings tenaciously to the archaic and irrelevant spirit that made that ancestor powerful, and resists the new bottles for the new wine that its health as a modern society so desperately needs. So sweeping a conclusion might have been doubted concerning the American State had it not been for the war, which has provided a long and beautiful series of examples of the tenacity of the State ideal and its hold on the significant classes of the American nation. War is the health of the State, and it is during war that one best understands the nature of that institution. If the American democracy during wartime has acted with an almost incredible trueness to form, if it has resurrected with an almost joyful fury the somnolent State, we can only conclude that that tradition from the past has been unbroken, and that the American republic is the direct descendant of the early English State.

And what was the nature of this early English State? It was first of all a mediæval absolute monarchy, arising out of the feudal chaos, which had represented the first effort at order after the turbulent assimilation of the invading barbarians by the Christianizing Roman civilization. The feudal lord evolved out of the invading warrior who had seized or been granted land and held it, souls and usufruct thereof, as fief to some higher lord whom he aided in war. His own serfs and vassals were exchanging faithful service for the protection which the warrior with his organized band could give them. Where one invading chieftain retained his power over his lesser lieutenants, a petty kingdom would arise, as in England, and a restless and ambitious king might extend his power over his neighbors and consolidate the petty kingdoms only to fall before the armed power of an invader like William the Conqueror, who would bring the whole realm under his heel. The modern State begins when a prince secures almost undisputed sway over fairly homogeneous territory and people and strives to fortify his power and maintain the order that will conduce to the safety and influence of his heirs. The State in its inception is pure and undiluted monarchy; it is armed power, culminating in a single head, bent on one primary object, the reducing to subjection, to unconditional and unqualified loyalty of all the people of a certain territory. This is the primary striving of the State, and it is a striving that the State never loses, through all its myriad transformations.

When this subjugation was once acquired, the modern State had begun. In the King, the subjects found their protection and their sense of unity. From his side, he was a redoubtable, ambitious, and stiff-necked warrior, getting the supreme mastery which he craved. But from theirs, he was a symbol of the herd, the visible emblem of that security which they needed and for which they drew gregariously together. Serfs and villains, whose safety under their petty lords had been rudely shattered in the constant conflicts for supremacy, now drew a new breath under the supremacy, that wiped out all this local anarchy. King and people agreed in the thirst for order, and order became the first healing function of the State. But in the maintenance of order, the King needed officers of justice; the old crude group-rules for dispensing justice had to be codified, a system of formal law worked out. The King needed ministers, who would carry out his will, extensions of his own power, as a machine extends the power of a man's hand. So the State grew as a gradual differentiation of the King's absolute power, founded on the devotion of his subjects and his control of a military band, swift and sure to smite. Gratitude for protection and fear of the strong arm sufficed to produce the loyalty of the country to the State.

The history of the State, then, is the effort to maintain these personal prerogatives of power, the effort to convert more and more into stable law the rules of order, the conditions of public vengeance, the distinction between classes, the possession of privilege. It was an effort to convert what was at first arbitrary usurpation, a perfectly apparent use of unjustified force, into the taken for granted and the divinely established. The State moves inevitably along the line from military dictatorship to the divine right of Kings. What had to be at first rawly imposed becomes through social habit to seem the necessary, the inevitable. The modern unquestioning acceptance of the State comes out of long and turbulent centuries when the State was challenged and had to fight its way to prevail. The King's establishment of personal power—which was the early State—had to contend with the impudence of hostile barons, who saw too clearly the adventitious origin of the monarchy and felt no reason why they should not themselves reign. Feuds between the King and his relatives, quarrels over inheritance, quarrels over the devolution of property, threatened constantly the existence of the new monarchical State. The King's will to power necessitated for its absolute satisfaction universality of political control in his dominions, just as the Roman Church claimed universality of spiritual control over the whole world. And just as rival popes were the inevitable product of such a pretension of sovereignty, rival kings and princes contended for that dazzling jewel of undisputed power.

Not until the Tudor régime was there in England an irresponsible absolute personal monarchy on the lines of the early State ideal, governing a fairly well-organized and prosperous nation. The Stuarts were not only too weak-minded to inherit this fruition of William the Conqueror's labors, but they made the fatal mistake of bringing out to public view and philosophy the idea of Divine Right implicit in the State, and this at a time when a new class of country gentry and burghers were attaining wealth and self-consciousness backed by the zeal of a theocratic and individualistic religion. Cromwell might certainly, if he had continued in power, have revised the ideal of the State, perhaps utterly transformed it, destroying the concepts of personal power, and universal sovereignty, and substituting a sort of Government of Presbyterian Soviets under the tutelage of a celestial Czar. But the Restoration brought back the old State under a peculiarly frivolous form. The Revolution was the merest change of monarchs at the behest of a Protestant majority which insisted on guarantees against religious relapse. The intrinsic nature of the monarchy as the symbol of the State was not in the least altered. In place of the inept monarch who could not lead the State in person or concentrate in himself the royal prerogatives, a coterie of courtiers managed the State. But their direction was consistently in the interest of the monarch and of the traditional ideal, so that the current of the English State was not broken.

The boasted English Parliament of lords and commoners possessed at no time any vitality which weakened or threatened to weaken the State ideal. Its original purpose was merely to facilitate the raising of the King's revenues. The nobles responded better when they seemed to be giving their consent. Their share in actual government was subjective, but the existence of Parliament served to appease any restiveness at the autocracy of the King. The significant classes could scarcely rebel when they had the privilege of giving consent to the King's measures. There was always outlet for the rebellious spirit of a powerful lord in private revolt against the King. The only Parliament that seriously tried to govern outside of and against the King's will precipitated a civil war that ended with the effectual submission of Parliament in a more careless and corrupt autocracy than had yet been known. By the time of George III Parliament was moribund, utterly unrepresentative either of the new bourgeois classes or of peasants and laborers, a mere frivolous parody of a legislature, despised both by King and people. The King was most effectively the State and his ministers the Government, which was run in terms of his personal whim, by men whose only interest was personal intrigue. Government had been for long what it has never ceased to be—a series of berths and emoluments in Army, Navy and the different departments of State, for the representatives of the privileged classes.

The State of George III was an example of the most archaic ideal of the English State, the pure, personal monarchy. The great mass of the people had fallen into the age-long tradition of loyalty to the crown. The classes that might have been restive for political power were placated by a show of representative government and the lucrative supply of offices. Discontent showed itself only in those few enlightened elements which could not refrain from irony at the sheer irrationality of a State managed on the old heroic lines for so grotesque a sovereign and by so grotesque a succession of courtier-ministers. Such discontent could by no means muster sufficient force for a revolution, but the Revolution which was due came in America where even the very obviously shadowy pigment of Parliamentary representation was denied the colonists. All that was vital in the political thought of England supported the American colonists in their resistance to the obnoxious government of George III.

The American Revolution began with certain latent hopes that it might turn into a genuine break with the State ideal. The Declaration of Independence announced doctrines that were utterly incompatible not only with the century-old conception of the Divine Right of Kings, but also with the Divine Right of the State. If all governments derive their authority from the consent of the governed, and if a people is entitled, at any time that it becomes oppressive, to overthrow it and institute one more nearly conformable to their interests and ideals, the old idea of the sovereignty of the State is destroyed. The State is reduced to the homely work of an instrument for carrying out popular policies. If revolution is justifiable a State may be even criminal sometimes in resisting its own extinction. The sovereignty of the people is no mere phrase. It is a direct challenge to the historic tradition of the State. For it implies that the ultimate sanctity resides not in the State at all or in its agent, the government, but in the nation, that is, in the country viewed as a cultural group and not specifically as a king-dominated herd. The State then becomes a mere instrument, the servant of this popular will, or of the constructive needs of the cultural group. The Revolution had in it, therefore, the makings of a very daring modern experiment—the founding of a free nation which should use the State to effect its vast purposes of subduing a continent just as the colonists' armies had used arms to detach their society from the irresponsible rule of an overseas king and his frivolous ministers. The history of the State might have ended in 1776 as far as the American colonies were concerned, and the modern nation which is still striving to materialize itself have been born.

For a while it seemed almost as if the State was dead. But men who are freed rarely know what to do with their liberty. In each colony the fatal seed of the State had been sown; it could not disappear. Rival prestiges and interests began to make themselves felt. Fear of foreign States, economic distress, discord between classes, the inevitable physical exhaustion and prostration of idealism which follows a protracted war—all combined to put the responsible classes of the new States into the mood for a regression to the State ideal. Ostensibly there is no reason why the mere lack of a centralized State should have destroyed the possibility of progress in the new liberated America, provided the inter-state jealousy and rivalry could have been destroyed. But there were no leaders for this anti-State nationalism. The sentiments of the Declaration remained mere sentiments. No constructive political scheme was built on them. The State ideal, on the other hand, had ambitious leaders of the financial classes, who saw in the excessive decentralization of the Confederation too much opportunity for the control of society by the democratic lower-class elements. They were menaced by imperialistic powers without and by democracy within. Through their fear of the former they tended to exaggerate the impossibility of the latter. There was no inclination to make the new

State a school where democratic experiments could be worked out as they should be. They were unwilling to give reconstruction the term that might have been necessary to build up this truly democratic nationalism. Six years is a short time to reconstruct an agricultural country devastated by a six years' war. The popular elements in the new States had time only to show their turbulence; they were given no time to grow. The ambitious leaders of the financial classes got a convention called to discuss the controversies and maladjustments of the States, which were making them clamor for a revision of the Articles of Confederation, and then, by one of the most successful *coups d'état* in history, turned their assembly into the manufacture of a new government on the strongest lines of the old State ideal.

This new constitution, manufactured in secret session by the leaders of the propertied and ruling classes, was then submitted to an approval of the electors which only by the most expert manipulation was obtained, but which was sufficient to override the indignant undercurrent of protest from those popular elements who saw the fruits of the Revolution slipping away from them. Universal suffrage would have killed it forever. Had the liberated colonies had the advantage of the French experience before them, the promulgation of the Constitution would undoubtedly have been followed by a new revolution, as very nearly happened later against Washington and the Federalists. But the ironical ineptitude of Fate put the machinery of the new Federalist constitutional government in operation just at the moment that the French Revolution began, and by the time those great waves of Jacobin feeling reached North America, the new Federalist State was firmly enough on its course to weather the gale and the turmoil.

The new State was therefore not the happy political symbol of a united people, who in order to form a more perfect union, etc., but the imposition of a State on a loose and growing nationalism, which was in a condition of unstable equilibrium and needed perhaps only to be fertilized from abroad to develop a genuine political experiment in democracy. The preamble to the Constitution, as was soon shown in the hostile popular vote and later in the revolt against the Federalists, was a pious hope rather than actuality, a blessedness to be realized when by the force of government pressure, the creation of idealism, and mere social habit, the population should be welded and kneaded into a State. That this is what has actually happened is seen in the fact that the somewhat shockingly undemocratic origins of the American State have been almost completely glossed over and the unveiling is bitterly resented, by none so bitterly as the significant classes who have been most industrious in cultivating patriotic myth and legend. American history, as far as it has entered into the general popular emotion, runs along this line: The Colonies are freed by the Revolution from a tyrannous King and become free and independent States; there follow six years of impotent peace, during which the Colonies quarrel among themselves and reveal the hopeless weakness of the principle under which they are working together; in desperation the people then create a new instrument, and launch a free and democratic republic, which was and remains—especially since it withstood the shock of civil war—the most perfect form of democratic government known to man, perfectly adequate to be promulgated as an example in the twentieth century to all people, and to be spread by propaganda, and, if necessary, the sword, in all unregenerately Imperial regions. Modern historians reveal the avowedly undemocratic personnel and opinions of the Convention. They show that the members not only had an unconscious economic interest but a frank political interest in founding a State which should protect the propertied classes against the hostility of the people. They show how, from one point of view, the new government became almost a mechanism for overcoming the repudiation of debts, for putting back into their place a farmer and small trader class whom the unsettled times of reconstruction had threatened to liberate, for reëstablishing on the securest basis of the sanctity of property and the State, their class-supremacy menaced by a democracy that had drunk too deeply at the fount of Revolution. But all this makes little impression on the other legend of the popular mind, because it disturbs the sense of the sanctity of the State and it is this rock to which the herd-wish must cling.

Every little school boy is trained to recite the weaknesses and inefficiencies of the Articles of Confederation. It is taken as axiomatic that under them the new nation was falling into anarchy and was only saved by the wisdom and energy of the Convention. These hapless articles have had to bear the infamy cast upon the untried by the radiantly successful. The nation had to be strong to repel invasion, strong to pay to the last loved copper penny the debts of the propertied and the provident ones, strong to keep the unpropertied and improvident from ever using the government to ensure their own prosperity at the expense of moneyed capital. Under the Articles the new States were obviously trying to reconstruct themselves in an alarming tenderness for the common man impoverished by the war. No one suggests that the anxiety of the leaders of the heretofore unquestioned ruling classes desired the revision of the Articles and labored so weightily over a new instrument not because the nation was failing under the Articles but because it was succeeding only too well. Without intervention from the leaders, reconstruction threatened in time to turn the new nation into an agrarian and proletarian democracy. It is impossible to predict what would have been worked out in time, whether the democratic idealism implicit in the Declaration of Independence would have materialized into a form of society very much modified from the ancient State. All we know is that at a time when the current of political progress was in the direction of agrarian and proletarian democracy, a force hostile to it gripped the nation and imposed upon it a powerful form against which it was never to succeed in doing more than blindly struggle. The liberating virus of the Revolution was definitely expunged, and henceforth if it worked at all it had to work against the State, in opposition to the armed and respectable power of the nation.

The propertied classes, seated firmly in the saddle by their Constitutional *coup d'état*, have, of course, never lost their ascendancy. The particular group of Federalists who had engineered the new machinery and enjoyed the privilege of setting it in motion, were turned out in a dozen years by the "Jeffersonian democracy" whom their manner had so deeply offended. But the Jeffersonian democracy never meant in practice any more than the substitution of the rule of the country gentleman for the rule of the town capitalist. The true hostility between their interests was small as compared with the hostility of both towards the common man. When both were swept away by the irruption of the Western democracy under Andrew Jackson and the rule of the common man appeared for a while in its least desirable forms, it was comparatively easy for the two propertied classes to form a tacit coalition against them. The new West achieved an extension of suffrage and a jovial sense of having come politically into its own, but the rule of the ancient classes was not seriously challenged. Their squabbles over the tariff were family affairs, for the tariff could not materially affect the common man of either East or West. The Eastern and Northern capitalists soon saw the advantage of supporting Southern country gentleman slave-power as against the free-soil pioneer. Bad generalship on the part of this coalition allowed a Western free-soil minority President to slip into office and brought on the Civil War, which smashed the slave power and left Northern capital in undisputed possession of a field against which the pioneer could make only sporadic and ineffective revolts.

From the Civil War to the death of Mark Hanna, the propertied capitalist industrial classes ran a triumphal career in possession of the State. At various times, as in 1896, the country had to be saved for them from disillusioned, rebellious hordes of small farmers and traders and democratic idealists, who had in the overflow of prosperity been squeezed down into the small end of the horn. But except for these occasional menaces, business, that is to say, aggressive expansionist capitalism, had nearly forty years in which to direct the American republic as a private preserve, or laboratory, experimenting, developing, wasting, subjugating, to its heart's content, in the midst of a vast somnolence of complacency such as has never been seen and contrasts strangely with the spiritual dissent and constructive revolutionary thought which went on at the same time in England and the Continent.

That era ended in 1904 like the crack of doom, which woke a whole people into a modern day which they had far overslept, and for which they had no guiding principles or philosophy to conduct them about. They suddenly became acutely and painfully aware of the evils of the society in which they had slumbered and they snatched at one after the other idea, programme, movement, ideal, to uplift them out of the slough in which they had slept. The glory of those shining figures—captains of industry—went out in a sulphuric gloom. The head of the State, who made up in dogmatism what he lacked in philosophy, increased the confusion by reviving the Ten Commandments for political purposes, and belaboring the wicked with them. The American world tossed in a state of doubt, of reawakened social conscience, of pragmatic effort for the salvation of society. The ruling classes—annoyed, bewildered, harassed—pretended with much bemoaning that they were losing their grip on the State. Their inspired prophets uttered solemn warnings against political novelty and the abandonment of the tried and tested fruits of experience.

These classes actually had little to fear. A political system which had been founded in the interests of property by their own spiritual and economic ancestors, which had become ingrained in the country's life through a function of 120 years, which was buttressed by a legal system which went back without a break to the early English monarchy was not likely to crumble before the anger of a few muck-rakers, the disillusionment of a few radical sociologists, or the assaults of proletarian minorities. Those who bided their time through the Taft interregnum, which merely continued the Presidency until there could be found a statesman to fill it, were rewarded by the appearance of the exigency of a war, in which business organization was imperatively needed. They were thus able to make a neat and almost noiseless coalition with the Government. The mass of the worried middle-classes, riddled by the campaign against American failings, which at times extended almost to a skepticism of the American State itself, were only too glad to sink back to a glorification of the State ideal, to feel about them in war, the old protecting arms, to return to the old primitive robust sense of the omnipotence of the State, its matchless virtue, honor and beauty, driving away all the foul old doubts and dismays.

That the same class which imposed its constitution on the nascent proletarian and agrarian democracy has maintained itself to this day indicates how slight was the real effect of the Revolution. When that political change was consolidated in the new government, it was found that there had been a mere transfer of ruling-class power across the seas, or rather that a ruling commercial class in the colonies had been able to remove through a war fought largely by the masses a vexatious over-lordship of the irresponsible coterie of ministers that surrounded George III. The colonies merely exchanged a system run in the interest of the overseas trade of English wealth for a system run in the interest of New England and Philadelphia merchanthood, and later of Southern slavocracy. The daring innovation of getting rid of a king and setting up a kingless State did not apparently impress the hard headed farmers and small traders with as much force as it has their patriotic defenders. The animus of the Convention was so obviously monarchical that any executive they devised could be only a very thinly disguised king. The compromise by which the presidency was created proved but to be the means by which very nearly the whole mass of traditional royal prerogatives was brought over and lodged in the new State.

The President is an elected king, but the fact that he is elected has proved to be of far less significance in the course of political evolution than the fact that he is pragmatically a king. It was the intention of the founders of the Constitution that he be elected by a small body of notables, representing the ruling propertied classes, who could check him up every four years in a new election. This was no innovation. Kings have often been selected in this way in European history, and the Roman Emperor was regularly chosen by election. That the American President's term was limited merely shows the confidence which the founders felt in the buttressing force of their instrument. His election would never pass out of the hands of the notables, and so the office would be guaranteed to be held by a faithful representative of upper-class demands. What he was most obviously to represent was the interests of that body which elected him, and not the mass of the people who were still disfranchised. For the new State started with no Quixotic belief in universal suffrage. The property qualifications which were in effect in every colony were continued. Government was frankly a function of those who held a concrete interest in the public weal, in the shape of visible property. The responsibility for the security of property rights could safely lie only with those who had something to secure. The "stake" in the commonwealth which those who held office must possess was obviously larger.

One of the larger errors of political insight which the sage founders of the Constitution committed was to assume that the enfranchised watchdogs of property and the public order would remain a homogeneous class. Washington, acting strictly as the mouthpiece of the unified State ideal, deprecated the growth of parties and of factions which horridly keep the State in turbulence or threaten to rend it asunder. But the monarchical and repressive policies of Washington's own friends promptly generated an opposition democratic party representing the landed interests of the ruling classes, and the party system was fastened on the country. By the time the electorate had succeeded in reducing the electoral college to a mere recorder of the popular vote, or in other words, had broadened the class of notables to the whole property-holding electorate, the parties were firmly established to carry on the selective and refining and securing work of the electoral college. The party leadership then became, and has remained ever since, the nucleus of notables who determine the presidency. The electorate having won an apparently democratic victory in the destruction of the notables, finds itself reduced to the rôle of mere ratification or selection between two or three candidates, in whose choice they have only a nominal share. The electoral college which stood between even the propertied electorate and the executive with the prerogatives of a king, gave place to a body which was just as genuinely a bar to democratic expression, and far less responsible for its acts. The nucleus of party councils which became, after the reduction of the Electoral College, the real choosers of the Presidents, were unofficial, quasi-anonymous, utterly unchecked by the populace whose rulers they chose. More or less self-chosen, or chosen by local groups whom they dominated, they provided a far more secure guarantee that the State should remain in the hands of the ruling classes than the old electoral college. The party councils could be loosely organized entirely outside of the governmental organization, without oversight by the State or check from the electorate. They could be composed of the leaders of the propertied classes themselves or their lieutenants, who could retain their power indefinitely, or at least until they were unseated by rivals within the same charmed domain. They were at least entirely safe from attack by the officially constituted electorate, who, as the party system became more and more firmly established, found they could vote only on the slates set up for them by unknown councils behind an imposing and all-powerful "Party."

As soon as this system was organized into a hierarchy extending from national down to state and county politics, it became perfectly safe to broaden the electorate. The clamors of the unpropertied or the less propertied to share in the selection of their democratic republican government could be graciously acceded to without endangering in the least the supremacy of those classes which the founders had meant to be supreme. The minority were now even more effectually protected from the majority than under the old system, however indirect the election might be. The electorate was now reduced to a ratifier of slates, and as a ratifier of slates, or a chooser between two slates, both of which were pledged to upper-class domination, the electorate could have the freest, most universal suffrage, for any mass-desire for political change, any determined will to shift the class-balance, would be obliged to register itself through the party machinery. It could make no frontal attack on the Government. And the party machinery was directly devised to absorb and neutralize this popular shock, handing out to the disgruntled electorate a disguised stone when it asked for political bread, and effectually smashing any third party which ever avariciously tried to reach government except through the regular two-party system.

The party system succeeded, of course, beyond the wildest dreams of its creators. It relegated the founders of the Constitution to the rôle of doctrinaire theorists, political amateurs. Just because it grew up slowly to meet the needs of ambitious politicians and was not imposed by ruling-class fiat, as was the Constitution, did it have a chance to become assimilated, worked into the political intelligence and instinct of the people, and be adopted gladly and universally as a genuine political form, expressive both of popular need and ruling-class demand. It satisfied the popular demand for democracy. The enormous sense of victory which followed the sweeping away of property qualifications of suffrage, the tangible evidence that now every citizen was participating in public affairs, and that the entire manhood democracy was now self-governing, created a mood of political complacency that lasted uninterruptedly into the twentieth century. The party system was thus the means of removing political grievance from the greater part of the populace, and of giving to the ruling classes the hidden but genuine permanence of control which the Constitution had tried openly to give them. It supplemented and repaired the ineptitudes of the Constitution. It became the unofficial but real government, the instrument which used the Constitution as its instrument.

Only in two cases did the party system seem to lose its grip, was it thrown off its base by the inception of a new party from without—in the elections of Jackson and of Lincoln. Jackson came in as the representative of a new democratic West which had no tradition of suffrage qualifications, and Lincoln as a minority candidate in a time of factional and sectional strife. But the discomfiture of the party politicians was short. The party system proved perfectly capable of assimilating both of these new movements. Jackson's insurrection was soon captured by the old machinery and fed the slavocracy, and Lincoln's party became the property of the new bonanza capitalism. Neither Jackson nor Lincoln made the slightest deflection in the triumphal march of the party-system. In practically no other contests has the electorate had for all practical purposes a choice except between two candidates, identical as far as their political rôle would be as representatives of the significant classes in the State. Campaigns such as Bryan's, where one of the parties is captured by an element which seeks a real transference of power from the significant to the less significant classes, split the party, and sporadic third party attacks merely throw the scale one way or the other between the big parties, or, if threatening enough, produce a virtual coalition against them. . . .

Trans-National America

Trans-National America

8

Trans-National America[1]

No reverberatory effect of the great war has caused American public opinion more solicitude than the failure of the 'melting-pot.' The discovery of diverse nationalistic feelings among our great alien population has come to most people as an intense shock. It has brought out the unpleasant inconsistencies of our traditional beliefs. We have had to watch hard-hearted old Brahmins virtuously indignant at the spectacle of the immigrant refusing to be melted, while they jeer at patriots like Mary Antin[2] who write about 'our forefathers.' We have had to listen to publicists who express themselves as stunned by the evidence of vigorous nationalistic and cultural movements in this country among Germans, Scandinavians, Bohemians, and Poles, while in the same breath they insist that the alien shall be forcibly assimilated to that Anglo-Saxon tradition which they unquestioningly label 'American.'

As the unpleasant truth has come upon us that assimilation in this country was proceeding on lines very different from those we had marked out for it, we found ourselves inclined to blame those who were thwarting our prophecies. The truth became culpable. We blamed the war, we blamed the Germans. And then we discovered with a moral shock that these movements had been making great headway before the war even began. We found that the tendency, reprehensible and

---

[1] *Atlantic Monthly,* cxviii (July 1916), 86–97.

[2] Mary Antin, Russian-born American author. Her autobiography, *The Promised Land* (1912), described the hardships encountered by Jewish immigrants. It was also a paean to America as the land of opportunity.

paradoxical as it might be, has been for the national clusters of immigrants, as they became more and more firmly established and more and more prosperous, to cultivate more and more assiduously the literatures and cultural traditions of their homelands. Assimilation, in other words, instead of washing out the memories of Europe, made them more and more intensely real. Just as these clusters became more and more objectively American, did they become more and more German or Scandinavian or Bohemian or Polish.

To face the fact that our aliens are already strong enough to take a share in the direction of their own destiny, and that the strong cultural movements represented by the foreign press, schools, and colonies are a challenge to our facile attempts, is not, however, to admit the failure of Americanization. It is not to fear the failure of democracy. It is rather to urge us to an investigation of what Americanism may rightly mean. It is to ask ourselves whether our ideal has been broad or narrow—whether perhaps the time has not come to assert a higher ideal than the 'melting-pot.' Surely we cannot be certain of our spiritual democracy when, claiming to melt the nations within us to a comprehension of our free and democratic institutions, we fly into panic at the first sign of their own will and tendency. We act as if we wanted Americanization to take place only on our own terms, and not by the consent of the governed. All our elaborate machinery of settlement and school and union, of social and political naturalization, however, will move with friction just in so far as it neglects to take into account this strong and virile insistence that America shall be what the immigrant will have a hand in making it, and not what a ruling class, descendant of those British stocks which were the first permanent immigrants, decide that America shall be made. This is the condition which confronts us, and which demands a clear and general readjustment of our attitude and our ideal.

I

Mary Antin is right when she looks upon our foreign-born as the people who missed the Mayflower and came over on the first boat they could find. But she forgets that when they did come it was not upon other Mayflowers, but upon a 'Maiblume,' a 'Fleur de Mai,' a 'Fior di Maggio,' a 'Majblomst.' These people were not mere arrivals from the same family, to be welcomed as understood and long-loved, but strangers to the neighborhood, with whom a long process of settling down had to take place. For they brought with them their national and racial characters, and each new national quota had to wear slowly away the contempt with which its mere alienness got itself greeted. Each had to make its way slowly from the lowest strata of unskilled labor up to a level where it satisfied the accredited norms of social success.

We are all foreign-born or the descendants of foreign-born, and if distinctions are to be made between us they should rightly be on some other ground than indigenousness. The early colonists came over with motives no less colonial than the later. They did not come to be assimilated in an American melting-pot. They did not come to adopt the culture of the American Indian. They had not the smallest intention of 'giving themselves without reservation' to the new country. They came to get freedom to live as they wanted to. They came to escape from the stifling air and chaos of the old world; they came to make their fortune in a new land. They invented no new social framework. Rather they brought over bodily the old ways to which they had been accustomed. Tightly concentrated on a hostile frontier, they were conservative beyond belief. Their pioneer daring was reserved for the objective conquest of material resources. In their folkways, in their social and political institutions, they were, like every colonial people, slavishly imitative of the mother-country. So that, in spite of the 'Revolution,' our whole legal and political system remained more English than the English, petrified and unchanging, while in England law developed to meet the needs of the changing times.

It is just this English-American conservatism that has been our chief obstacle to social advance. We have needed the new peoples—the order of the German and Scandinavian, the turbulence of the Slav and Hun—to save us from our own stagnation. I do not mean that the illiterate Slav is now the equal of the New Englander of pure descent. He is raw material to be educated, not into a New Englander, but into a socialized American along such lines as those thirty nationalities are being educated in the amazing schools of Gary.[3] I do not be-

[3] In 1907, Gary, Indiana, began a through reorganization of its school system, applying John Dewey's theories. Within a few years Gary's schools became the leading example of progressive education in the United States. Bourne's articles in the *New Republic*, eventually published as *The Gary Schools* (1916), were instrumental in publicising the experiment.

lieve that this process is to be one of decades of evolution. The spectacle of Japan's sudden jump from mediævalism to post-modernism should have destroyed that superstition. We are not dealing with individuals who are to 'evolve.' We are dealing with their children, who, with that education we are about to have, will start level with all of us. Let us cease to think of ideals like democracy as magical qualities inherent in certain peoples. Let us speak, not of inferior races, but of inferior civilizations. We are all to educate and to be educated. These peoples in America are in a common enterprise. It is not what we are now that concerns us, but what this plastic next generation may become in the light of a new cosmopolitan ideal.

We are not dealing with static factors, but with fluid and dynamic generations. To contrast the older and the newer immigrants and see the one class as democratically motivated by love of liberty, and the other by mere money-getting, is not to illuminate the future. To think of earlier nationalities as culturally assimilated to America, while we picture the later as a sodden and resistive mass, makes only for bitterness and misunderstanding. There may be a difference between these earlier and these later stocks, but it lies neither in motive for coming nor in strength of cultural allegiance to the homeland. The truth is that no more tenacious cultural allegiance to the mother country has been shown by any alien nation than by the ruling class of Anglo-Saxon descendants in these American States. English snobberies, English religion, English literary styles, English literary reverences and canons, English ethics, English superiorities, have been the cultural food that we have drunk in from our mothers' breasts. The distinctively American spirit—pioneer, as distinguished from the reminiscently English—that appears in Whitman and Emerson and James, has had to exist on sufferance alongside of this other cult, unconsciously belittled by our cultural makers of opinion. No country has perhaps had so great indigenous genius which had so little influence on the country's traditions and expressions. The unpopular and dreaded German-American of the present day is a beginning amateur in comparison with those foolish Anglophiles of Boston and New York and Philadelphia whose reversion to cultural type sees uncritically in England's cause the cause of Civilization, and, under the guise of ethical independence of thought, carries along European traditions which are no more 'American' than the German categories themselves.

It speaks well for German-American innocence of heart or else for its lack of imagination that it has not turned the hyphen stigma into a 'Tu quoque!'[4] If there were to be any hyphens scattered about, clearly they should be affixed to those English descendants who had had centuries of time to be made American where the German had had only half a century. Most significantly has the war brought out of them this alien virus, showing them still loving English things, owing allegiance to the English Kultur, moved by English shibboleths and prejudice. It is only because it has been the ruling class in this country that bestowed the epithets that we have not heard copiously and scornfully of 'hyphenated English-Americans.' But even our quarrels with England have had the bad temper, the extravagance, of family quarrels. The Englishman of to-day nags us and dislikes us in that personal, peculiarly intimate way in which he dislikes the Australian, or as we may dislike our younger brothers. He still thinks of us incorrigibly as 'colonials.' America—official, controlling, literary, political America—is still, as a writer recently expressed it, 'culturally speaking, a self-governing dominion of the British Empire.'

The non-English American can scarcely be blamed if he sometimes thinks of the Anglo-Saxon predominance in America as little more than a predominance of priority. The Anglo-Saxon was merely the first immigrant, the first to found a colony. He has never really ceased to be the descendant of immigrants, nor has he ever succeeded in transforming that colony into a real nation, with a tenacious, richly woven fabric of native culture. Colonials from the other nations have come and settled down beside him. They found no definite native culture which should startle them out of their colonialism, and consequently they looked back to their mother-country, as the earlier Anglo-Saxon immigrant was looking back to his. What has been offered the new-comer has been the chance to learn English, to become a citizen, to salute the flag. And those elements of our ruling classes who are responsible for the public schools, the settlements, all the organizations for amelioration in the cities, have every reason to be proud of the care and labor which they have devoted to absorbing the immigrant. His opportunities the immigrant has taken to gladly, with almost a pathetic eagerness to make his way in the new land without friction or disturbance. The common language has made not only for the necessary communication, but for all the amenities of life.

If freedom means the right to do pretty much as one pleases, so

[4] 'Thou too!' A retort accusing an adversary for doing the same as oneself.

long as one does not interfere with others, the immigrant has found freedom, and the ruling element has been singularly liberal in its treatment of the invading hordes. But if freedom means a democratic cooperation in determining the ideals and purposes and industrial and social institutions of a country, then the immigrant has not been free, and the Anglo-Saxon element is guilty of just what every dominant race is guilty of in every European country: the imposition of its own culture upon the minority peoples. The fact that this imposition has been so mild and, indeed, semi-conscious does not alter its quality. And the war has brought out just the degree to which that purpose of 'Americanizing,' that is, 'Anglo-Saxonizing,' the immigrant has failed.

For the Anglo-Saxon now in his bitterness to turn upon the other peoples, talk about their 'arrogance,' scold them for not being melted in a pot which never existed, is to betray the unconscious purpose which lay at the bottom of his heart. It betrays too the possession of a racial jealousy similar to that of which he is now accusing the so-called 'hyphenates.' Let the Anglo-Saxon be proud enough of the heroic toil and heroic sacrifices which moulded the nation. But let him ask himself, if he had had to depend on the English descendants, where he would have been living to-day. To those of us who see in the exploitation of unskilled labor the strident red *leit-motif* of our civilization, the settling of the country presents a great social drama as the waves of immigration broke over it.

Let the Anglo-Saxon ask himself where he would have been if these races had not come? Let those who feel the inferiority of the non-Anglo-Saxon immigrant contemplate that region of the States which has remained the most distinctively 'American,' the South. Let him ask himself whether he would really like to see the foreign hordes Americanized into such an Americanization. Let him ask himself how superior this native civilization is to the great 'alien' states of Wisconsin and Minnesota, where Scandinavians, Poles, and Germans have self-consciously labored to preserve their traditional culture, while being outwardly and satisfactorily American. Let him ask himself how much more wisdom, intelligence, industry and social leadership has come out of these alien states than out of all the truly American ones. The South, in fact, while this vast Northern development has gone on, still remains an English colony, stagnant and complacent, having progressed culturally scarcely beyond the early Victorian era. It is culturally sterile because it has had no advantage of cross-fertilization like the Northern states. What has happened in states such as Wisconsin and Minnesota is that strong foreign cultures have struck root in a new and fertile soil. America has meant liberation, and German and Scandinavian political ideas and social energies have expanded to a new potency. The process has not been at all the fancied 'assimilation' of the Scandinavian or Teuton. Rather has it been a process of their assimilation of us—I speak as an Anglo-Saxon. The foreign cultures have not been melted down or run together, made into some homogeneous Americanism, but have remained distinct but coöperating to the greater glory and benefit, not only of themselves but of all the native 'Americanism' around them.

What we emphatically do not want is that these distinctive qualities should be washed out into a tasteless, colorless fluid of uniformity. Already we have far too much of this insipidity,—masses of people who are cultural half-breeds, neither assimilated Anglo-Saxons nor nationals of another culture. Each national colony in this country seems to retain in its foreign press, its vernacular literature, its schools, its intellectual and patriotic leaders, a central cultural nucleus. From this nucleus the colony extends out by imperceptible gradations to a fringe where national characteristics are all but lost. Our cities are filled with these half-breeds who retain their foreign names but have lost the foreign savor. This does not mean that they have actually been changed into New Englanders or Middle Westerners. It does not mean that they have been really Americanized. It means that, letting slip from them whatever native culture they had, they have substituted for it only the most rudimentary American—the American culture of the cheap newspaper, the 'movies,' the popular song, the ubiquitous automobile. The unthinking who survey this class call them assimilated, Americanized. The great American public school has done its work. With these people our institutions are safe. We may thrill with dread at the aggressive hyphenate, but this tame flabbiness is accepted as Americanization. The same moulders of opinion whose ideal is to melt the different races into Anglo-Saxon gold hail this poor product as the satisfying result of their alchemy.

Yet a truer cultural sense would have told us that it is not the self-conscious cultural nuclei that sap at our American life, but these fringes. It is not the Jew who sticks proudly to the faith of his fathers and boasts of that venerable culture of his who is dangerous to America, but the Jew who has lost the Jewish fire and become a mere elementary, grasping animal. It is not the Bohemian who supports the Bohemian schools in Chicago whose influence is sinister, but the Bohemian who has made money and has got into ward politics. Just so surely as we tend to disintegrate these nuclei of nationalistic culture do we tend to create hordes of men and women without a spiritual country, cultural outlaws, without taste, without standards but those of the mob. We sentence them to live on the most rudimentary planes of American life. The influences at the centre of the nuclei are centripetal. They make for the intelligence and the social values which mean an enhancement of life. And just because the foreign-born retains this expressiveness is he likely to be a better citizen of the American community. The influences at the fringe, however, are centrifugal, anarchical. They make for detached fragments of peoples. Those who came to find liberty achieve only license. They become the flotsam and jetsam of American life, the downward undertow of our civilization with its leering cheapness and falseness of taste and spiritual outlook, the absence of mind and sincere feeling which we see in our slovenly towns, our vapid moving pictures, our popular novels, and in the vacuous faces of the crowds on the city street. This is the cultural wreckage of our time, and it is from the fringes of the Anglo-Saxon as well as the other stocks that it falls. America has as yet no impelling integrating force. It makes too easily for this detritus of cultures. In our loose, free country, no constraining national purpose, no tenacious folk-tradition and folk-style hold the people to a line.

The war has shown us that not in any magical formula will this purpose be found. No intense nationalism of the European plan can be ours. But do we not begin to see a new and more adventurous ideal? Do we not see how the national colonies in America, deriving power from the deep cultural heart of Europe and yet living here in mutual toleration, freed from the age-long tangles of races, creeds, and dynasties, may work out a federated ideal? America is transplanted Europe, but a Europe that has not been disintegrated and scattered in the transplanting as in some Dispersion. Its colonies live here inextricably mingled, yet not homogeneous. They merge but they do not fuse.

America is a unique sociological fabric, and it bespeaks poverty of imagination not to be thrilled at the incalculable potentialities of so novel a union of men. To seek no other goal than the weary old nationalism,—belligerent, exclusive, inbreeding, the poison of which we are witnessing now in Europe,—is to make patriotism a hollow sham, and to declare that, in spite of our boastings, America must ever be a follower and not a leader of nations.

II

If we come to find this point of view plausible, we shall have to give up the search for our native 'American' culture. With the exception of the South and that New England which, like the Red Indian, seems to be passing into solemn oblivion, there is no distinctively American culture. It is apparently our lot rather to be a federation of cultures. This we have been for half a century, and the war has made it ever more evident that this is what we are destined to remain. This will not mean, however, that there are not expressions of indigenous genius that could not have sprung from any other soil. Music, poetry, philosophy, have been singularly fertile and new. Strangely enough, American genius has flared forth just in those directions which are least understood [sic] of the people. If the American note is bigness, action, the objective as contrasted with the reflective life, where is the epic expression of this spirit? Our drama and our fiction, the peculiar fields for the expression of action and objectivity, are somehow exactly the fields of the spirit which remain poor and mediocre. American materialism is in some way inhibited from getting into impressive artistic form its own energy with which it bursts. Nor is it any better in architecture, the least romantic and subjective of all the arts. We are inarticulate of the very values which we profess to idealize. But in the finer forms —music, verse, the essay, philosophy—the American genius puts forth work equal to any of its contemporaries. Just in so far as our American genius has expressed the pioneer spirit, the adventurous, forward-looking drive of a colonial empire, is it representative of that whole America of the many races and peoples, and not of any partial or traditional enthusiasm. And only as that pioneer note is sounded can we really speak of the American culture. As long as we thought of Americanism in terms of the 'melting-pot,' our American cultural tradition lay in the past. It was something to which the new Americans were to be moulded. In the light of our changing ideal of Americanism, we must perpetrate the paradox that our American cultural tradition lies in the future. It will be what we all together make out of this incomparable opportunity of attacking the future with a new key.

Whatever American nationalism turns out to be, it is certain to become something utterly different from the nationalisms of twentieth-century Europe. This wave of reactionary enthusiasm to play the orthodox nationalistic game which is passing over the country is scarcely vital enough to last. We cannot swagger and thrill to the same national self-feeling. We must give new edges to our pride. We must be content to avoid the unnumbered woes that national patriotism has brought in Europe, and that fiercely heightened pride and self-consciousness. Alluring as this is, we must allow our imaginations to transcend this scarcely veiled belligerency. We can be serenely too proud to fight if our pride embraces the creative forces of civilization which armed contest nullifies. We can be too proud to fight if our code of honor transcends that of the schoolboy on the playground surrounded by his jeering mates. Our honor must be positive and creative, and not the mere jealous and negative protectiveness against metaphysical violations of our technical rights. When the doctrine is put forth that in one American flows the mystic blood of all our country's sacred honor, freedom, and prosperity, so that an injury to him is to be the signal for turning our whole nation into that clan-feud of horror and reprisal which would be war, then we find ourselves back among the musty schoolmen of the Middle Ages, and not in any pragmatic and realistic America of the twentieth century.

We should hold our gaze to what America has done, not what mediæval codes of dueling she has failed to observe. We have transplanted European modernity to our soil, without the spirit that inflames it and turns all its energy into mutual destruction. Out of these foreign peoples there has somehow been squeezed the poison. An America, 'hyphenated' to bitterness, is somehow non-explosive. For, even if we all hark back in sympathy to a European nation, even if the war has set every one vibrating to some emotional string twanged on the other side of the Atlantic, the effect has been one of almost dramatic harmlessness.

What we have really been witnessing, however unappreciatively, in this country has been a thrilling and bloodless battle of Kulturs. In that arena of friction which has been the most dramatic—between the hyphenated German-American and the hyphenated English-American —there have emerged rivalries of philosophies which show up deep traditional attitudes, points of view which accurately reflect the gigantic issues of the war. America has mirrored the spiritual issues. The vicarious struggle has been played out peacefully here in the mind. We have seen the stout resistiveness of the old moral interpretation of history on which Victorian England thrived and made itself great in its own esteem. The clean and immensely satisfying vision of the war as a contest between right and wrong; the enthusiastic support of the Allies as the incarnation of virtue-on-a-rampage; the fierce envisaging of their selfish national purposes as the ideals of justice, freedom and democracy—all this has been thrown with intensest force against the German realistic interpretations in terms of the struggle for power and the virility of the integrated State. America has been the intellectual battleground of the nations.

III

The failure of the melting-pot, far from closing the great American democratic experiment, means that it has only just begun. Whatever American nationalism turns out to be, we see already that it will have a color richer and more exciting than our ideal has hitherto encompassed. In a world which has dreamed of internationalism, we find that we have all unawares been building up the first international nation. The voices which have cried for a tight and jealous nationalism of the European pattern are failing. From that ideal, however valiantly and disinterestedly it has been set for us, time and tendency have moved us further and further away. What we have achieved has been rather a cosmopolitan federation of national colonies, of foreign cultures, from whom the sting of devastating competition has been removed. America is already the world-federation in miniature, the continent where for the first time in history has been achieved that miracle of hope, the peaceful living side by side, with character substantially preserved, of the most heterogeneous peoples under the sun. Nowhere else has such contiguity been anything but the breeder of misery. Here, notwithstanding our tragic failures of adjustment, the outlines are already too clear not to give us a new vision and a new orientation of the American mind in the world.

It is for the American of the younger generation to accept this cosmopolitanism, and carry it along with self-conscious and fruitful purpose. In his colleges, he is already getting, with the study of modern history and politics, the modern literatures, economic geography, the privilege of a cosmopolitan outlook such as the people of no other nation of to-day in Europe can possibly secure. If he is still a colonial, he is no longer the colonial of one partial culture, but of many. He is a colonial of the world. Colonialism has grown into cosmopolitanism, and his motherland is no one nation, but all who have anything life-enhancing to offer to the spirit. That vague sympathy which the France of ten years ago was feeling for the world—a sympathy which was drowned in the terrible reality of war—may be the modern American's, and that in a positive and aggressive sense. If the American is parochial, it is in sheer wantonness or cowardice. His provincialism is the measure of his fear of bogies or the defect of his imagination.

Indeed, it is not uncommon for the eager Anglo-Saxon who goes to a vivid American university to-day to find his true friends not among his own race but among the acclimatized German or Austrian, the acclimatized Jew, the acclimatized Scandinavian or Italian. In them he finds the cosmopolitan note. In these youths, foreign-born or the children of foreign-born parents, he is likely to find many of his old inbred morbid problems washed away. These friends are oblivious to the repressions of that tight little society in which he so provincially grew up. He has a pleasurable sense of liberation from the stale and familiar attitudes of those whose ingrowing culture has scarcely created anything vital for his America of to-day. He breathes a larger air. In his new enthusiasms for continental literature, for unplumbed Russian depths, for French clarity of thought, for Teuton philosophies of power, he feels himself citizen of a larger world. He may be absurdly superficial, his outward-reaching wonder may ignore all the stiller and homelier virtues of his Anglo-Saxon home, but he has at least found the clue to that international mind which will be essential to all men and women of good-will if they are ever to save this Western world of ours from suicide. His new friends have gone through a similar evolution. America has burned most of the baser metal also from them. Meeting now with this common American background, all of them may yet retain that distinctiveness of their native cultures and their national spiritual slants. They are more valuable and interesting to each other for being different, yet that difference could not be creative were it not for this new cosmopolitan outlook which America has given them and which they all equally possess.

A college where such a spirit is possible even to the smallest degree, has within itself already the seeds of this international intellectual world of the future. It suggests that the contribution of America will be an intellectual internationalism which goes far beyond the mere exchange of scientific ideas and discoveries and the cold recording of facts. It will be an intellectual sympathy which is not satisfied until it has got at the heart of the different cultural expressions, and felt as they feel. It may have immense preferences, but it will make understanding and not indignation its end. Such a sympathy will unite and not divide.

Against the thinly disguised panic which calls itself 'patriotism' and the thinly disguised militarism which calls itself 'preparedness' the cosmopolitan ideal is set. This does not mean that those who hold it are for a policy of drift. They, too, long passionately for an integrated and disciplined America. But they do not want one which is integrated only for domestic economic exploitation of the workers or for predatory economic imperialism among the weaker peoples. They do not want one that is integrated by coercion or militarism, or for the truculent assertion of a mediæval code of honor and of doubtful rights. They believe that the most effective integration will be one which coördinates the diverse elements and turns them consciously toward working out together the place of America in the world-situation. They demand for integration a genuine integrity, a wholeness and soundness of enthusiasm and purpose which can only come when no national colony within our America feels that it is being discriminated against or that its cultural case is being prejudged. This strength of coöperation, this feeling that all who are here may have a hand in the destiny of America, will make for a finer spirit of integration than any narrow 'Americanism' or forced chauvinism.

In this effort we may have to accept some form of that dual citizenship which meets with so much articulate horror among us. Dual citizenship we may have to recognize as the rudimentary form of that international citizenship to which, if our words mean anything, we aspire. We have assumed unquestioningly that mere participation in the political life of the United States must cut the new citizen off from all sympathy with his old allegiance. Anything but a bodily transfer of devotion from one sovereignty to another has been viewed as a sort of moral treason against the Republic. We have insisted that the immigrant whom we welcomed escaping from the very exclusive nationalism of his European home shall forthwith adopt a nationalism just as exclusive, just as narrow, and even less legitimate because it is founded on no warm traditions of his own. Yet a nation like France is said to permit a formal and legal dual citizenship even at the present time. Though a citizen of hers may pretend to cast off his allegiance in favor of some other sovereignty, he is still subject to her laws when he returns. Once a citizen, always a citizen, no matter how many new citizenships he may embrace. And such a dual citizenship seems to us sound and right. For it recognizes that, although the Frenchman may accept the formal institutional framework of his new country and indeed become intensely loyal to it, yet his Frenchness he will never lose. What makes up the fabric of his soul will always be of this Frenchness, so that unless he becomes utterly degenerate he will always to some degree dwell still in his native environment.

Indeed, does not the cultivated American who goes to Europe practice a dual citizenship, which, if not formal, is no less real? The American who lives abroad may be the least expatriate of men. If he falls in love with French ways and French thinking and French democracy and seeks to saturate himself with the new spirit, he is guilty of at least a dual spiritual citizenship. He may be still American, yet he feels himself through sympathy also a Frenchman. And he finds that this expansion involves no shameful conflict within him, no surrender of his native attitude. He has rather for the first time caught a glimpse of the cosmopolitan spirit. And after wandering about through many races and civilizations he may return to America to find them all here living vividly and crudely, seeking the same adjustment that he made. He sees the new peoples here with a new vision. They are no longer masses of aliens, waiting to be 'assimilated,' waiting to be melted down into the indistinguishable dough of Anglo-Saxonism. They are rather threads of living and potent cultures, blindly striving to weave themselves into a novel international nation, the first the world has seen. In an Austria-Hungary or a Prussia the stronger of these cultures would be moving almost instinctively to subjugate the weaker. But in America those wills-to-power are turned in a different direction into learning how to live together.

Along with dual citizenship we shall have to accept, I think, that free and mobile passage of the immigrant between America and his native land again which now arouses so much prejudice among us. We shall have to accept the immigrant's return for the same reason that we consider justified our own flitting about the earth. To stigmatize the alien who works in America for a few years and returns to his own land, only perhaps to seek American fortune again, is to think in narrow nationalistic terms. It is to ignore the cosmopolitan significance of this migration. It is to ignore the fact that the returning immigrant is often a missionary to an inferior civilization.

This migratory habit has been especially common with the unskilled laborers who have been pouring into the United States in the last dozen years from every country in southeastern Europe. Many of them return to spend their earnings in their own country or to serve their country in war. But they return with an entirely new critical outlook, and a sense of the superiority of American organization to the primitive living around them. This continued passage to and fro has already raised the material standard of living in many regions of these backward countries. For these regions are thus endowed with exactly what they need, the capital for the exploitation of their natural resources, and the spirit of enterprise. America is thus educating these laggard peoples from the very bottom of society up, awakening vast masses to a new-born hope for the future. In the migratory Greek, therefore, we have not the parasitic alien, the doubtful American asset, but a symbol of that cosmopolitan interchange which is coming, in spite of all war and national exclusiveness.

Only America, by reason of the unique liberty of opportunity and traditional isolation for which she seems to stand, can lead in this cosmopolitan enterprise. Only the American—and in this category I include the migratory alien who has lived with us and caught the pioneer spirit and a sense of new social vistas—has the chance to become that citizen of the world. America is coming to be, not a nationality but a trans-nationality, a weaving back and forth, with the other lands, of many threads of all sizes and colors. Any movement which attempts to thwart this weaving, or to dye the fabric any one color, or disentangle the threads of the strands, is false to this cosmopolitan vision. I do not mean that we shall necessarily glut ourselves with the raw product of humanity. It would be folly to absorb the nations faster than we could weave them. We have no duty either to admit or reject. It is purely a question of expediency. What concerns us is the fact that the strands are here. We must have a policy and an ideal for an actual situation. Our question is, What shall we do with our America? How are we likely to get the more creative America—by confining our imaginations to the ideal of the melting-pot, or broadening them to some such cosmopolitan conception as I have been vaguely sketching?

The war has shown America to be unable, though isolated geo-graphically and politically from a European world-situation, to remain aloof and irresponsible. She is a wandering star in a sky dominated by two colossal constellations of states. Can she not work out some posi-tion of her own, some life of being in, yet not quite of, this seething and embroiled European world? This is her only hope and promise. A trans-nationality of all the nations, it is spiritually impossible for her to pass into the orbit of any one. It will be folly to hurry herself into a premature and sentimental nationalism, or to emulate Europe and play fast and loose with the forces that drag into war. No Americani-zation will fulfill this vision which does not recognize the uniqueness of this trans-nationalism of ours. The Anglo-Saxon attempt to fuse will only create enmity and distrust. The crusade against 'hyphenates' will only inflame the partial patriotism of trans-nationals, and cause them to assert their European traditions in strident and unwholesome ways. But the attempt to weave a wholly novel international nation out of our chaotic America will liberate and harmonize the creative power of all these peoples and give them the new spiritual citizenship, as so many individuals have already been given, of a world.

Is it a wild hope that the undertow of opposition to metaphysics in international relations, opposition to militarism, is less a cowardly provincialism than a groping for this higher cosmopolitan ideal? One can understand the irritated restlessness with which our proud pro-British colonists contemplate a heroic conflict across the seas in which they have no part. It was inevitable that our necessary inaction should evolve in their minds into the bogey of national shame and dishonor. But let us be careful about accepting their sensitiveness as final arbiter. Let us look at our reluctance rather as the first crude beginnings of assertion on the part of certain strands in our nationality that they have a right to a voice in the construction of the American ideal. Let us face realistically the America we have around us. Let us work with the forces that are at work. Let us make something of this trans-national spirit instead of outlawing it. Already we are living this cos-mopolitan America. What we need is everywhere a vivid consciousness of the new ideal. Deliberate headway must be made against the sur-vivals of the melting-pot ideal for the promise of American life.

We cannot Americanize America worthily by sentimentalizing and moralizing history. When the best schools are expressly renouncing the questionable duty of teaching patriotism by means of history, it is not the time to force shibboleth upon the immigrant. This form of Americanization has been heard because it appealed to the vestiges of our old sentimentalized and moralized patriotism. This has so far held the field as the expression of the new American's new devotion. The inflections of other voices have been drowned. They must be heard. We must see if the lesson of the war has not been for hundreds of these later Americans a vivid realization of their trans-nationality, a new consciousness of what America meant to them as a citizenship in the world. It is the vague historic idealisms which have provided the fuel for the European flame. Our American ideal can make no progress until we do away with this romantic gilding of the past.

All our idealisms must be those of future social goals in which all can participate, the good life of personality lived in the environment of the Beloved Community. No mere doubtful triumphs of the past, which redound to the glory of only one of our trans-nationalities, can satisfy us. It must be a future America, on which all can unite, which pulls us irresistibly toward it, as we understand each other more warmly.

To make real this striving amid dangers and apathies is work for a younger *intelligentsia* of America. Here is an enterprise of integration into which we can all pour ourselves, of a spiritual welding which should make us, if the final menace ever came, not weaker, but infinitely strong.

9

The Jew and Trans-National America[1]

Before the American people at the present time there are two ideals of American nationalism, sharply focussed and emphasized by the war. One is that of the traditional melting-pot, the other is that of a co-operation of cultures. The first is congenial to the ruling class, the nativist element of our population; the second appeals, however vaguely, to the leaders of the various self-conscious European national groups which have settled here. The idealism of the melting-pot would assimilate all Europeans, as they are received into the American social and economic scheme, to a very definite type, that of the prevailing Anglo-Saxon. For however much this desire may be obscured, what the Anglicized American prophets of the melting-pot really mean shall happen to the immigrant is that he shall acquire, along with the new common English language, the whole stock of English political and social ideals. When they attempt to judge how far any group has been Americanized, it is by this standard that they judge them.

The effect of the melting-pot ideal is either to influence this Angliciz-ing, or to obliterate the distinctive racial and cultural qualities, and work the American population into a colorless, tasteless, homogeneous mass. With large masses of our foreign-born of the second generation this latter process is far advanced, and the result is that cultural point-lessness and vacuity which our critics of American life are never weary

[1] *The Menorah Journal,* II (Dec. 1916), 277–284. Originally an address before the Harvard Menorah Society.

of deploring. Both effects of the melting-pot idealism, I believe, are highly undesirable. Both make in the long run for exactly that terrible unity of pride, chauvinism, and ambition that has furnished the popular fuel in the armed clash of nationalism in Europe. To preach a pure and undiluted Americanism with the spectacle of suicidal Europe before us is to invite disaster and destruction. American idealism is face to face with a crucial dilemma. Cultural self-consciousness, concentrated, inspiring vigor of intellectual and personal qualities such as the French possess, for instance, is the most precious heritage a nation can have. Yet apparently this intense national feeling leads straight into chauvinistic self-assertion, into conflict with other nationalisms, into a belligerency which drags the world down in mutual ruin. Who can doubt that, if we ever obtained this homogeneous Americanism that our Rooseveltian prophets desire, the latent imperialism of our ruling class would flame forth and America would follow the other States in their plunge to perdition? America's only hope is in the development of a democratic and pacific way of life. We have an opportunity at last to try to make good that old boast of our being a model to the nations. We can at least make the effort to show that a democratic civilization founded on peace is a possibility in this portentous twentieth century.

I

Wherein the "Hyphenate" Has Been a Blessing

I feel so strongly on this subject that I am willing to believe that the so-called "hyphenate," by keeping us from being swept into a premature and nebulous cohesion, has actually been our salvation. I believe that almost anything that keeps us from being welded together into a terrible national engine which powerful political or financial interests may wield at will, flinging the entire nation's strength in a moment to any cause or movement that seems to advance their will or their private class-sense of honor or justice—I say that anything that keeps us from being thus used is a salvation. I do not say that division and confusion are good for long. I do not say that we do not need a unity of purpose and sympathy. But I do say that any confusion which results in giving time for the weak democratic, radical and pacific forces in this country to struggle to their feet and become strong is a beneficent confusion. Such, I believe, is our present confusion, which even that present evil genius of the American people, ————² has been unable to dispel. We want no national unity that is not based on democratic and socialized and international goals.

That is why I am almost fanatically against the current programs of Americanism, with their preparedness, conscription, imperialism, integration issues, their slavish imitation of the European nationalisms which are slaying each other before our eyes. The current war is the terrible price which European nationalism has had to pay for its hard, bright, inspiring integrity. By welding themselves into a spiritual and patriotic cohesion, these peoples have handed themselves over to their rulers as single, compact, all-powerful weapons for those rulers to wield. America is still an industrial oligarchy. Were America to get that cohesion which is urged upon us before democratic forces developed, would it not be wielded in exactly the same way? In defense of so-called "rights," what could prevent our own rulers from brandishing our strength and using the nation as a hammer to wage needless war? Nothing will save us but the firmest insistence on a different kind of Americanism. We must somehow acquire this intensity and vigor of cultural self-consciousness without paying the price of terrible like-mindedness.

II

Shall the Immigrant Give Up His Cultural Allegiance?

Now it is exactly this gradual solution of the dilemma which I look to the ideal of co-operative Americanism to achieve. If America is to be nationalistic without being chauvinistic, we need new conceptions of the state, of nationality, of citizenship, of allegiance. The war, to my mind, has proved the utter obsolescence of the old conceptions. Even without the war the old conceptions would have been obsolete. For the development of backward countries, the growth of population in Europe, the demand for labor and colonists in all parts of the globe, the ease and cheapness of travel, have set in motion vast currents of immigration which render impossible the old tight geographical group-

² The deletion was made by the editors of the *Menorah Journal*.

ings of nationality. The political ideas of the future will have to be adjusted to a shifting world-population, to the mobility of labor, to all kinds of new temporary mixings of widely diverse peoples, as well as to their permanent mixings.

The Jews have lost their distinctiton of being a peculiar people. Dispersion is now the lot of every race. The Jewish ghetto in America is matched by the Italian, by the Slovac ghetto. The war will intensify this setting in motion of wandering peoples. The age-long problems of Jewish nationalism have become the burning problems of other dispersed nationalities. America has become a vast reservoir of dispersions. The adjustment which the Jew has had to make throughout the ages is a pattern of what other nationals have to make to-day. From their point of view, the same dilemmas of assimilation and absorption, of cultural and racial allegiance, beset them. In the new country they have often the same alternatives of disintegration or sub-national life. To the intelligent and enthusiastic emigré from the Teuton or Slavic or Latin lands, it seems no more desirable that his cultural soul should be washed out of him than it seems to the Jew. America puts to him the same problem of becoming assimilated to New World life, of meeting his new political freedom and vague expansion of economic opportunity, without becoming a mere colorless unit in a gray mass. And the immigrant puts to America the problem of finding a place for him to make his peculiar and whole-hearted contribution to the upbuilding of the America which is still in process of creation. The problem of the Jew in the modern world is identical. As a Jew has said, "The modern world sets the Jew the problem of maintaining some sort of distinctive existence without external props of territorial sovereignty and a political machine; the Jew sets the modern world the problem of finding for him a place in its social structure which shall enable him to live as a human being without demanding that he cease to be a Jew."

III

How Jewish Idealism Solves the Problem

If then this co-operative Americanism is an ideal which meets at once the demands of a native American like myself who wishes to see America kept from militarization and feudalization, and also the demands of the foreign immigré who wishes freedom to preserve his heritage at the same time that he co-operates loyally with all other nationals in the building-up of America, I believe we shall find in the current Jewish ideal of Zionism the purest pattern and the most inspiring conceptions of trans-nationalism. I used to think, as many Americans still do, that Zionism was incompatible with Americanism, that if your enthusiasm and energy went into creating a Jewish nation in the Orient, you could not give yourself to building up the State in which you lived. I have since learned that however flawless such a logical antithesis would be, nothing could be falser than this idea. This dilemma of dual allegiance must be solved in America, it must be solved by the world, and it is in the fertile implications of Zionism that I veritably believe the solution will be found.

To the orthodox Jew, I presume the ideas clustering about the founding of Zion will seem only the realization of age-long Jewish hopes. To me they represent an international idealism almost perilously new. They furnish just those new conceptions that I said this new American idealism would need. Indeed my own mind was set working on the whole idea of American national ideals by the remarkable articles of Dr. Kallen in *The Nation* last year,[3] and the very phrase, "trans-nationalism," I stole from a Jewish college mate of mine who, I suspect, is now a member of your Menorah Society here. The idea is a Jewish idea, and the great contribution of Jewish intelligence in America I conceive to be to clarify and spread these new conceptions.

It may be daring of me to assume that the Jew, with his traditional segregation, his intense fusion of racial and religious egoism, will contribute hopefully to the foundations of a new spiritual internationalism. But has it not always been the anomaly of the Jew that he was at once the most self-conscious of beings—feels himself, that is, religiously, culturally, racially, a being peculiar in his lot and signally blessed—and yet has proven himself perhaps the most assimilable of all races to other and quite alien cultures? Which is cause and which is effect? Is he assimilable because he has had no national centre, no geographical and political basis for his religion and his mode of life, or has he not had his Jewish nation because he has been so readily assimilated? Is it not just this in the Jewish personality that has piqued and irritated and attracted other peoples, that it is at once so congenial and so alien?

[3] See Horace M. Kallen, "Democracy Versus the Melting-Pot," *The Nation*, C (1915), 219–220.

And can we not connect the so very recent flowering of the hopes of Jewish nationalism with the fact that Zionistic ideals now for the first time seem to be making towards internationalism? They move in line with the world's best hope. For as I understand it, the Jewish State which Zionists are building is a non-military, a non-chauvinistic State. Palestine is to be built as a Jewish centre on purely religious and cultural foundations. It is not to be the home of all the Jewish people. Zionism does not propose to prevent Jews from living in full citizenship in other countries. The Zionist does not believe that there is a necessary conflict between a cultural allegiance to the Jewish centre and political allegiance to a State.

IV

A Dual Citizenship—A Spiritual Internationalism

This distinction between State and nationality is a very modern conception. The successful State to-day is a federation of autonomous units, or a federation of different peoples living in justice and amity. The State becomes more and more a coalition of people for the realization of common social ends. It is becoming more and more difficult to identify State and nationality. The modern world, with its mixings and shiftings of peoples, its differences of potential between large and small national groups, simply will not fit into these terms. Cultural allegiance will not necessarily coincide with political allegiance. A sort of dual citizenship becomes possible and desirable, if fullest expression is to be given to those feelings of racial sympathy, similar traditions, cultural distinction, which make peoples cling so fiercely together and sacrifice so much for political unity. The world has thought that it must have its culture and its political unity coincide. Witness the strivings of Italy for Italia Irredenta, of Greece for its Islands and Asiatic shore, of Serbia for the greater Serbia. But suppose these unreclaimed nationalities autonomous and unoppressed within their larger Empire. Does not the example of trans-national Belgium and Switzerland imply that in such peaceful and just States these irredentist problems would disappear, and is it not oppression that causes the egotism of small nationalities to swell unwholesomely? The Zionist philosophy, I take it, assumes that with a national centre for the Jewish race in Palestine to which the oppressed might flee, and to which, as the place where the type of life corresponding to the character and ideals of the Jewish people, the eyes of all Jews might turn, cultural allegiance and political allegiance might automatically strike a balance and a Jew might remain a complete Jew and at the same time be a complete citizen of any modern political State where he happened to live and where his work and interests lay.

If this interpretation of mine is correct, then the modern world, and above all America, needs these Zionist conceptions. What I mean by co-operative Americanism—that is, an ideal of a freely mingling society of peoples of very different racial and cultural antecedents, with a common political allegiance and common social ends but with free and distinctive cultural allegiances which may be placed anywhere in the world that they like—is simply a generalization of the practical effect of the Zionist ideal. I see no other way by which international sympathy may be created and the best human expressivenesses and distinctive attitudes and traits preserved. And if the Jews have been the first international race, I look to America to be the first international nation.

V

Two Real Dangers of Misdirected Trans-Nationalism

Groups of identical culture must find some way of leading a national life that is neither belligerently egotistic like the hectic nationalism of Europe nor sub-national like that of the Jews of the Russian Pale. The American ideal must make possible such an ideal national life within our own country if the peoples who came here are to be enriched and enriching.

My argument for Trans-National America has seemed to be vitiated by two considerations. One is that this trans-nationalism of the foreign national groups in America is too often colored by political as well as cultural allegiance to the homeland. Deutschtum is not only a movement for the keeping alive of a noble German tongue and literature, which is desirable, but it has become at times suspiciously like a Kaisertum, which is wholly undesirable. Another dangerous corollary to trans-nationalism is that the national groups, if this patriotic and cultural emphasis are too great, if their Deutschtum and their Kaisertum become too intensified, might tend to become actual political groups of racial rivalry within the American nation. This is a consummation even more sinister. I do not argue for an artificial stimulation of trans-national feeling. I only argue for its freedom, believing that when it is free it will fertilize and enhance the common American life. But even when it is free, there is another danger. The *Kultur* that an expatriated group of nationals cultivate may be one that has already been superseded at home. This has happened repeatedly in America. The contemporary official German-American element, for instance, seems to reproduce a fussy, transitory stage of the German bourgeoisie of the seventies and eighties, and very little the peculiar Nietzschean flair of the present-day Germany. The English South is still mid-Victorian, though English culture has been revolutionized. The official Irish-American is rather wierdly [*sic*] different from his expressive Irish brother. These groups, transplanted to America, are victims of arrested development, in spite of their fierce trans-national cultural patriotism. They fondly imagine that they are keeping the faith. But in merely not changing, these expatriated groups have not really kept the faith. This faith is a certain way of facing the world, of accepting experience. It is a spirit and not any particular forms. A genuine trans-nationalism would be modern, reflecting not only the peculiar gifts and temperament of the people, but reflecting it in its contemporary form. America runs a very real danger of becoming not the modern cosmopolitan grouping that we desire, but a queer conglomeration of the prejudices of past generations, miraculously preserved here, after they have mercifully perished at home.

VI

But the Jewish Aspiration is Wholesome

Jewish trans-nationalism, on the other hand, seems to me just to avoid these very pitfalls. The Zionist's lack of chauvinistic and dynastic aims for his new nation removes the fear of Jewish political groupings in this country. And the fact that the Jewish national life is in the future avoids that danger of the petrifying of outworn expressions of the national ideal. The Zionist's outlook is intensely modern. The nation that he is building in Palestine is clearly designed to work out the Jewish mode of life on the most scientific modern lines. Scientific agriculture, the protection of health, education, equitable taxation, economic justice between individuals—all this indicates a union between the noble old Law and the most enlightened spirit of modern social welfare. As I read of the admirable features of the suburban settlement at Jaffa, or of some of the other colonies, I realize that the trans-national Jew will have a nation to look to which he can really adore as no other trans-national, forced to look at vexing compromises between the medieval and the new, will be able to adore. An ancient spirit of justice and sobriety, expressed with all the technique of modern science and sense of social welfare—what could more perfectly symbolize the nationalism which will keep our old earth rich, sweet and varied?

If I take this Zionism, which seems to me to contain the best current Jewish idealism, as a pattern for American trans-nationalism, I may unwittingly be doing it injustice. It will seem to you that I have ignored the religious aspect, and I have perhaps unknowingly caricatured its political conceptions. But I am looking at Zionism from the outside and not from within. My interest is in the question how far do Jewish ideals contribute to that larger internationalism of which America might be the exponent? There is very real danger that a reactionary idealism may force a fatally narrow patriotic spirit upon us. In new conceptions, such as those which this Jewish idealism seems to contribute, I see our salvation. The Jew in America is proving every day the possibility of this dual life. To clinch one's argument one would need no other evidence than the figure of Justice Brandeis, at once an ardent Zionist and at the same time an incomparable American leader in economic and social reconstruction. And what shall we say of the younger generation of Jewish intelligents, which includes such men as Felix Frankfurter, Horace M. Kallen, Morris R. Cohen, Walter Lippmann? The intellectual service which such writers are doing us with their clarity of expression, their radical philosophy, their masterly fibre of thought, can hardly be over-valued. Their contribution is so incomparably greater than that of any other American group of foreign cultural affiliations that one can scarcely get one's perspective. A large majority of this younger generation is, I understand, Zionist in its sympathy. Yet that Jewish idealism has not in the least vitiated their peculiarly intimate insight into American problems, their gift of picking a way through the tangled social and economic maze. In their light we all see light. They are my last proof of the practicability of the co-operative American ideal. And they suggest that an ardent Zionism involves the responsibility for an equally ardent effort for that progressive democratic reconstruction in America which is the ideal of all true Americans, no matter what their heritage or trans-nationality.

10

What is Exploitation?[1]

My western friend who runs a prosperous stove-factory has been finding fault with my insistent use of the word "exploitation." My outlook on life is not sufficiently cheerful, and I am inclined to see malevolence where everything is, as they say at college, healthy, hearty and happy. Our quarrel rose over the Mesaba strike,[2] and my acceptance of an I. W. W. pamphlet as a plausible account of what was going on there. The accounts of the insecurity of pay, the petty robberies, the reeking houses, the bigoted opposition to labor organization, seemed to me to smell of truth, because I had read the maddening tales of Colorado and West Virginia, and seen with my own eyes in Scranton and Gary and Pittsburgh the way workers live, not in crises of industrial war but in brimming times of peace.

My friend, however, is more robust. He would make no such hasty impassioned judgments. He would judge nothing without "going to the mines, working in them for a year or two, being one of the men, getting their free confidence, then working for a couple of years as confidential auditor for the company." Such Olympian judiciality fills me with envy and dismay. I feel that his serenity is the normal mood of healthy activity, facing the modern world. Could he find anything but scorn for those of us who go around with the vestiges of what it is now priggish to call a "social conscience"? To him an industrial strike

[1] *The New Republic,* IX (Nov. 4, 1916), 12–14.
[2] A current strike of iron workers in the Mesabi Range, led by the International Workers of the World.

is like an exciting political contest or the recriminations between "two kid baseball teams." Both sides, he says, "squawk a good deal about the raw stuff the other side is trying to pull off," but deep down, his experience convinces him, "they are very uniformly a pretty human bunch." He hasn't been to Mesaba, but his friend the Duluth bread-dealer assures him that agitators were the cause of all the trouble. They always are. Trouble, to my friend, is a personal matter. He sees individuals, laboring as happily as they can expect to labor on this far from perfumed earth. He sees their contentment disturbed by "outsiders," individuals, bitter envious mischievous men who make a business of setting workmen against their employers. He sees the "outsiders" deluding, persuading, intimidating honest workers into stopping work and engaging in careers of lawlessness. He sees the individual employer in natural self-defense fighting for his rights, defending his property, ousting the agitators, carrying the war into his laborers' camp. From the busy office of his stove-factory, it all looks like a personal quarrel between free and equal individuals. When the state interferes with its militia and its injunctions, it is not flouting individuality, but merely doing its business of maintaining order and defending private property.

Our argument really hinges on whether to the workman all this excitement and deprivation and delusion is not part of the daily business of living. I am too tender-minded. What is at the back of my confused hints that there is "something shameful, something consciously brutal" about industrial relations? My friend admits that he has in his shop men who work in places that are noisy and dusty, in hot places, in rooms where paint is being sprayed. He has workmen who do their work at night the year round. He is sorry. He wishes these things did not have to be, and he is remedying them as fast as he can. What he will not admit is that any one is "specifically to blame." He does not imprison his men. They come freely to him and ask for employment. He "gives them such compensation as makes the jobs attractive to them, in competition with all other jobs in city and country." He is fair and scrupulous. His company is in business to produce goods at such cost that people can afford to buy them. He cannot make his plant a sanatorium—and when he says this the faintest note of irony steals into his robust voice—for his wage-earners. The stockholders have built a factory and not a philanthropic institution. If the workers did not like his factory, would they send for their brothers and cousins from the old country across the sea? If these "hunkies" in stove-factory and iron mine were being "exploited," would they not drift speedily away to jobs where they were content? My friend cannot imagine a man being willingly exploited. There are, no doubt, heartless employers; workmen here and there are perhaps subject to oppression. But systematic, prevalent industrial exploitation—and he has worked in all parts of the country and at every level of skill—my stove-factory friend has never seen. And he turns aside from my abstract philosophy to the daily manipulation of stoves and men.

What then do I mean by exploitation? And I have to remind my friend that my very first industrial experience was one of those rudimentary patterns of life which, if they are imprinted on your mind early enough, remain to fix the terms in which you interpret the world. The experience was leaving school to work for a musician who had an ingenious little machine on which he cut perforated music-rolls for the players which were just then becoming popular. His control of the means of production consisted in having the machine in his house, to which I went every morning at eight and stayed till five. He provided the paper and the music and the electric power; I worked as a wage-earner, serving his skill and enterprise. I was on piece-work, and everything suggested to my youthful self that it depended only upon my skill and industry how prosperous I should become. But what startled me was my employer's lack of care to conceal from me the fact that for every foot of paper which I made he received fifteen cents from the manufacturer with whom he had his contract. He paid me five, and while I worked, spent his time composing symphonies in the next room. As long as I was learning the craft, I had no more feeling about our relation than that there was a vague injustice in the air. But when I began to be dangerously clever and my weekly earnings mounted beyond the sum proper for a young person of eighteen who was living at home, I felt the hand of economic power. My piece-rate was reduced to four and a half cents. My innocence blazed forth in rebellion. If I was worth five cents a foot while I was learning, I was worth more, not less, after I had learned. My master folded his arms. I did not have to work for him. There were neighbors who would. I could stay or go. I was perfectly free. And then fear smote me. This was my only skill, and my timorous inexperience filled the outside world with horrors. I returned cravenly to my bench, and when my employer, flushed with his capitalistic ardor, built another machine and looked about for a young musician to work it, I weakly suggested to an old playmate of mine that he apply for the position.

Enlarge my musician into the employing class of owners and managers and shareholders of factory and mine and railroad, and myself into the class of wage-earners in all these enterprises, and you have the picture of the industrial system which the I. W. W. agitator has in his mind when he writes the Mesaba pamphlet to which my friend took such exception. With my five cents making that huge differential of profit for my employer, and with my four and a half cents giving his enterprise a productiveness which, if he had incorporated himself, he could have turned into additional capitalization, I was a crude symbol of the industrial system as my mind gradually took in the fact that there was an industrial system. This was my first experience in "exploitation." If there had been fewer musicians available I should have gotten more pay, and if there had been more available I should probably have had even less. But there would always have been a surplus, and I should have always felt the power of my employer to skim it, to pull it towards himself. As long as I continued at work, nothing could have removed my sense of helplessness. Any struggle I might have made would have been only towards weakening his pull, and lessening the amount he was able to skim. He was not robbing me, and no person of sense would have said he was, but our very relation was an exploitation. There was no medium way between exploitation and philanthropy.

My stove-factory friend, however, will have none of this theory. If it is a question of power, he says, then Mike Solomon exploits the stove company when he is able to get three dollars a day, on account of the present demand for labor, when two dollars was wealth to him a year ago. Then I admit that local groups of workers are able—either through lack of competition or clever politics or display of force—to exercise temporarily a decisive pull on the surplus and divert most of it to themselves. It is all a question of power. But as long, I tell him, as the employer is entrenched in property rights with the armed state behind him, the power will be his, and the class that does the diverting will not be labor. My friend, however, does not like these Nietzschean terms. He is sure that his workmen have just as much power to exploit him as he has of exploiting them. This is where we differ, and this is why thought will buzz in an angry murky haze over eight-hour bills and individual contracts and collective bargaining as long as millions agree with him. He trusts rights, I trust power. He recognizes only individuals, I recognize classes.

That is why I can never make him understand what I mean by "exploitation." He thinks of it as something personally brutal. He does not see it inherent in a system, for which no one is "specifically to blame" only because all are equally guilty of short vision and flimsy analysis. And yet as I read his letters and clippings, I wonder if he is not the realist and I the mystic. He punctures my phrases of power and class with a coarse satisfied hunky to whom work and disease and riot are all in the day's work and who would despise the philosophy which I am so anxiously weaving for him. It seems a long way from my dainty music-bench to the iron range, or the stove-factory. One has to feel exploitation perhaps before one understands it. I console myself with the thought that power is itself mystic, and that my friend will have to get hit with some invisible threat of class-force, as some of his frightened friends are now getting hit, before he will analyze any deeper that industrial system of which he is so efficient and loyal an officer.

11

The Price of Radicalism[1]

M r. Seymour Deming follows his eloquent "Message to the Middle Class" with an assault upon the colleges. His book he calls "a profane baccalaureate," and it rips along as from one who is overturning the altars of Baal. No one has a style quite like this, with its mixture of Greek classicism and Broadway slang, with its cheap sardonic kicks and its sudden flashes of insight. Mr. Deming moves you, but he leaves you in the end more entertained than persuaded. His prophetic fire is so much fire and so little light. The first part of the book is devoted to picturesque denunciation of the colleges for not training a man to make a living. The second glorifies the radical as the man who scorns success, and has turned from everything which the world thinks of value. Such logic dims the force of his blast.

I quite agree with Mr. Deming that the object of an education is to know a revolution when you see one. Colorado, Calumet, and West Virginia should make the college sky much more lurid than they do. But something more is needed for this "class unconscious of class-consciousness" than clarion calls summoning it to be radical. Mr. Deming has too much of the martyr-complex. He talks as if the radical of to-day occupied the position of social outlawry that the Abolitionist of 1850 occupied. To be radical, he says, is to be thrust out of the society of cultivated men, and to seek one's companionship among the meek

[1] *The New Republic,* VI (March 11, 1916), 161. A review of Seymour Deming, *The Pillar of Fire* (Boston: Small, Maynard & Co., 1915).

and lowly. He speaks too always as if this little group of early Christians living in catacombs were all of the saintliest breed, the foolish who have confounded the sayings of the wise. Most of us used to believe both of these things. But most of us have given up looking on ourselves as heroes and martyrs because we blaspheme the "property-god of Things-As-They-Are." We have climbed out of the catacombs, and we find many radicals disillusioning. We have either grown up or the world has moved on.

The real trouble with middleclass radicalism in this country to-day is that it is too easy. It is becoming too popular. It is not the heroic abnegation which Mr. Deming pictures, but something which almost anybody can encompass. The ranks are full of the unfocussed and the unthinking. Let the college man or girl who listens to Mr. Deming's sermon join the Intercollegiate Socialist Society or some similar institution, and discover how discouragingly respectable they are. The only way by which middle-class radicalism can serve is by being fiercely and concentratedly intellectual. This is something which these organizations have so far failed to do. The labor movement in this country needs a philosophy, a literature, a constructive socialist analysis and criticism of industrial relations. How very far even the most intelligent accredited representatives of labor are still from such a goal is shown by the Manly report.[2] Labor will scarcely do this thinking for itself. Unless middle-class radicalism threshes out its categories and interpretations and undertakes this constructive thought it will not be done. Mr. Deming must add to his message of fire the clear cold determination to be intolerantly intellectual.

Given the prophetic fire, the young middle-class radical to whom Mr. Deming appeals should be able to find himself in an intellectual movement which is struggling to clarify its ideas and use them as tools for turning up the layers and interpreting the changes in the social world about them. Intellectual radicalism should not mean repeating stale dogmas of Marxism. It should not mean "the study of socialism." It had better mean a restless, controversial criticism of current ideas, and a hammering out of some clear-sighted philosophy that shall be this pillar of fire. The young radical to-day is not asked to be a martyr,

[2] Report of the United States Commission on Industrial Relations, Basil M. Manly, Director of Research and Investigation (Washington, Government Printing Office, 1916). The report emphasized the poverty existing among large numbers of industrial workers and their failure to improve their lot.

but he is asked to be a thinker, an intellectual leader. So far as the official radicals deprecate such an enterprise they make their movement sterile. Yet how often when attempts are made to group radicals on an intellectual basis does not some orthodox elder of the socialist church arise and solemnly denounce such intellectual snobbishness. Let these young men and women, he will say, go down into the labor unions and the socialist locals and learn of the workingman. Let them touch the great heart of the people. Let them put aside their university knowledge and hear that which is revealed unto babes. Only by humbly working up through the actual labor movement will the young radical learn his job. His intellectualism he must disguise. The epithet "intellectual" must make him turn pale and run.

And so this middle-class radicalism tends to drift, destitute of intellectual light. The pugnacious thinkers who want to thresh things out find themselves labelled heterodox and esoteric. There is little controversy because nobody will quarrel about ideas. The workers must not be offended and the movement must not be split. The young radical soon learns to be ashamed of his intellectual bias, and after an ineffectual effort to squeeze himself into the mind of the workingman drifts away disillusioned from his timid collegiate radicals. His energy evaporates, because intellectual radicalism was afraid to be itself.

Mr. Deming ignores this practical postlude to his challenges. The pillar of fire was not an exciting alarm but a guide which led the way towards the Promised Land. A cloud by day, its mission by night was to give forth no heat but light. Just so far as such messages as Mr. Deming's are real pillars of fire they are the needfullest we could have.

12

A Moral Equivalent for Universal
Military Service[1]

The current agitation for preparedness has set hosts of Americans to thinking out for the first time what a real national strength and readiness would mean. We suddenly realize that if we are to defeat that militaristic trend which we loathe we shall have to offer some kind of action more stirring and more creative. The call now upon every citizen is to be not nebulously patriotic, but clear and lucid as to America's aims, so that our national energy shall not be squandered and misused. There looms up as a crucial need that "moral equivalent for war" with which William James first roused our imaginations. It seems no longer so academic a proposal. Confronted with the crisis, we see that he analyzed the situation with consummate accuracy.

All around us we feel a very genuine craving for unity of sentiment, for service, for some new national lift and broadening which shall keep us out of the uneasy pettiness into which the American conscience has threatened to fall. In our hearts we know that to crystallize this desire into a meaningless sentiment, or into a piling-up of armaments or a proscribing of alien cultures, would not satisfy us. We want action, but we do not want military action. Even the wildest patriots know that America would have to go through the most pernicious and revolutionary changes to accept the universal military service which they advo-

[1] *The New Republic*, VII (July 1, 1916), 217–219.

cate. We wish to advance from where we stand. We begin to suspect that military service, flag-reverence, patriotic swagger, are too much the weary old deep-dug channels into which national feeling always runs and is lost. The flooding river fills again its archaic and forsaken paths. Our present confusion expresses the dilemma we find ourselves in, when our instincts impel us into courses that our intelligence tells us we ought not to follow.

Our American danger is not so much that we become militarists as that we grope along, fretting and harrying each other into a unity which is delusive, and expressing our "Americanism" in activities that are not creative. The best will in America at the present time seems to crave some kind of national service but it veers off from military service. Until we satisfy that craving, we shall run at half-power, and suffer all the dissatisfaction and self-despising that comes from repressed energy. The question which all are asking, in the varied and disguised forms, is: How can we all together serve America by really enhancing her life?

To more and more of us the clue has come through James's conception of a productive army of youth, warring against nature and not against men, finding in drudgery and toil and danger the values that war and preparation for war had given. Ten years ago such an army seemed Utopian. We had neither the desire nor the technique. It seemed a project not to be realized without a reorganization of our life so radical as to make the army itself unnecessary. To-day, however, a host of new attitudes seem to give us the raw material out of which such a national service could be created. We hear much of universal military service as "education." The Plattsburgs[2] are sugar-coated as "civic training camps," "schools for citizenship." Universal service no longer stands on its old ground of mere preparation for war. It is frankly trying to get itself recognized as an indispensable mode of education. The next pertinent step is evidently to ask why, if universal service is valuable because it is educational, it should not be constructed on a strict educational foundation.

James's proposal sounded Utopian because it would require an entirely new and colossal national organization to put it into action. Universal military service in this country would certainly mean such a

[2] "Plattsburgs" were training camps for civilians. They were widely publicized in 1915 when at Plattsburg, N.Y. General Leonard Wood advocated their use as part of the preparedness movement.

task. But if our national service is to be educational, we already have the organization in existence. The rapidly consolidating public school systems in the states provide the machinery for such an organization. As the public schools become better places for children to spend their time in, we are growing less tolerant of the forms of schooling outside of the public system. The tendency is towards the inclusion of all children in the public school. And the progressive states are requiring schooling up to the full age of sixteen years. We are rapidly creating a public school system, effectively administered by the states, which gives us the one universally national, compulsory service which we possess or are ever likely to consent to.

Education is the only form of "conscription" to which Americans have ever given consent. Compulsory military service would require decades of Napoleonic political evangelism to introduce. Compulsory education is universally accepted. For a national service which shall be educational you would have to convert nobody. The field is sown. No one denies the right of the state to conscript the child for education. But coupled with this assent is the insistence that the educaion shall be the freest, fullest and most stimulating that we know how to give. The current educational interest arises largely from the indignant demand that a state which takes all the children must meet the needs of every child. The very recent enthusiasm for "vocational education" means that we want a schooling that shall issue in capacity for fruitful occupation. A national educational service could give training for work at the same time that it gave opportunity for service.

It is only a national service of this kind that would really be universal. Military service is a sham universality. It omits the feminine half of the nation's youth. And of the mascuine half it uses only the physically best. France is the only country where the actual levy on men for military service has approximated the number liable. But worst of all, military service irons out all differences of talent and ability. It does not even tap the resources it enlists. It makes out of an infinitely varied group a mere machine of uniform, obeying units. The personal qualities, the individual powers of the youth it trains, are of no relevance whatever. Men are valuable exactly to the degree that they crush out these differences.

A national service for education would not be a sham. It would actually enlist the coöperation of every youth and girl. It would aim at stimulation, not obedience. It would call out capacity and not submerge it. It would organize varied tasks adapted to the capacities and strengths of its young citizenry. It would be universal, but it would be compulsory only in the sense that it called every one to the service. The tasks would not be enforced drudgery, but work that enlisted the will and toned up the aspirations.

Such a national service would be the logical outgrowth of our public school system. Suppose the state said: All children shall remain in school till the age of sixteen years. Between the ages of sixteen and twenty-one they shall spend two years in national service. This service shall be organized and administered by the state educational administrations, but supervised and subsidized by the national government. The service would be performed as national service, but its work would be constructive and communal in its purposes and not military. Special military training could be given as a branch of this service to those who were best fitted for it. But defense would be but an incident in our constructive life, and not the sinew of our effort.

The tasks for such a national service would evidently be different from those contemplated by James. He thought of turning his army of youth into the drudgery of the world, where they might win in heroic toil and self-sacrifice the moral rewards which war had formerly given. But if our service is to be universal, it cannot be mere unskilled labor in mines and farms and forests. A large proportion of our youth would be disqualified. Furthermore, a service which made such frontal attack on industry would be bitterly resisted by those with whom its work competed. We are not prepared for a service which clashes too suddenly and harshly with the industrial system. What we need is a service which shall not so much do the old work of the world as create new demands and satisfy them. This national service could do the things which need to be done, but which are not now being done. It could have for its aim the improvement of the quality of our living. Our appalling slovenliness, the ignorance of great masses in city and country as to the elementary technique of daily life—this should be the enemy of the army of youth. I have a picture of a host of eager young missionaries swarming over the land, spreading the health knowledge, the knowledge of domestic science, of gardening, of tastefulness, that they have learned in school.

Such a service would provide apprentices for communal services in town and country, as many schools and colleges are already actually providing. Food inspection, factory inspection, organized relief, the care of dependents, playground service, nursing in hospitals—all this would be a field for such an educational service. On a larger scale, tree-planting, the care and repair of roads, work on conservation projects, the care of model farms, would be tasks for this army. As I was burning caterpillars' nests the other day in New Jersey and saw the trees sinister with grey webs, I thought of the destroying army of youth that should be invading the land clearing it of all insect pests. We might even come to the forcible rebuilding of the slovenly fences and outhouses which strew our landscape, and to an imposition of cleanness upon our American countryside. With an army of youth we could perform all those services of neatness and mercy and intelligence which our communities now know how to perform and mean to perform, but have not the weapons to wield.

The army could be organized in flying squadrons, so that its youth could travel widely and see and serve all kinds of men and communities. For its direction we would need that new type of teacher-engineer-community worker that our best school systems are already producing. Scientific schools, schools of philanthropy, are turning out men and women who could step into their places as non-commissioned officers for such an army. The service could be entirely flexible. Boys and girls could learn the rudiments of their trade or profession in actual service with the army. Book studies could be carried on, and college learning could come to its own as the intellectual fertilizer of a wholesome and stimulating life. Athletics and sports would be an integral part of the two years' service. There would be long periods of camping in the national parks or upon ocean beaches. The Boy Scouts and Camp-Fire Girls already give the clue to such an enterprise.

If objection is made that this national educational service would fail to bring out the sterner qualities of heroism and self-sacrifice, and would not be a genuine moral equivalent for war, the answer is that the best kind of a moral equivalent is a moral sublimation. We want to turn the energies of youth away from their squandering in mere defense or mere drudgery. Our need is to learn how to live rather than die; to be teachers and creators, not engines of destruction; to be inventors and pioneers, not mere defenders. Our cities and isolated farms alike are mute witnesses that Americans have never learned how to live. Suppose we had a national service which was making a determined assault for the enhancement of living. Would its standards and discipline be less rigorous? Rather would the ingenuity and imagination have to be of the finest.

Some such conception of national service is the only one which will give us that thrill of unity and vigor which we seek. An educational service built on the public school system puts the opportunity in our hands. The raw material in attitudes and desires is here. Every task that an army of youth might perform is already being done in some school or college or communal service. All we need to do is to coördinate and make universal what is now haphazard and isolated. An army of youth which focused school work would provide just that purpose that educators seek. The advocates of "preparedness" are willing to spend billions on a universal military service which is neither universal nor educational nor productive. Cannot we begin to organize a true national service which will let all serve creatively towards the toning up of American life?

13

Education as Living[1]

What is the current broadening of the public school—the bringing in of gymnasiums and pools, shops and gardens, dramatics and organized play—but a new effort to realize the school as more a life and less an institution? Are we not getting a little restless over the resemblance of our schools to penitentiaries, reformatories, orphan asylums, rather than to free and joyous communities? A school system whose object was little more than to abolish illiteracy and prepare the more fortunate for college was bound to fall an easy prey to the mechanical organizer. Education in this country has been one-sidedly professionalized. The machinery was developed before the moving ideals were worked out. Professional educators have worked too much for a logical system rather than an experimental adjustment to the life needs of individual children. We have achieved a democratic education in the sense that common schooling is practically within the reach of every one. But a democratic education, in the sense of giving equal opportunities to each child of finding in the school that life and training which he peculiarly needs, has still to be generally worked for. The problem of American education is now to transform an institution into a life.

Let us not deny the value of that emphasis on administration. The slow progress from the diffuse district school to the well organized state system represents the welding of a powerful instrument for a

[1] *The New Republic,* VIII (Aug. 5, 1916), 10–12.

future democracy to use. Centralized and efficient administration is indispensable for insuring educational benefits to all. But there is a danger that we shall create capable administrators faster than we create imaginative educators. It is so easy to forget that this tightening of the machinery is only in order that the product may be finer and richer. Unless it does so result in more creative life it will be a detriment rather than a good. For it is too easy to make the running of the machine, the juggling with schedules and promotions and curricula and courses and credits, the end. To institutionalize a social function is always the line of least resistance.

We are becoming used to the impressive schoolhouses that tower over the unkempt and fragile houses of our American towns. The school already overshadows the church. If this means that the school is the most important place in the community, then it is a hopeful sign. But if its slightly forbidding bulk means simply that there is another institution to put people through a uniform process, or indeed through any kind of process, then we are no further along. The educators of the last generation, whether from false ideas of democracy or from administrative convenience or necessity, imposed deadly uniformities of subject matter and method on the children in the schools. They assumed that a uniform process would give uniform results. But children are infinitely varied in temperament and capacity and interests. So the uniform process gave the most wildly heterogeneous results. And the present unrest arises from our amazed dissatisfaction that so admirable and long-continued a public-school education should have left the masses of children so little stimulated and trained.

The pseudo-science of education under which most of us were brought up assumed that children were empty vessels to be filled by knowledge. Teachers and parents still feel that to cut down an arithmetic hour to forty-five minutes is to deprive the child of a fourth of his education. But children are not empty vessels, nor are they automatic machines which can be wound up and set running on a track by the teacher. They are pushing wills and desires and curiosities. They are living, growing things, and they need nothing so much as a place where they can grow. They live as wholes far more than older people do, and they cannot be made to become minds and minds alone for four or five hours a day—that is, without stultification. The school forgets that we are only accidentally intellectual, that our other impulses are far more imperious. Because a teacher can secure outward order, it does not mean that she has harmonized the child's personality. She has not the least clue to riot or apathy or delusion that may be going on inside him. She may easily become a drill-sergeant, but she must not think that she has thereby become an educational scientist.

To become that she will have to think of the school as a place where children spend their time living not as artificially segregated minds but as human things. She would have to judge their activities in terms of an interesting life. And that involves good health, play, sport, constructive work, talk, questioning, exercise, friendship, personal expression, as well as reading and learning. A place where children really lived would be a place that gave opportunities for all these activities to just the extent that children were individually capable of expressing themselves. Children want to be busy together, they want to try their hand at tools and materials, they want to find out what older people do and watch them at it. They have to flounder about and have all sorts of experiences before they touch their spring of interest and face their real direction. All their education is really acquired in the same random way that the baby learns to control his movements and respond to his environment. No matter how the school tries to organize their learning, and feed it to them in graduated doses, this way of trial and error is really the one by which they will learn. You have no way of guaranteeing that they will learn what you think you are teaching them. What you can do is to put them in a controlled environment where they will most frequently strike the electric contact of curiosity and response, and get experiences that thrill with meaning for them.

Life in its lowest terms is a matter of passing the time. It would be well if educators would more often remember this. If they did, would they not examine more carefully the life which they provide for growing youth? College and high school life is reasonably antiseptic, it is not oppressive, it is not particularly arbitrary or shabby. But compared abstractly with what might be a good life, given the interests and outlook and needed training of youth, would it not seem a little sorry? Is it not a travesty, except for the few, on a really stimulating and creative way of spending time? Suppose educators seriously measured their schools by this standard of the good life. Suppose we really tried to carry out the principle that the secret of life is to pass time worthily.

Most of this current educational interest is another stab at the age-long problem of making education synonymous with living. We are rediscovering the fact that we learn only as we desire, as we seek to understand or as we are busy. We are trying to make the school a place where children cannot escape doing these things. We see now that education has grown up in this country in a separate institutional compartment, jealously apart from the rest of the community life. It has developed its own technique, its own professional spirit. Its outlines are cold and logical. It is far the best ordered of our institutions. Its morale is the nearest thing we have to compulsory military service. There is something remote and antiseptic about even our best schools. They contrast strangely with the color and confusion of the rest of our American life. The bare class-rooms, the stiff seats, the austere absence of beauty, suggest a hospital where painful if necessary intellectual operations are going on. Additions of gymnasiums and shops and studios to such a school will do little to set the current of life flowing again. The whole school must be loosened up, the stiff forms made flexible, children thought of as individuals and not as "classes." Thus new activities must be woven into a genuine child-community life. These things must be the contacts with experience that waken and focus children's interests. They must be opportunities for spontaneous living.

The school constantly encroaches on the home. It provides play and work opportunities that even well-to-do homes cannot provide. It must take over too the free and comradely atmosphere of the homes and the streets where children play. Let teachers face the fact that they cannot teach masses of children anything with the assurance that they will really assimilate it. What they can do is to fill the school with all kinds of typical experiences, and see that children are exposed to them. They can see that children have a chance to dabble in them, touch tools and growing things, read books, draw, swim, play and sing. Let the teacher cleverly supervise and coördinate, see that the children's interests are drawn out, and that what they do contributes toward their growth. In the last analysis, each child will have to educate himself up to his capacity. He can only educate himself by living. The school will be the place where he lives most worthily.

Our best American public schools are already in sight of such an ideal. Americans need more than anything to learn how to live. This is the first business of education.

14

The Idea of a University[1]

Every American college and university is affected by the issue raised in Professor Beard's dramatic resignation from Columbia as a protest against trustee autocracy.[2] For the conditions which he found intolerable spring from a ruling conception held by university trustees and a portion of conservative public opinion as to the nature of the modern university. The methods taken at Columbia to secure the expulsion of Professors Cattell and Dana are very revealing as to the status of professors and the nature of university prestige. The excuses, causes, and reasons given by the university authorities and the current comment of the newspapers show how frankly the American university has become a financial corporation, strictly analogous, in its motives and responses, to the corporation which is concerned in the production of industrial commodities. Trustees who are business men, who hold positions as directors or executives in large financial or industrial corporations, carry over into the management of the university the attitudes and sensitivities learned in the corporate world. The university produces learning instead of steel or rubber, but the nature of the academic commodity has become less and less potent in ensuring for the

---

[1] *The Dial,* LXIII (Nov. 22, 1917), 509–510.

[2] In September, 1917, Professor J. McKeen Cattell of the psychology department and Professor Henry W. L. Dana, an assistant professor of comparative literature, were dismissed by the trustees of Columbia University. Both teachers had expressed publicly their opposition to the war. In protest against this breach of academic freedom, Charles Beard resigned from the University.

academic workman a status materially different from that of any other kind of employee.

As directors in this corporation of learning, trustees seem to regard themselves primarily as guardians of invested capital. They manage as a sacred trust the various bequests, gifts, endowments which have been made to the university by men and women of the same orthodoxies as themselves. Their obligation is to see that the quality of the commodity which the university produces is such as to seem reputable to the class which they represent. And in order to maintain the flow of capital and the general credit of the institution they must keep the stock above par. In the minds apparently of the trustees, and of the executives and professors who work with them, the reputation of a university is comparable to the standing of a corporation's securities on the street, the newspapers taking the place of the stock exchange. The real offence of Professors Cattell and Dana seems to have been not so much that they were unpatriotic as that they had lowered the prestige of the university in the public mind. Neither the president nor the trustees nor the faculty committees brought forward any evidence besides epithet that either professor had, in the language of President Butler's warning, actually "opposed or counselled opposition to the laws of the United States, or had acted, spoken, or written treason." What these professors had done was to associate themselves with organizations which were enjoying infamy in the irresponsible press. No attempt was made to discover whether the newspaper accounts were true. Chatter and rumor were sufficient to convict them. Why? Because on the stock exchange it is by rumor and prejudice that the value of securities is hit, not by evidence. When your stock is depressed by an alarming rumor, it is irrelevant whether the rumor is true or not. The mischief lies in what people think, not in the actual facts. And for this purpose newspaper chatter is authoritative. Your object then becomes not to discover the truth but to combat the rumor. If the fall in your stock is due to a suspicion of the value of your commodity, you renew your efforts to convince the public of its soundness. If it is due to an offending employee, you dismiss the employee. Having removed the cause of the prejudice, you may then expect your securities to resume their former level.

Only on such an interpretation can we explain the tendency of university authorities to rely on newspaper opinion and upon the complaints of persons whom they would not take seriously on any other question whatever. One is often amazed at the callousness of university trustees towards the indignation that follows these arbitrary dismissals of professors. But this corporate attitude naturally discounts the opinions of the non-investing public. It is not the discontent of idealists that matters, but the vague complaints from parents that their sons are being taught irreligion and sedition within the university, complaints from business men that a professor is tainted with economic heresy, indignation of prominent alumni at the connection of the university's name with unpopular movements. These are the attitudes that depress the credit of the university in the investing world, and these are the attitudes that carry weight, therefore, with the university president and the trustees. Vested interests presumably receive dividends in the form of orthodox graduates. Whatever interferes with the supply of such a revenue is therefore a serious assault on the stability of the corporation.

In any such system of ideas, the professor becomes inevitably a mere employee of a company which has a standing to maintain in the corporate world. His intellectual freedom is extremely precarious, because a chance remark, or any public activity, may bring him that newspaper censure which causes the grave damage the university is likely to incur in the minds of the significant classes. An "institution of learning," administered even on autocratic principles, might be expected to move always with the most scrupulous regard for the dignity of the teacher and for the principles of legal evidence in any cases of dismissal or censure. The professor might be expected to have a status more secure and more respected than that of the employee, holding his position from day to day, and might be expected to be dismissed only after formal charges, and after conviction on evidence which would satisfy an impersonal and judicial mind. None of the circumstances connected with the latest expulsions at Columbia shows that any such standards prevail in our largest and wealthiest university. They show, on the contrary, that under trustee control the American university has been degraded from its old, noble ideal of a community of scholarship to a private commercial corporation. And the situation at Columbia is merely a sharpened form of what has gone on in other colleges and universities throughout the country.

Professor Beard's stirring gesture has raised the issue whether this reigning corporate idea of a university shall any longer prevail. If that reigning idea is making it impossible for a man of Charles Beard's intellectual distinction, courage, and democratic idealism to serve our largest university, we have come to the time when Americans will have to choose between the current philosophy of university government and the presence in the university of independent and vigorous minds. If a man like Professor Beard is to be forced to cut short his academic career because the status of the college teacher is becoming intolerable, a revolution in the idea of a university cannot come too quickly. The present agitation for at least a constitutional form of government by which control over all academic matters is turned over to the faculties is an advance. But to ensure the instructor's freedom, both university authorities and the newspaper public must learn to distinguish between his academic functions and his private opinions and activities. He will scarcely be free as long as he is vulnerable for activities which in no way concern his academic work, or as long as he is considered to implicate the university in everything he says or does. The partisan of "academic freedom" will also want to see worked out an entirely new status for both the instructor, who is now an employee, and for the student, who is now partly ward and partly consumer. State control is no solution, so long as directorship is given to men with the current corporate attitudes. State ownership of universities, with control vested in the "guild" of professors, is probably the ideal solution. Meanwhile what is most needed is a clear realization of the hostility between the present system of ideas which governs university control, and the functional and coöperative ideals which should govern a community devoted to learning. That hostility is almost complete, and Professor Beard has done a great service by making a dramatic issue of it at the present time.

15

The Puritan's Will to Power[1]

To the modern young person who tries to live well there is no type so devastating and harassing as the puritan. We cannot get away from him. In his sight we always live. We finish with justifying our new paganism against him, but we never quite lose consciousness of his presence. Even Theodore Dreiser, who always revolted from the puritan clutch, finds it necessary now and then to tilt a lance against him. If there were no puritans we should have to invent them. And if the pagan Mr. Dreiser has to keep on through life fighting puritans, how much more intrigued must we be who are only re-formed puritans, and feel old dangers stirring at every aggressive gesture of righteousness? For the puritan is the most stable and persistent of types. It is scarcely a question of a puritanical age and a pagan age. It is only a question of more puritans or less puritans. Even the most emancipated generation will find that it has only broken its puritanism up into compartments, and balances sexual freedom—or better perhaps a pious belief in sexual freedom—with a cult of efficiency and personal integrity which is far more coercive than the most sumptuary of laws. Young people who have given up all thought of "being good" anxiously celebrate a cult of "making good." And a superstition like eugenics threatens to terrorize the new intelligentsia.

Every new generation, in fact, contrives to find some new way of

[1] *The Seven Arts*, I (April 1917), 631–637.

being puritanical. Every new generation finds some new way of sacrifice. Every new triumphant assertion of life is counterbalanced by some new denial. In Europe this most proud and lusty young generation goes to its million-headed slaughter, and in America the social consciousness arises to bewilder and deflect the *essor* towards life. Just when convention seemed to be on the run, and youth seemed to be facing a sane and candid attitude towards sex, we find idealistic girls and men coming out of the colleges to tell us of our social responsibility towards the race. This means not only that our daily living is to be dampened by the haunting thought of misery that we cannot personally prevent, but that our thirst towards love-experience is to be discouraged and turned aside into a concern for racial perfection. That is, we are subtly persuaded against merely growing widely and loving intensely. We become vague and mystified means toward nebulous and unreal ends. This new puritanism will not let us be ends in ourselves, or let personality be the chief value in life. It will almost let us sometimes. But it always pulls us up somewhere. There is always a devil of inhibition to interpose before our clean and naive grasping of life. (You see, my puritanism takes the form of a suspicion that there may be a personal devil lurking in the universe.)

This is why the puritan always needs to be thoroughly explained and exposed. We must keep him before our eyes, recognize him as the real enemy, no matter in what ideal disguise he lurks. We must learn how he works, and what peculiar satisfactions he gets from his activity. For he must get satisfaction or he would not be so prevalent. I accept the dogma that to explain anybody we have to do little more than discover just what contentment people are getting from what they do, or from what they are permitting to have happen to them, or even from what they are flinging their will into trying to prevent have happen to them. For, if life is anything positive, it is the sense of control. In the puritan, of course, we have the paradox how he can get satisfaction from ruggedly and sternly subjecting himself and renouncing the world, the flesh and the devil. There is a popular superstition that the puritan has an extra endowment of moral force, that he reverses the natural current of life, that he resists the drag of carnality down toward hell, that his energy is thrown contra-satisfaction, that his control is a real straddling of the nefarious way. But, of course, it is just this superstition that gives the puritan his terrific prestige. In the light of the will-to-power dogma, however, this superstition fades. The puritan becomes just as much of a naturalistic phenomenon as the most carnal sinner. Instincts and impulses, in the puritan, are not miraculously cancelled, but have their full play. The primitive currents of life are not blocked and turned back on their sources, but turned into powerful and usually devastating channels. The puritan is just as much of a "natural" man as you or I.

But we still have to explain how this lustful, headstrong creature called man, spilling with greed, could so unabatedly throughout the ages give up the primitive satisfactions of sex and food and drink and gregariousness and act the ascetic and the glumly censorious. How could an animal whose business was to feel powerful get power from being in subjection and deprivation? Well, the puritan gets his sense of power from a very cunningly organized satisfaction of two of his strongest impulses,—the self-conscious personal impulses of being regarded and being neglected. The puritan is no thwarted and depleted person. On the contrary, he is rather a complete person, getting almost the maximum of satisfaction out of these two apparently contradictory sentiments,—the self-regarding and self-abasing. The pure autocrat would feed himself wholly on the first, the pure slave would be only a human embodiment of the second. But the pure puritan manages to make the most powerful amalgam of both.

What we may call the puritan process starts with the satisfaction of the impulse for self-abasement, (an impulse as primitive as any, for in the long struggle for survival, it was often just as necessary for life to cower as it was to fight.) It is only the puritan's prestige that has attached moral values to self-sacrifice, for there is nothing intrinsic in it that makes it any more praiseworthy than lust. But its pragmatic value is immense. When the puritan announces himself as the least worthy of men, he not only predisposes in his favor the naturally slavish people around him, but he neutralizes the aggressive and self-regarding who would otherwise be moved to suppress him. He renounces, he puts on meekness, he sternly regiments himself, he makes himself unhappy in ways that are just not quite severe enough to excite pity and yet run no risk of arousing any envy. If the puritan does all this unconsciously, the effect is yet the same as if he were deliberately plotting. To give his impulses of self-abasement full play, he must, of course, exercise a certain degree of control. This control, however, gives him little of that sense of power that makes for happiness. Puritan moralists have always tried to make us believe in this virtue of self-control. They forget to point out, however, that it does not become a virtue until it has become idealized. Control over self gives us little sense of control. It is the dreariest of all satisfactions of the will-to-power. Not until we become *proud* of our self-control do we get satisfaction. The puritan only begins to reap his satisfaction when the self-regarding impulse comes into play.

Having given his self-abasing impulse free rein, he is now in a position to exploit his self-regard. He has made himself right with the weak and slavish. He has fortified himself with their alliance. He now satisfies his self-regard by becoming proud of his humility and enjoining it on others. If it were self-control alone that made the puritan, he would not be as powerful as he is. Indeed he would be no more than the mild ascetic, who is all abnegation because his self-regarding mechanism is weak. But in the puritan, both impulses are strong. It is control over others that yields him his satisfactions of power. He may stamp out his sex-desire, but his impulse to shatter ideas that he does not like will flourish wild and wanton. To the true puritan the beauty of unselfishness lies in his being able to enforce it on others. He loves virtue not so much for its own sake as for its being an instrument of his terrorism.

The true puritan is at once the most unselfish and the most self-righteous of men. There is nothing he will not do for you, give up for you, suffer for you. But at the same time there is no cranny of your world that he will not illuminate with the virtue of this doing of his. His real satisfaction comes not from his action of benevolence but from the moral of the tale. He need not boast about his renunciation or his altruism. But in any true puritan atmosphere, that pride will be prevalent. Indeed, it is the oxygen of that atmosphere. Wherever you come across that combination of selfless devotion with self-righteousness, you have the essence of the puritan. Should you come across the one without the other you would find not the puritan but the saint.

The puritan then gets the satisfaction of his will-to-power through the turning of his self-abasement into purposes of self-regard. Renunciation is the raw material for his positive sense of power. The puritan gets his satisfaction exactly where the most carnal of natural men gets his, out of the stimulation of his pride. And in a world where renunciation has to happen to us whether we want it or not, the puritan is in the most impressive strategic position. In economy of energy he has it all over the head that is bloody but unbowed. For the puritan is so efficient morally that he can bow his head and yet extract control both out of the bowing and out of the prestige which his bowing gives him, as well as out of the bowing which he can enforce on others. The true puritan must become an evangelist. It is not enough to renounce the stimulus to satisfaction which is technically known as a "temptation." The renouncing must be made into an ideal, the ideal must be codified, promulgated, and, in the last analysis, enforced. In the compelling of others to abstain, you have the final glut of puritanical power. For in getting other people to renounce a thing, you thereby get renewed justification for your own renouncing. And so the puritan may go on inexhaustibly rolling up his satisfaction, one impulse reinforcing the other. The simultaneous play of these two apparently inconsistent personal impulses makes the puritan type one of the stablest in society. While the rest of us are longing for power, the puritan is enjoying his. And because the puritan is so well integrated, he almost always rules. The person whose satisfactions of control are more various and more refined is on the defensive against him.

The puritan gets his sense of power not in the harmless way of the artist or the philosopher or the lover or the scientist, but in a crude assault on that most vulnerable part of other people's souls, their moral sense. He is far more dangerous to those he converts than to those he intimidates. For he first scares them into abandoning the rich and sensuous and expressive impulses in life, and then teaches them to be proud of having done so. We all have the potentiality of the puritan within us. I remember suffering agonies at the age of ten because my aunt used to bring me candy that had been wickedly purchased on the Sabbath day. I forget whether I ate it or not, but that fact is irrelevant. What counted was the guilt with which the whole universe seemed to be stained. I need no other evidence for the irrational nature of morality than this fact that children can be such dogged little puritans, can be at the age of ten so sternly and intuitively righteous.

The puritan is a case of arrested development. Most of us do grow beyond him and find subtler ways of satisfying our desire for power. And we do it because we never can quite take that step from self-abasement to self-regard. We never can quite become proud of our humility. Renunciation remains an actual going without, sacrifice a real thwarting. If we value an experience and deliberately surrender it, we are too naive to pretend that there are compensations. There *is* a loss. We are left with a vacuum. There is only depression and loss of control. Our self-regard is not quite elemental enough to get stimulation from wielding virtue over others. I never feel so degraded as when I have renounced. I had rather beat my head rhythmically and endlessly against an unyielding wall. For the pagan often breaks miraculously through the wall. But the puritan at his best can only strut outside.

Most of us, therefore, after we have had our puritan fling, sown our puritan wild oats as it were, grow up into devout and progressing pagans, cultivating the warmth of the sun, the deliciousness of love-experience, the high moods of art. The puritans remain around us, a danger and a threat. But they have value to us in keeping us acutely self-conscious of our faith. They whet our ardor. Perhaps no one can be really a good appreciating pagan who has not once been a bad puritan.

16

H. L. Mencken[1]

M r. Mencken gives the impression of an able mind so harried and
irritated by the philistinism of American life that it has not been
able to attain its full power. These more carefully worked-over critical
essays are, on the whole, less interesting and provocative than the irresponsible comment he gives us in his magazine. How is it that so robust
a hater of uplift and puritanism becomes so fanatical a crusader himself? One is forced to call Mr. Mencken a moralist, for with him
appraisement has constantly to stop while he tilts against philistine
critics and outrageous puritans. In order to show how good a writer
is, he must first show how deplorably fatuous, malicious or ignorant are
all those who dislike him. Such a proof is undoubtedly the first impulse of any mind that cares deeply about artistic values. But Mr.
Mencken too often permits it to be his last, and wastes away into a
desert of invective. Yet he has all the raw material of the good critic—
moral freedom, a passion for ideas and for literary beauty, vigor and
pungency of phrase, considerable reference and knowledge. Why have
these intellectual qualities and possessions been worked up only so par-
tially into the finished attitude of criticism? Has he not let himself be
the victim of that paralyzing Demos against which he so justly rages?
As you follow his strident paragraphs, you become a little sorry that
there is not more of a contrast in tone between his illumination of the

[1] *The New Republic,* XIII (Nov. 24, 1917), 102–103. This is a review of
H. L. Mencken, *A Book of Prefaces* (New York: A. A. Knopf, 1917).

brave, the free and the beautiful, and the peevish complaints of the superannuated critics of the old school. When are we going to get anything critically curative done for our generation, if our critical rebels are to spend their lives cutting off hydra-heads of American stodginess?

Mr. Mencken's moralism infects the essay on Conrad perhaps the least. With considerable effort the critic shakes himself loose from the clutches of his puritan enemies and sets Conrad very justly in relation to his time. "What he sees and describes in his books," Mr. Mencken says, "is not merely this man's aspiration or that woman's destiny, but the overwhelming sweep and devastation of universal forces, the great central drama that is at the heart of all other dramas, the tragic struggles of the soul of man under the gross stupidity and obscene joking of the gods." He likes Dreiser for the same reason, because "he puts into his novels a touch of the eternal Weltschmerz. They get below the drama that is of the moment and reveal the greater drama that is without end." Mr. Mencken discusses Dreiser with admirable balance, and his essay is important because it criticizes him more harshly and more searchingly than many of us dare to do when we are defending him against the outrageous puritan. The essay on Huneker is perhaps the most entertaining. If "to be a civilized man in America is measurably less difficult, despite the war, than it used to be, say, in 1890" (when Mr. Mencken, by the way, was ten years old), it is to Mr. Huneker's gallant excitement that part of the credit is due.

Dreiser and Huneker Mr. Mencken uses with the utmost lustiness, as Samson used the jaw-bone, to slay a thousand Philistines, and his zeal mounts to a closing essay on Puritanism as a Literary Force, which employs all the Menckenian artillery. Here Mr. Mencken, as the moralist contra moralism, runs amuck. It is an exposure that should stir our blood, but it is so heavily documented and so stern in its conviction of the brooding curtain of bigotry that hangs over our land, that its effect must be to throw paralyzing terror into every American mind that henceforth dares to think of not being a prude. Mr. Mencken wants to liberate, but any one who took his huge concern seriously would never dare challenge in any form that engine of puritanism which derives its energy from the history and soul of the American people. Mr. Mencken is much in earnest. His invective rises above the tone of scornful exaggeration. But his despair seems a little forced. I cannot see that the younger writers—particularly the verse-writers—are conscious of living under any such cultural terrorism as he describes. Mr. Mencken admits that the puritan proscription is irrational and incalculable in its operation. Surely as long as there are magazines and publishers—as there are in increasing numbers—who will issue vigorous and candid work, comstockery in art must be seen as an annoying but not dominating force. Mr. Mencken queerly shows himself as editor, bowing meekly under the puritan proscription, acting as censor of "a long list of such things by American authors, well-devised, well-imagined, well-executed, respectable as human documents and as works of art—but never to be printed in mine or any other American magazine." But what is this but to act as busy ally to that very comstockery he denounces? If the Menckens are not going to run the risk, in the name of freedom, they are scarcely justified in trying to infect us with their own caution.

The perspective is false that sees this persecution as peculiar to America. Was not Lemonnier prosecuted in Paris? Did not Baudelaire, Flaubert, Zola suffer? Did not Zola's publisher in England die in prison? Has not D. H. Lawrence's latest novel been suppressed in England before it had even a chance to be prosecuted here? It is England not America that has an official censorship of plays. Comstockery is not so much a function of American culture as it is of the current moralism of our general middle-class civilization. The attack must be, as Nietzsche made it, on that moralism rather than on its symptoms. But Mr. Mencken is not particularly happy in his understanding of Nietzsche. He wrote the book from which a majority of the Americans who know about Nietzsche seem to have gotten their ideas. How crude a summary it is may be seen by comparing it with the recent study of Nietzsche by another American, W. M. Salter. One wishes Mr. Mencken had spent more time in understanding the depth and subtleties of Nietzsche, and less on shuddering at puritanism as a literary force, and on discovering how the public libraries and newspaper reviewers are treating Theodore Dreiser.

Mr. Mencken's mode of critical attack thus plays into the hands of the philistines, demoralizes the artist, and demoralizes his own critical power. Why cannot Demos be left alone for a while to its commercial magazines and its mawkish novels? All good writing is produced in serene unconsciousness of what Demos desires or demands. It cannot be created at all if the artist worries about what Demos will think of him or do to him. The artist writes for that imagined audience of perfect comprehenders. The critic must judge for that audience too.

17

Paul Elmer More[1]

The author of "Aristocracy and Justice" is more than an essayist, more than a critic. He is an American institution, the ablest spokesman for the idealism of our intellectual plutocracy. If his books are not read, at least his ideas are thought, and if our plutocracy has become too timid in the face of a growling Demos to express itself so uncompromisingly, at least it continues to act just as if it had this social and moral philosophy which Mr. More expounds.

Human life, says Mr. More, is a very primitive thing, prone without control to degenerate into savagery. In preventing society from crumbling beneath the aggressive passions of the present, artificial institutions are required to curb the restive and self-seeking nature of man. These institutions make up civilization, and property is its bulwark. In the struggle for life and goods, the strong and cruel will conquer, and nature will not gainsay their irrational victory. Order requires that a controlling power over will and appetite be placed somewhere. Man must recognize nature's rigid hierarchy and subordination of her creatures, but sublimate it into justice, which is right distribution of power and privilege. Society must seek justice after the pattern of the moral

[1] *The New Republic,* vi (April 1, 1916), 245–247. A review of P. E. More, *Aristocracy and Justice* (Boston and New York: Houghton Mifflin Co., 1916). More, former literary editor of the New York *Evening Post* and editor of the *Nation* (1909–14), was beginning his twenty years' teaching career at Princeton University. After Irving Babbitt he was the chief representative of the literary movement known as the "New Humanism."

individual soul, in which the reason and feelings are reconciled. The strong must have the privilege of imposing their will upon those who are inferior to them, but only in a way that at once satisfies the distinctions of reason among the superior, and does not outrage the feelings of the inferior. This is social justice, and its operation requires a natural aristocracy. This natural aristocracy will be found in the class whose views are broadened by the inherited possession of privilege and honors. In a democracy inherited wealth replaces aristocracy. Property is the symbol and instrument of these privileges, and is therefore the very foundation of society. The dollar must always be more than the man and the right to property more sacred than the right to life.

A natural aristocracy is spiritually supported through the exercise of the moral imagination working in all classes of society. This moral imagination which accepts the powerful everywhere as the good and wise, if an illusion, is a most pleasing and beneficent one, for it makes power gentle and obedience liberal and harmonizes the different shades of life. Church and university are ever the strongest stimulators of this imagination, the strongest reactionaries against innovations which threaten the intrenched rights of property, and this not because of greed of possession, but because the safety and usefulness of institutions is bound up with the inviolability of property by which a leisure class, by character destined more specifically to be the creators and transmitters of the world's intellectual and spiritual heritage, retains its stability and its capacity for governing the masses.

That training of the disciplined mind by which a natural aristocracy cultivates this heritage is one of the most important tasks of society. Only the liberal studies—Greek, Latin, philosophy, mathematics—perform this office of discipline. On these the college must concentrate. Any attempt to make education an industrial social training for the masses stabs deep at the vitals of society. The true aim of a state is to make possible the high friendship of those who have raised themselves to a vision of the supreme good. To care for mediocrity is to destroy that just inequality of Nature, and open the gates to warring class-passions and the revolt of the unfit.

To the neglect of these principles, Mr. More attributes our present discontents. Under the rising tide of democracy, our intellectual plutocrats themselves have faltered and paled. A new morality has arisen which renounces personal responsibility in favor of social responsibility. We have become enfeebled by humanitarianism. We give full liberty to human nature to follow its own impulsive desire of expansion. Sympathy in place of justice saps the fibre of character and gives free rein to egoistic impulses. The release of the inhibitions of reason and conscience have plunged us into the savagery of a world war. The envious many have broken down the securities of property rights, and imperiled social order. Even Mr. Rockefeller and the New York *Sun* have come to defending the right to work, rather than the inalienable right of property. In the new social ideals the intellectual class has been guilty of a moral treason. Unless it returns to the eternal principles of justice, restoring harmony in the individual breast and a just and contented subordination in society, our civilization is doomed.

Such a philosophy is, of course, its own best self-satirization. A piece of *a priori* reasoning in the classic style, it is a mere apologia for the modern legal reactionary. The calm of Mr. More's style cannot keep the claws of class-exploitation from showing through.

Granting the power of his classic social analysis, he makes two gratuitous assumptions. One assumption, that modern America, before it was sapped by the new morality, was a Platonic Republic, betrays the extent of his inductive studies. The other is that the only choice is between a contented plutocracy and anarchy.

His misunderstanding of modern radicalism is complete. His major premises are exactly those of that modern social and psychological science which he so deplores, and of the modern pragmatic philosophy. Any book of statistics or sociological survey would show him curves of distribution which are nothing more or less than his "inequality of nature" made graphic and explicit. And any modern philosopher of force from Nietzsche to Dewey will show him our full appreciation of the philosophy of will-to-power. It is not in his premises but in his conclusions that Mr. More is flatly out of touch with the driving and creative thought of the day. He assumes the very question he ought to prove—that a "natural aristocracy" of inherited wealth does produce in society that harmony of reason and emotion which is justice. He has canonized the particular denouement of a non-moral struggle of group wills-to-power which our time most passionately rebels against, and which has been most productive of disorder and intellectual chaos— the rule of an industrial plutocracy.

For what we have learned in our American experience is that property rights cannot be put above human rights unless humanity itself becomes property. Mr. More's ideal is a slave-society, as the Greek state to which he always reverts was a slave-state. Any society which works towards such a social goal works towards a society based on slavery or on serfdom.

What Mr. More sees as a sentimental humanitarianism is really a growing general disinclination to live longer in a semi-servile society. What he sees as the materializing of life is rather a determined effort to understand the forces and goods of nature so that they may become the tools of a genuine all-nourishing humanism such as has never before been remotely possible in the world.

To have missed all this, and to have seen the modern democratic movement as merely an invidious mob-desire to level life to mediocrity or as the mere drift of sentiment, is to have betrayed a dearth of imagination far more sinister than that want of the Burkian reverence for the established which Mr. More so much deplores in us. This continuing to live in the America of 1915 among the political and moral problems of an Attic Deme would be comic if it were not pathetic. Mr. More is ignorant of the fact that we live in a new age of surplus value, economic and spiritual. The kernel of our problems is the use of that surplus energy. It is this changed orientation that has destroyed the old antithesis. Equilibrium can no longer be the ideal. We find that we are not dealing with economic or social forces which can be balanced against each other, and society and the individual reduced to a harmonious and static design. Our psychology shows us life not as an arrangement of emotions, sensations, judgments, which can be treated kaleidoscopically to produce certain effects of character. We see life now rather as an incalculable and importunate stream of desire, which rises in the adult to a will-to-power. The problem of the soul becomes the direction of this desire and energy into creative channels, not its suppression or even control by that reason which is so often a mere disguise of another and more acceptable desire. In such a world, personality becomes more desirable than character, creative expressiveness than self-control, coöperation than justice, social freedom than rights. Mr. More's ethics is the ethics of a parsimonious world. It has no place in a world of surplus energy or of possible surplus energy. Only by repressing this energy, only by turning it back to its latent state, could the modern world be put back to the tight little Greek frame in which Mr. More and his friends would find themselves most at home and their rights and privileges least disturbed. And that would mean a serfdom, of both person and group, for which the time is too late.

The social purpose no longer means the sentimentality of a social conscience which is mere sympathy, but work towards a creative, imaginative and inter-stimulating community life, in which personality and expressiveness shall flourish as they cannot flourish under present institutions. The enterprises which seem to the conservative mere enervating fads and fancies are experimental means towards this end. This readjustment, this progressive re-shaping, is the work of the modern radical movements. It is an audacious and Promethean task, as far as possible removed from drift or vagueness. At its lowest, it stems "the amorous and vehement drift of man's herd to hell." At its best, it tones up society, giving to great masses vigor, skill and outlook, endowing institutions with new purpose, adjusting them to the best wills and powers of the men and women affected by them. Industrial education, town-planning, labor legislation, social insurance and the rest are not ends in themselves, but means of social technique toward this great social end.

Mr. More met this century in its childish years, and he has neglected to observe its growing up. His misinterpretation of the modern spirit which is so bold in desire to substitute mastery for drift betrays either an ignorance or a callousness. It is probably both, for his philosophy was hammered together in its perfect form fifteen years ago, and no word of the movement of men and minds has since penetrated his studied isolation. It is not only an insensitiveness that he betrays, but since the modern political and social vision is so largely an aesthetic one, a genuine anesthesia. His narrow preoccupation with the Greek classics has prevented him from seeing the color and forms of that sociological world which men are now eagerly studying and in which they seem to find all the imaginative lift and intellectual discipline which their fathers got from the classics. If he looked about the world, he would find his orthodox classical scholars the stalest and most stagnant of men, their fire passed to pragmatic philosophers or the realistic publicists. He would find Gilbert Murray, the greatest Greek scholar of his age, gone with all his students over into the sociological camp, delving into mana and initiation ceremonies and primitive magic in order to explain his Greek tragedy, or else making the abhorrent classical compromise by popularizing Euripides in English verse. One wonders of what classics and of what discipline Mr. More is talking when his greatest scholars, his natural aristocracy, are finding his lovely archaic poems a tangled tissue of social myth rather than the naïve outpourings of the human heart.

The world has grown too wide and too adventurous for Mr. More's tight little categories. We are becoming too conscious of vast economic forces which control the destinies of society. We cannot believe that our salvation lies in the resolution of Mr. More and his anxious friends to put a harsh stop to those dangerous modern ideas that are undermining the sober virility of our minds.

18

The Heart of the People[1]

As a would-be democrat, I should like to believe passionately in the movies. I am told constantly of their great educational possibilities. By the innocent and ubiquitous movies we are to be made over, insensibly led to higher things. Buoyed by such hopes, I go with ever-renewed courage. But into that democrat that I long to be I shall never be made by such exhibitions as "The White Terror," "an educational feature film in four reels," sponsored by the National Association for the Prevention of Tuberculosis. Experience it seems has proved that the public does not take kindly to pure "education" in the movies. The "education" has had to be smeared on in the spots where was thought it would best stick. The first object of the deviser of this film had been to tell a dramatic story, and from the meticulous care with which it was presented one could not doubt that every detail had been ingeniously arranged to meet some deep public hunger.

It was exciting. Love, crime, political corruption, industrial exploitation, social service, redemption, pathos and personal hygiene were woven into an unforgettable work of art. The climax came when, after a long and blissful kiss between the happily healed and reconciled daughter of the ruthless but reformed patent-medicine magnate and her valiant lover, this hopeful quotation from Pasteur was thrown upon our gaze: "It is possible to banish from the earth all such parasitic germ diseases within a generation." Although our sophisticated social-

[1] *The New Republic,* III (July 3, 1915), 233.

worker group burst into unanimous glee, there lingered the horrible suspicion that that fifty per cent of the public who would see it were not supposed to laugh.

But when my mirth had flowed away from me I realized that I could not put the thing down to the low intelligence of a dear deluded public. This is what comes of being a democrat. You have to take a great many things seriously that your fathers would have been quite serene about. I wanted to find this drama natural and moving, shot through with personal and social motives that represented for me, as they must for my "fifty per cent of the people" my interpretations of life. And to find it not only not harmless but all crooked and unreal, was to fall into a very unpleasant embarrassment. My conscience would have been appeased, I think, if the acting had been good. I seem to recall Italian melodramas in Rome that were done with such verve on the cinema as to be quite passionately convincing. But these Americans were quite wooden. Only the little children were appealing as they ran to their mother, lying dead from too much devotion to "Sacc-Ozone, Nature's Only Cure for Consumption." Otherwise emotion such as Brand's, whom the daughter of the masterful president will not marry until he has performed some good deed which will render him worthy of her, is expressed by rolling the eyeballs. The good deed is to buy up the newspaper which is exposing the rotten labor conditions in the mills and the poisonous shams of "Nature's Only Cure." A war of masterful men ensues, done through much stalking about with high hats and long cigars, much sticking of powerful jaws into one another's faces, and a final realistic dynamiting scene in which the faithful partner of the president blows up the newspaper office and himself with it.

Swift upon the crime follows nemesis. The lovely daughter contracts the dread disease. I hope the movies don't see many such scenes of bathos as this in which the father comes with a touching smile and presents his daughter with a bottle of his interesting compound of opium and arsenic. Fortunately the doctor intervenes. Enter "education," with its sanatoriums and open-air schools and all the proper ways to cure consumption. The father falls upon his desk, a broken man, while lines of skeletons pouring over his advertisements pass before his eyes, and serried rows of gravestones haunt him, each marking the effect of a bottle of his poison. But presto! all is redeemed. A sumptuous banquet is given the reconciled pair, the father announces a gift of a tuberculosis sanatorium to the city, the bad man is redeemed into a philanthropist, the daughter is healed, the lover rewarded, and excellent moral and hygienic lessons are implanted in the heart of the American people.

After "The White Terror," I begin to feel like an esoteric little bubble on a great stream of the common life. What makes me laugh or blush doesn't make my fifty per cent of the people laugh or blush. But I do not like to have my democracy thus assailed. I should like to dismiss it all as mere old-fashioned melodrama in a modern setting. But "The White Terror" didn't seem to have even the virtues of melodrama. Melodrama was essentially the heroism of the child's Big-Injun age, tainted with calf-love, but at least untainted with current moral and social issues. It had an element of the timeless. And it was passionately believed in. It represented a genuine stage in the development of the soul. Melodrama was not quackery, but this current rubbish is. It catches the social cant of the day. It crudely parodies ideals. See how our fifty per cent interprets graft. The still unredeemed magnate and his lieutenant stride into the mayor's office with their hats on and say, "We have decided to make you mayor next year. But you will have to do what we tell you!" Out goes at once to the local tuberculosis committee a very ungrammatical letter announcing that the city's funds forbid the erection of the proposed municipal sanatorium. No time can be lost in the movies or in the movie interpretation of life.

I have to take "The White Terror" seriously, because it is as scientific a record as a statistical graph. Like the popular novel, it marks the norm of what happy and hearty America is attending to. Melodrama used to be bad form, but the movies are good form for almost all classes. This is the great public of a generation which has had universal common school education, free libraries, museums, cheap journals, and books, on a scale known to no generation in history. This is what we get out of it all.

I don't mean that it would have been any better if they had all chosen Renaissance pictures or Ibsen plays or Dante. I feel even a certain unholy glee at this wholesale rejection of what our fathers reverenced as culture. But I don't feel any glee about what is substituted for it. We seem to be witnessing a lowbrow snobbery. In a thousand ways it is as tyrannical and arrogant as the other culture of universities and millionaires and museums. I don't know which ought to be more offensive to a true democrat—this or the cheapness of the current life that so sadly lacks any raciness or characteristic savor. It looks as if we should have to resist the stale culture of the masses as we resist the stale culture of the aristocrat. It is very easy to be lenient and pseudo-human, and call it democracy. Perhaps there is no third alternative. But if there is—if there are moods and values in our current life which are at once native and significant—we can scarcely pursue them too avidly or express them too loudly. Such an enterprise of thought would be the democratic thing that the current popularities are emphatically not.

19

Sociologic Fiction[1]

You must judge the American sociological novelist by standards of sociological pertinency rather than of literary art. Whether it is Winston Churchill exposing the capitalistic taint in the church, or Ernest Poole extending the family into the Gary school,[2] or Upton Sinclair revealing the bestialities of the stockyards, you never look for those subtleties of personal life or for those living and breathing people that make the good novelist's art. The sociological raconteur uses people, but only as bricks to build his institutional edifice. It is the family, church, industry, that the story is really about. It is the institution that is the hero or villain, and the institution either in process of reformation or in shrieking need of it. The purpose of the story is to "show conditions," and the significance is frankly the message that something ought to be done about it. Where the literary artist would let the institution and its "message" play insistently out of the palpitating life of the individuals, caught in the struggle with it and busy with a thousand personal desires and adjustments, the sociological novelist sharply isolates institutional consciousness and denies his people thoughts and feelings that do not contribute directly to the missionary effect he

[1] *The New Republic*, XII (Oct. 27, 1917), 359–360. A review of Upton Sinclair's *King Coal* (New York: The Macmillan Co., 1917).

[2] Winston Churchill and Ernest Poole, like Upton Sinclair, were writing novels in the naturalist genre and from a vaguely socialist point of view. The references are to one of Churchill's most popular novels, *The Inside of the Cup* (1912) which "muckraked" the churches, and to Poole's *His Family* (1917) which won the Pulitzer Prize.

wants to produce. Zola still lives because, though the master of the sociological novelist, he laboriously painted in every segment of his canvas, documenting sensual impression and confused aspiration, as well as institutional circumstance, so as to produce, through sheer massiveness and breadth, a feeling of personal life.

The Americans are less industrious, and consequently they are under a certain responsibility of showing that their work "shows conditions" better than would a sober report or generalized narrative. The theory is, of course, that the fictional form will make them more widely read. So they throw their material into dramatic shape, arrange the incidents cumulatively, give their characters fictitious names, endow them with conversation, and presumably get a more brilliant effect. All we have a right to ask, therefore, of such a novel is that its sociology be sound and true, and its "message" urgent. Such a story should not pretend to be more than a movie transcription of life. It is sociological observation "filmed." There is no claim to artistic value, and we do not ask for any. All we say is, Does the novel make visible conditions as they are and as they ought to be speedily altered?

Judged from this standard, I should say that Upton Sinclair's King Coal was a most satisfactory effort at fictional sociology. Technically it reads like a stenographic report run through the mould of a melodrama. All the same, it is far superior to a book like Ernest Poole's His Family, which, although constructed with more literary tact, had its sociology of both education and the family so lamentably strained and off the key. Ernest Poole erred in attempting art. You have the irritating task of disentangling the sociology from the well meant but clumsy personal characterization, and when you get it disentangled you find it is neither sound nor true. Upton Sinclair pleases because he makes it so easy to unwarp the melodrama from this picture of the servitude of unorganized labor in a great mining camp of the American West. The soundness and truth of the sociology are fortified by "eight million words of evidence" collected in the investigations of the great Colorado coal strike of 1913–14. Upton Sinclair slaps melodrama and sociology together so honestly as to make it easy for you to believe that "practically all the characters are real persons, and every incident which has social significance is not merely a true incident but a typical one."

You discard the rich young hero who, fresh from his sociological courses at college, goes to work incognito in a coal mine to test out what he has learned, but you retain the brutal intrigue, the almost Turkish oppression, the terrorism of suspicion and fear which compose life within the armed camp of the "Pine Creek Coal Co." You discard his sensational escape into the private car of his friend, the son of the owner of the mines, and the ineptitude of the little plutocratic party, but you retain a sense of the callous indifference with which the owners hand over labor troubles to the slave driving foremen. You discard the decayed gentility of the company official to whom the hero, in disgrace, makes appeal, but you retain a vivid insight into that crew of petty helots, and provocateurs into whose hands these industrial helots, the mine workers, are delivered. You discard the amorous troubles of Red Mary and her confrontation with the dainty capitalistic sweetheart, but you do not lose the horror of the crushing out of hope in these grim and terrible camps. Throughout the book, the "social significance" of the incidents seems as impressive as the dramatic invention is unconvincing. You smile at the plot, but you say, These are conditions as they are, in all their almost incredible detail of exploitation.

Upton Sinclair does his work so well, however, as to leave you undecided whether an honest generalized summary of the labor camp life, such as that Colorado judicial decision which he prints in his postscript as proof of the accuracy of his work, would not have carried just as much dramatic conviction. Yet King Coal is an exceedingly vivacious narrative, boyishly sincere. If it proves to carry its "message" further than did the "eight million words," it will have to be preferred to any unfictional account. Other writers, however, might not strike so good a balance, might not make their fiction so easy to unwind. Their invention might grotesquely distort the conditions they were trying to render vivid. We are left with the question whether there is really any place for anything between the straightforward social document and the work of literary art in which the writer not only keeps the faith towards his sociological material, but creates also a drama of personal life. But if we are to have something else, King Coal is perhaps as good a compromise as we are likely ever to get.

The "message" needs no paraphrasing. The total impression the reader gets is one of outraged wonder that Assyrian centers of iniquity like these camps should have grown up in a country with any intuition whatever for democracy. Where political boundaries have been made to coincide with the limits of corporation property, these camps have become actual little industrial principalities within the state, armed and barricaded against the world, and "justified" in any oppression by the plea of an "industrial necessity" which parodies the "military necessity" of the state. These camps represent the systematic squeezing of the worker almost to the last detail that human ingenuity could suggest. The system shows the will-to-exploit almost gone insane and run amuck. Scruple, legality, tradition, humaneness, have collapsed, and brutal power acts unrestrained. King Coal shows step by step the ingenuity of extortion, the difficulty of protest or revolt, the organized espionage which crushes any effort at organization. The direction of the industrially subjugated has become an engineering task like the mining of coal. The workers are so much wood and stone to be manipulated into the mine, and so much human slag to be destroyed with the other refuse. Only because the human instrument shows animal perversity and resistance has this technique of subjugation been turned over by corporations not to engineers but to the terrorism of criminaloid foremen. Will the war do anything to this terrible industrial slavery? King Coal provides a lurid but convincing background against which to understand the present industrial revolt.

20

Traps for the Unwary[1]

W hat place is there to be for the younger American writers who have broken the "genteel" tradition with a sudden violence that elicits angry cries of pain from the critics, so long regarded by the significant classes as guardians of our cultural faith? Read Mr. Brownell[2] on standards and see with what a bewildered contempt one of the most vigorous and gentlemanly survivals from the genteel tradition regards the efforts of the would-be literary artists of today. Read Stuart P. Sherman[3] on contemporary literature, and see with what a hurt panic a young gentleman, perhaps the very last brave offshoot of the genteel tradition, regards those bold modern writers from whom his contemporaries derive. One can admire the intellectual acuteness and sound moral sense of both these critics, and yet feel how quaintly irrelevant for our purposes is an idea of the good, the true, and the beautiful, which culminates in a rapture for Thackeray (vide Mr. Brownell), or is a literary æsthetic (vide Mr. Sherman) which gives Mr. Arnold Bennett first place as an artist because of his wholesome theories of human conduct. Mr. Sherman has done us the service of showing us how very dead is the genteel tradition in our hearts, how

[1] *The Dial*, LXIV (March 28, 1918), 277–279.

[2] William Crary Brownell, literary advisor to Charles Scribner's Sons from 1888 to 1928, was one of the earliest spokesmen of the "humanist" literary movement. Bourne's reference is to Brownell's *Standards* (1917).

[3] Sherman was then professor of English at the University of Illinois and regarded himself as standing half-way between the naturalist and genteel traditions.

thoroughly the sense of what is desirable and absorbing has shifted in our younger American life.

But he has also shown us how gentility in literary attitude lingers on. Professors of literature still like it, and those pioneer rebels who hate it have tended to hate it not wisely but too well. Crusaders like Mr. Dreiser and Mr. Mencken have dealt loud enough blows, but they beat at a straw man of puritanism which, for the younger generation, has not even the vitality to be interesting. Art always has to struggle with the mob, and Mr. Mencken's discovery that it has to struggle in America is a little naïve. The philistine and the puritan are trouble-some, though never decisive, and in America today they seem less decisive than ever. Mr. Sherman, an arrant philistine, in that he de-fends the life lived through the conventions, is dangerous because he makes philistinism sound like belles-lettres. Mr. Mencken, on the other hand, deserves everything Mr. Sherman says about him, because in his rather self-conscious bluster he makes literary art sound like vul-garity. The best thing that can be done to these contending critics is to persuade them to kill each other off. Both are moralists before they are critics of literary art. Both have an exaggerated respect for Demos, which one expresses by means of a phobia, the other by a remarkable process of idealization. Mr. Mencken is as much a product of the genteel tradition as is Mr. Sherman, for he represents a moralism im-perfectly transcended.

Let us look for the enemy of the literary artist in America today not among the philistines or the puritans, among the animal-obsessed novelists or the dainty professors who make Mr. Mencken profane. The real enemy is still the genteel tradition which tends to smother the timid experiments of a younger generation that is not satisfied with husks. For the deadly virus of gentility is carried along by an up-to-date cultivated public—small perhaps, but growing—who are all the more dangerous because they are so hospitable. The would-be literary artist needs to be protected not so much from his enemies as from his friends. Puritan and professor may agree in their disgust at the creative imagination at work in America, but it is not their hos-tility which keeps it from being freer and more expressive. The con-fusing force is rather an undiscriminating approval on the part of a public who want the new without the unsettling. The current pop-ularity of verse, the vogue of the little theatres and the little magazines reveal a public that is almost pathetically receptive to anything which has the flavor or the pretension of literary art. The striving literary artist is faced by no stony and uncomprehending world. Almost anyone can win recognition and admiration. But where is the criticism that will discriminate between what is fresh, sincere, and creative and what is merely stagy and blatantly rebellious? The Brownells profess to find no nuances in this mob of young literary anarchists. The Shermans cannot degrade themselves to the level of treating seriously a crowd of naughty children. A new criticism has to be created to meet not only the work of the new artists but also the uncritical hospitality of current taste. If anything more than ephemeral is to come out of this younger school, outlawed by the older criticism, the new critic must intervene between public and writer with an insistence on clearer and sharper outlines of appreciation by the one, and the attainment of a richer artistry by the other.

That is why a study such as Miss Amy Lowell's[4] on recent tendencies in American verse is so significant. The intelligent reviewers who saw in the book only a puff for Imagism disclosed how very novel is an intelligent attempt to place our current literary art not merely against the spiritual background of tradition, but in the terms and in the spirit of the contemporary imagination itself. Her very tone is revolutionary. She is neither sentimental nor apologetic. Poetry appears for the first time on our critical horizon as neither a refined dessert to be consumed when the day's work is done, nor as a private hobby which the business man will deride if he hears about it, but as a sound and important activity of contemporary American life. Some people who habitually patronize Miss Lowell complain that in her book she patronizes Carl Sandburg. Actually she makes him a powerful figure, with his brave novelty of the America that is in the making. Her sound intuition gets the better of her class-feeling even in her attitude towards the war. For, having orthodoxly registered her sense of the complete *bouleversement* which it is making in the spiritual life of the world, she calmly proceeds as if it were not. Neither in her criticism nor in her verse is the slightest evidence that into the domain of literary art has the war penetrated, or will it penetrate. Nothing shows better than her attitude how very far the younger generation is beyond those older counselors

[4] Amy Lowell, the imagist poet and literary biographer, spent summers near Dublin, N.H. where Bourne made her acquaintance. She at once captured his admiration but did not appear to respond to his invitation to carry on a correspondence. The reference is to her *Tendencies in Modern American Poetry* (1917).

who hope that the war will "get under our skins"—perhaps to make a few bad poets write worse poems, and to give many mediocre writers a momentary patriotic and social glamor, but not to touch a "young world" which has its treasures for other heavens!

The problem of the literary artist is how to obtain more of this intelligent, pertinent, absolutely contemporaneous criticism, which shall be both severe and encouraging. It will be obtained when the artist himself has turned critic and set to work to discover and interpret in others the motives and values and efforts he feels in himself. The "high seriousness" of Miss Lowell's own critical attitude towards the artistic problems of the six poets suggests, I think, that there is a promise of a rich and vibrant literary era before us. No one pretends to be satisfied with the novels and plays and interpretations now being turned out by the younger intellectuals. Least of all must they themselves be satisfied. After all, very little of their work really gives voice to the ambitions, desires, discontents, and spiritual adventures of the all too self-conscious young American world. Moreover, there is for this healthy dissatisfaction an insidious trap—the terrible glamor of social patronage which so easily blunts idealism in the young prophet. The other day, reading "My Literary Friends and Acquaintances," I shuddered at Howells's glee over the impeccable social tone of Boston and Cambridge literary life. He was playful enough about it, but not too playful to conceal the enormity of his innocence. He does not see how dreadful it is to contrast Cambridge with ragged vagabonds and unpresentable authors of other ages. To a younger generation which feels that the writer ought to be at least a spiritual vagabond, a de-classed mind, this gentility of Mr. Howells and his friends has come to seem more alien than Sologub. We are acquiring an almost Stendhalian horror for those correctnesses and tacts which wield such hypnotic influence over our middle-class life. "Society," we say, whether it be in the form of the mob or the cultivated dinner-circle, is the deadly enemy of the literary artist. Literary promises can be seen visibly fading out in the warm beams of association with the refined and the important. And social glamor was never so dangerous as it is today when it is anxious to be enlightened and liberal. Timidity is still the reigning vice of the American intellect, and the terrorism of "good taste" is yet more deadly to the creation of literary art than is sheer barbarism. The literary artist needs protection from the liberal audience that will accept him though he shock them, but that subtly tame him even while they appreciate.

If this literary promise does not fulfill itself, it will be because our younger writers have pleased a public too easy to please. As we look around at those who have ideas, our proper mood is not pleasure that their work is so good, but discontent that it is not better. It will not be better unless certain values are felt more intensely. Those Americans who are fortunate enough to see Copeau's theatre seem to remark there a fusion of fervor and simplicity with finished workmanship, a sort of sensuous austerity of tone—an effort of creative novelty working with all that is vital in a tradition. Do we not want these values in our American effort? Should we not like to see from this younger generation a literary art which will combine a classical and puritan tradition with the most modern ideas? Do we not want minds with a touch of the apostolic about them and a certain edge—a little surly, but not embittered—with an intellectual as well as an artistic conscience, with a certain tentative superciliousness towards Demos and an appalling hatred for everything which savors of the bourgeois or the sentimental? Now while everything that is respectable in America seems to be putting its effort, with a sort of joyful perversity, into the technique of destruction, are there no desperate spiritual outlaws with a lust to create?

The History of a Literary Radical[1]

For a man of culture, my friend Miro began his literary career in a singularly unpromising way. Potential statesmen in log-cabins might miraculously come in touch with all the great books of the world, but the days of Miro's young school life were passed in innocence of Homer or Dante or Shakespeare, or any of the other traditional mind-formers of the race. What Miro had for his nourishment, outside the Bible, which was a magical book that you must not drop on the floor, or his school-readers, which were like lightning flashes of unintelligible scenes, was the literature that his playmates lent him —exploits of British soldiers in Spain and the Crimea, the death-defying adventures of young filibusters in Cuba and Nicaragua. Miro gave them a languid perusing, and did not criticise their literary style. Huckleberry Finn and Tom Sawyer somehow eluded him until he had finished college, and no fresher tale of adventure drifted into his complacent home until the era of "Richard Carvel" and "Janice Meredith" sharpened his wits and gave him a vague feeling that there was such a thing as literary art. The classics were stiffly enshrined behind glass doors that were very hard to open—at least Hawthorne and Irving and Thackeray were there, and Tennyson's and Scott's poems —but nobody ever discussed them or looked at them. Miro's busy elders were taken up with the weekly "Outlook" and "Independent" and "Christian Work," and felt they were doing much for Miro when

[1] *The Yale Review,* VIII (April 1919), 468–484.

they provided him and his sister with "St. Nicholas" and "The Youth's Companion." It was only that Miro saw the black books looking at him accusingly from the case, and a rudimentary conscience, slipping easily over from calvinism to culture, forced him solemnly to grapple with "The Scarlet Letter" or "Marmion." All he remembers is that the writers of these books he browsed among used a great many words and made a great fuss over shadowy offences and conflicts and passions that did not even stimulate his imagination with sufficient force to cause him to ask his elders what it was all about. Certainly the filibusters were easier.

At school Miro was early impressed with the vast dignity of the literary works and names he was compelled to learn. Shakespeare and Goethe and Dante lifted their plaster heads frowningly above the teacher's, as they perched on shelves about the room. Much was said of the greatness of literature. But the art of phonetics and the complications of grammar swamped Miro's early school years. It was not until he reached the High School that literature began really to assume that sacredness which he had heretofore felt only for Holy Scripture. His initiation into culture was made almost a religious mystery by the conscientious and harassed teacher. As the Deadwood Boys and Henty and David Harum slipped away from Miro's soul in the presence of Milton's "Comus" and Burke's "On Conciliation," a cultural devoutness was engendered in him that never really died. At first it did not take Miro beyond the stage where your conscience is strong enough to make you uncomfortable, but not strong enough to make you do anything about it. Miro did not actually become an omnivorous reader of great books. But he was filled with a rich grief that the millions pursued cheap and vulgar fiction instead of the best that has been thought and said in the world. Miro indiscriminately bought cheap editions of the English classics and read them with a certain patient uncomprehendingness.

As for the dead classics, they came to Miro from the hands of his teachers with a prestige even vaster than the books of his native tongue. No doubt ever entered his head that four years of Latin and three years of Greek, an hour a day, were the important preparation he needed for his future as an American citizen. No doubt ever hurt him that the world into which he would pass would be a world where, as his teacher said, Latin and Greek were a solace to the aged, a quickener of taste, a refreshment after manual labor, and a clue to the general knowledge of all human things. Miro would as soon have doubted the rising of the sun as have doubted the wisdom of these serious, puckered women who had the precious manipulation of his cultural upbringing in their charge. Miro was a bright, if a rather vague, little boy, and a fusion of brightness and docility gave him high marks in the school where we went together.

No one ever doubted that these marks expressed Miro's assimilation of the books we pored over. But he told me later that he had never really known what he was studying. Caesar, Virgil, Cicero, Xenophon, Homer, were veiled and misty experiences to him. His mind was a moving present, obliterating each day what it had read the day before, and piercing into a no more comprehended future. He could at no time have given any intelligible account of Aeneas's wanderings or what Cicero was really inveighing against. The Iliad was even more obscure. The only thing which impressed him deeply was an expurgated passage, which he looked up somewhere else and found to be about Mars and Venus caught in the golden bed. Caesar seemed to be at war, and Xenophon wandering somewhere in Asia Minor, with about the same lengthiness and hardship as Miro suffered in reading him. The trouble, Miro thought afterwards, was that these books were to his mind flickering lights in a vast jungle of ignorance. He does not remember marvelling at the excessive dulness of the stories themselves. He plodded his faithful way, using them as his conscientious teachers did, as exercises in language. He looked on Virgil and Cicero as essentially problems in disentangling words which had unaccountably gotten into a bizarre order, and in recognizing certain rather amusing and ingenious combinations, known as "constructions." Why these words took so irritating an order Miro never knew, but he always connected the problem with those algebraic puzzles he had elsewhere to unravel. Virgil's words were further complicated by being arranged in lines which one had to "scan." Miro was pleased with the rhythm, and there were stanzas that had a roll of their own. But the inexorable translating that had to go on tore all this fabric of poetry to pieces. His translations were impeccable, but, as he never wrote them down, he had never before his eyes the consecutive story.

Translations Miro never saw. He knew that they were implements of deadly sin that boys used to cheat with. His horror of them was such as a saint might feel towards a parody of the Bible. Just before Miro left school, his sister in a younger class began to read a prose translation of the Odyssey, and Miro remembers the scorn with which he looked down on so sneaking an entrance into the temple of light. He knew that not everyone could study Latin and Greek, and he learned to be proud of his knowledge. When at last he had passed his examinations for college—his Latin composition and grammar, his syntax and his sight-reading, and his Greek composition and grammar, his Greek syntax and sight-reading, and his translation of Gallic battles and Anabasian frosts, and Dido's farewell and Cicero's objurgations—his zealous rage did not abate. He even insisted on reading the Bucolics, while he was away on his vacation, and a book or two in the Odyssey. His family was a little chilled by his studiousness, but he knew well that he was laying up cultural treasures in heaven, where moth and rust do not corrupt, neither do thieves break through and steal.

Arrived at college, Miro expanded his cultural interests on the approved lines. He read Horace and Plato, Lysias and Terence, impartially, with faithful conscience. Horace was the most exciting because of the parodies that were beginning to appear in the cleverer newspapers. Miro scarcely knew whether to be amused or shocked at "Odi Persicos" or "Integer Vitae" done into current slang. The professors, mild-mannered men who knew their place and kept it, never mentioned these impudent adventures, but for Miro it was the first crack in his Ptolemaic system of reverences. There came a time when his mind began to feel replete, when this heavy pushing through the opaque medium of dead language began to fatigue him. He should have been able to read fluently, but there were always turning up new styles, new constructions, to plague him. Latin became to him like a constant diet of beefsteak, and Greek like a constant diet of fine wheaten bread. They lost their taste. These witty poets and ostentatious orators—what were they all about? What was their background? Where did they fit into Miro's life? The professors knew some history but what did that history mean? Miro found himself surfeited and dissatisfied. He began to look furtively at translations to get some better English than he was able to provide. The hair-splittings of Plato began to bore him when he saw them in crystal-clear English, and not muffled in the original Greek. His apostasy had begun.

It was not much better in his study of English literature. Miro was given a huge anthology, a sort of press-clipping bureau of *belles-lettres*, from Chaucer to Arthur Symons. Under the direction of a professor who was laying out a career for himself as poet—or "modern singer," as he expressed it—the class went briskly through the centuries sampling their genius and tasting the various literary flavors. The enterprise reminded Miro of those books of woolen samples which one looks through when one is to have a suit of clothes made. But in this case, the student did not even have the pleasure of seeing the suit of clothes. All that was expected of him, apparently, was that he become familiar, from these microscopic pieces, with the different textures and patterns. The great writers passed before his mind like figures in a crowded street. There was no time for preferences. Indeed the professor strove diligently to give each writer his just due. How was one to appreciate the great thoughts and the great styles if one began to choose violently between them, or attempted any discrimination on grounds of the peculiar congeniality for one's own soul? Criticism had to spurn such subjectivity, scholarship could not be wilful. The neatly arranged book of "readings," with its medicinal doses of inspiration, became the symbol of Miro's education.

These early years of college did not deprive Miro of his cultural loyalty, but they deadened his appetite. Although almost inconceivably docile, he found himself being bored. He had come from school a serious boy, with more than a touch of priggishness in him, and a vague aspiration to be a "man of letters." He found himself becoming a collector of literary odds-and-ends. If he did not formulate this feeling clearly, he at least knew. He found that the literary life was not as interesting as he had expected. He sought no adventures. When he wrote, it was graceful lyrics or polite criticisms of William Collins or Charles Lamb. These canonized saints of culture still held the field for Miro, however. There was nothing between them and that popular literature of the day that all good men bemoaned. Classic or popular, "highbrow" or "lowbrow," this was the choice, and Miro unquestioningly took the orthodox heaven. In 1912 the most popular of Miro's English professors had never heard of Galsworthy, and another was creating a flurry of scandal in the department by recommending Chesterton to his classes. It would scarcely have been in college that Miro would have learned of an escape from the closed dichotomy of culture. Bored with the "classic," and frozen with horror at the "popular," his career as a man of culture must have come to a dragging end if he had not been suddenly liberated by a chance lecture which he happened to hear while he was home for the holidays.

The literary radical who appeared before the Lyceum Club of Miro's village was none other than Professor William Lyon Phelps, and it is to that evening of cultural audacity Miro thinks he owes all his later emancipation. The lecturer grappled with the "modern novel," and tossed Hardy, Tolstoi, Turgenev, Meredith, even Trollope, into the minds of the charmed audience with such effect that the virgin shelves of the village library were ravished for days to come by the eager minds upon whom these great names dawned for the first time. "Jude the Obscure" and "Resurrection" were of course kept officially away from the vulgar, but Miro managed to find "Smoke" and "Virgin Soil" and "Anna Karenina" and "The Warden" and "A Pair of Blue Eyes" and "The Return of the Native." Later at college he explored the forbidden realms. It was as if some devout and restless saint had suddenly been introduced to the Apocrypha. A new world was opened to Miro that was neither "classic" nor "popular," and yet which came to one under the most unimpeachable auspices. There was, at first, it is true, an air of illicit adventure about the enterprise. The lecturer who made himself the missionary of such vigorous and piquant doctrine had the air of being a heretic, or at least a boy playing out of school. But Miro himself returned to college a cultural revolutionist. His orthodoxies crumbled. He did not try to reconcile the new with the old. He applied pick and dynamite to the whole structure of the canon. Irony, humor, tragedy, sensuality, suddenly appeared to him as literary qualities in forms that he could understand. They were like oxygen to his soul.

If these qualities were in the books he had been reading, he had never felt them. The expurgated sample-books he had studied had passed too swiftly over the Elizabethans to give him a sense of their lustiness. Miro immersed himself voluptuously in the pessimism of Hardy. He fed on the poignant torture of Tolstoi. While he was reading "Resurrection," his class in literature was making an "intensive" study of Tennyson. It was too much. Miro rose in revolt. He forswore literary courses forever, dead rituals in which anemic priests mumbled their trite critical commentary. Miro did not know that to naughtier critics even Mr. Phelps might eventually seem a pale and timid Gideon, himself stuck in moral sloughs. He was grateful enough for that blast of trumpets which made his own scholastic walls fall down.

The next stage in Miro's cultural life was one of frank revolt. He became as violent a heretic as he had been docile a believer. Modern novels merely started the rift that widened into modern ideas. The professors were of little use. Indeed, when Miro joined a group of radicals who had started a new college paper, a relentless vendetta began with the teachers. Miro and his friends threw over everything that was mere literature. Social purpose must shine from any writing that was to rouse their enthusiasm. Literary flavor was to be permissible only where it made vivid high and revolutionary thought. Tolstoi became their god, Wells their high priest. Chesterton infuriated them. They wrote violent assaults upon him which began in imitation of his cool paradoxicality and ended in incoherent ravings. There were so many enemies to their new fervor that they scarcely knew where to begin. There were not only the old tables of stone to destroy, but there were new and threatening prophets of the eternal verities who had to be exposed. The nineteenth century which they had studied must be weeded of its nauseous moralists. The instructors consulted together how they might put down the revolt, and bring these sinners back to the faith of cultural scripture.

It was of no avail. In a short time Miro had been converted from an aspiration for the career of a cultivated "man of letters" to a fiery zeal for artistic and literary propaganda in the service of radical ideas. One of the results of this conversion was the discovery that he really had no standards of critical taste. Miro had been reverential so long that he had felt no preferences. Everything that was classic had to be good to him. But now that he had thrown away the books that were stamped with the mark of the classic mint, and was dealing with the raw materials of letters, he had to become a critic and make selection. It was not enough that a book should be radical. Some of the books he read, though impeccably revolutionary as to ideas, were clearly poor as literature. His muffled taste began to assert itself. He found himself impressionable where before he had been only mildly acquisitive. The literature of revolt and free speculation fired him into a state of spiritual explosiveness. All that he read now stood out in brighter colors and in sharper outlines than before. As he reached a better balance, he began to feel the vigor of literary form, the value of sincerity and freshness of style. He began to look for them keenly in everything he read. It was long before Miro realized that enthusiasm not docility had made him critical. He became a little proud of his sensitive and discriminating reactions to the modern and the unsifted.

This pursuit had to take place without any help from the college. After Miro graduated, it is true that it became the fashion to study literature as the record of ideas and not merely as a canon of sacred books to be analyzed, commented upon, and absorbed. But no dent was made upon the system in Miro's time, and, the inventory of English criticism not going beyond Stevenson, no college course went beyond Stevenson. The Elizabethans had been exhumed and fumigated, but the most popular attention went to the gallery of Victorians, who combined moral soundness with literary beauty, and were therefore considered wholesome food for young men. The instructors all remained in the state of reverence which saw all things good that had been immemorially taught. Miro's own teacher was a fragile, earnest young man, whose robuster parents had evidently seized upon his nature as a fortunate pledge of what the family might produce in the way of an intellectual flower that should surpass in culture and gentility the ambitions of his parents. His studiousness, hopeless for his father's career as grocer, had therefore been capitalized into education.

The product now shone forth as one of the most successful and promising younger instructors in the department. He knew his subject. Card-indexes filled his room, covering in detail the works, life, and death of the illustrious persons whom he expounded, as well as everything that had been said about them in the way of appreciation or interpretation. An endless number of lectures and courses could be made from this bountiful store. He never tried to write himself, but he knew all about the different kinds of writing, and when he corrected the boys' themes he knew infallibly what to tell them to avoid. Miro's vagaries scandalized his teacher all the more because during his first year in college Miro had been generally noticed as one with the proper sobriety and scholarly patience to graduate into a similar priestly calling. Miro found scant sympathy in the young man. To the latter, literary studies were a science not an art, and they were to be treated with somewhat the same cold rigor of delimitation and analysis as any other science. Miro felt his teacher's recoil at the idea that literature was significant only as the expression of personality or as interpretation of some social movement. Miro saw how uneasy he became when he was confronted with current literature. It was clear that Miro's slowly growing critical sense had not a counterpart in the scholastic mind.

When Miro and his friends abandoned literary studies, they followed after the teachers of history and philosophy, intellectual arenas of which the literary professors seemed scandalously ignorant. At this ignorance Miro boiled with contempt. Here were the profitable clues that would give meaning to dusty literary scholarship, but the scholars had not the wits to seize them. They lived along, playing what seemed to Miro a rather dreary game, when they were not gaping reverently at ideas and forms which they scarcely had the genuine personality to appreciate. Miro felt once and for all free of these mysteries and reverences. He was to know the world as it has been and as it is. He was to put literature into its proper place, making all "culture" serve its apprenticeship for him as interpretation of things larger than itself, of the course of individual lives and the great tides of society.

Miro's later cultural life is not without interest. When he had finished college and his architectural course, and was making headway in his profession, his philosophy of the intellectual life began to straighten itself out. Rapid as his surrender of orthodoxy had been, it had taken him some time to live down that early education. He found now that he would have to live down his heresies also, and get some coherent system of tastes that was his own and not the fruit of either docility or propaganda zeal.

The old battles that were still going on helped Miro to realize his modern position. It was a queer, musty quarrel, but it was enlisting minds from all classes and of all intellectual fibres. The "classics" were dying hard, as Miro recognized whenever he read, in the magazines, attacks on the "new education." He found that professors were still taken seriously who declared in passion that without the universal study of the Latin language in American schools all conceptions of taste, standards, criticism, the historic sense itself, would vanish from the earth. He found that even as late as 1917 professional men were gathering together in solemn conclave and buttressing the "value of the classics" with testimonials from "successful men" in a variety of vocations. Miro was amused at the fact that the mighty studies once pressed upon him so uncritically should now require, like the patent medicines, testimonials as to their virtue. Bank presidents, lawyers, and editors had taken the Latin language regularly for years, and had found its effects painless and invigorating. He could not escape the unconscious satire that such plump and prosperous Americans expressed when they thought it admirable to save their cherished intellectual traditions in any such fashion.

Other conservatives Miro saw to be abandoning the line of opposition to science, only to fall back on the line of a defensive against "pseudo-science," as they seemed to call whatever intellectual interests had not yet become indubitably reputable. It was a line which would hold them rather strongly for a time, Miro thought, because so many of the cultural revolutionists agreed with them in hating some of these arrogant and mechanical psychologies and sociologies that reduced life to figures or organisms. But Miro felt also how obstructive was their fight. If the "classics" had done little for him except hold his mind in an uncomprehending prison, and fetter his spontaneous taste, they seemed to have done little more for even the thorough scholars. When professors had devoted scholarly lives to the "classics" only to exhibit in their own polemics none of the urbanity and intellectual command which were supposed by the believer somehow to rub off automatically on the faithful student, Miro had to conclude an absence of causal connection between the "classics" and the able modern mind. When, moreover, critical power or creative literary work became almost extinct among these defenders of the "old education," Miro felt sure that a revolution was needed in the materials and attitudes of "culture."

The case of the defenders was all the weaker because their enemies were not wanton infidels, ignorant of the holy places they profaned. They were rather cultural "Modernists," reforming the church from within. They had the classic background, these young vandals, but they had escaped from its flat and unoriented surface. Abreast of the newer objective, impersonal standards of thinking, they saw the weakness of these archaic minds which could only appeal to vested interests in culture and testimonials from successful men.

The older critics had long since disavowed the intention of discriminating among current writers. These men, who had to have an Academy to protect them, lumped the younger writers of verse and prose together as "anarchic" and "naturalistic," and had become, in these latter days, merely peevish and querulous, protesting in favor of standards that no longer represented our best values. Every one, in Miro's time, bemoaned the lack of critics, but the older critics seemed to have lost all sense of hospitality and to have become tired and a little spitefully disconsolate, while the newer ones were too intent on their crusades against puritanism and philistinism to have time for a constructive pointing of the way.

Miro had a very real sense of standing at the end of an era. He and his friends had lived down both their old orthodoxies of the classics and their new orthodoxies of propaganda. Gone were the priggishness and self-consciousness which had marked their teachers. The new culture would be more personal than the old, but it would not be held as a personal property. It would be democratic in the sense that it would represent each person's honest spontaneous taste. The old attitude was only speciously democratic. The assumption was that if you pressed your material long enough and winningly enough upon your culturable public, they would acquire it. But the material was something handed down, not grown in the garden of their own appreciations. Under these conditions the critic and appreciator became a mere impersonal register of orthodox opinion. The cultivated person, in conforming his judgments to what was authoritatively taught him, was really a member of the herd—a cultivated herd, it is true, but still a herd. It was the mass that spoke through the critic and not his own discrimination. These authoritative judgments might, of course, have come—probably had come—to the herd through discerning critics, but in Miro's time judgment in the schools had petrified. One believed not because one felt the original discernment, but because one was impressed by the weight and reputability of opinion. At least so it seemed to Miro.

Now just as the artists had become tired of conventions and were breaking through into new and personal forms, so Miro saw the younger critics breaking through these cultural conventions. To the elders the result would seem mere anarchy. But Miro's attitude did not want to destroy, it merely wanted to rearrange the materials. He wanted no more second-hand appreciations. No one's cultural store was to include anything that one could not be enthusiastic about. One's acquaintance with the best that had been said and thought should be encouraged—in Miro's ideal school—to follow the lines of one's temperament. Miro, having thrown out the old gods, found them slowly and properly coming back to him. Some would always repel him, others he hoped to understand eventually. But if it took wisdom to write the great books, did it not also take wisdom to understand them? Even the Latin writers he hoped to recover, with the aid of translations. But why bother with Greek when you could get Euripides in the marvellous verse of Gilbert Murray? Miro was willing to believe that no education was complete without at least an inoculation of the virus of the two orthodoxies that he was transcending.

As Miro looked around the American scene, he wondered where

the critics were to come from. He saw, on the one hand, Mr. Mencken and Mr. Dreiser and their friends, going heavily forth to battle with the Philistines, glorying in pachydermous vulgarisms that hurt the polite and cultivated young men of the old school. And he saw these violent critics, in their rage against puritanism, becoming themselves moralists, with the same bigotry and tastelessness as their enemies. No, these would never do. On the other hand, he saw Mr. Stuart P. Sherman, in his youthful if somewhat belated ardor, revolting so conscientiously against the "naturalism" and crude expressions of current efforts that, in his defense of *belles-lettres,* of the fine traditions of literary art, he himself became a moralist of the intensest brand, and as critic plumped for Arnold Bennett, because that clever man had a feeling for the proprieties of human conduct. No, Mr. Sherman would do even less adequately. His fine sympathies were as much out of the current as was the specious classicism of Professor Shorey.[2] He would have to look for the critic among the young men who had an abounding sense of life, as well as a feeling for literary form. They would be men who had not been content to live on their cultural inheritance, but had gone out into the modern world and amassed a fresh fortune of their own. They would be men who were not squeamish, who did not feel the delicate differences between "animal" and "human" conduct, who were enthusiastic about Mark Twain and Gorki as well as Romain Rolland, and at the same time were thrilled by Copeau's theatre.

Where was a better programme for culture, for any kind of literary art? Culture as a living effort, a driving attempt both at sincere expression and at the comprehension of sincere expression wherever it was found! Appreciation to be as far removed from the "I know what I like!" as from the textbook impeccability of taste! If each mind sought its own along these lines, would not many find themselves agreed? Miro insisted on liking Amy Lowell's attempt to outline the tendencies in American poetry in a form which made clear the struggles of contemporary men and women with the tradition and against "every affectation of the mind." He began to see in the new class-consciousness of poets the ending of that old division which "culture" made between the chosen people and the gentiles. We were now to

---

[2] Paul Shorey, professor of Greek at the University of Chicago, whose defense of classical education against modern tendencies Bourne had attacked earlier as an example of "a professor angrily defending his lifelong business." See "An American Humorist," *The Dial,* August 30, 1917.

form little pools of workers and appreciators of similar temperaments and tastes. The little magazines that were starting up became voices for these new communities of sentiment. Miro thought that perhaps at first it was right to adopt a tentative superciliousness towards the rest of the world, so that both Mr. Mencken with his shudders at the vulgar Demos and Mr. Sherman with his obsession with the sanely and wholesomely American might be shut out from influence. Instead of fighting the Philistine in the name of freedom, or fighting the vulgar iconoclast in the name of wholesome human notions, it might be better to write for one's own band of comprehenders, in order that one might have something genuine with which to appeal to both the mob of the "bourgeois" and the ferocious vandals who have been dividing the field among them. Far better a quarrel among these intensely self-conscious groups than the issues that have filled "The Atlantic" and "The Nation" with their dreary obsolescence. Far better for the mind that aspired towards "culture" to be told not to conform or worship, but to search out its group, its own temperamental community of sentiment, and there deepen appreciations through sympathetic contact.

It was no longer a question of being hospitable towards the work of other countries. Miro found the whole world open to him, in these days, through the enterprise of publishers. He and his friends felt more sympathetic with certain groups in France and Russia than they did with the variegated "prominent authors" of their own land. Winston Churchill as a novelist came to seem more of an alien than Artzybachev. The fact of culture being international had been followed by a sense of its being. The old cultural attitude had been hospitable enough, but it imported its alien culture in the form of "comparative literature." It was hospitable only in trying to mould its own taste to the orthodox canons abroad. The older American critic was mostly interested in getting the proper rank and reverence for what he borrowed. The new critic will take what suits his community of sentiment. He will want to link up not with the foreign canon, but with that group which is nearest in spirit with the effort he and his friends are making. The American has to work to interpret and portray the life he knows. He cannot be international in the sense that anything but the life in which he is soaked, with its questions and its colors, can be the material for his art. But he can be international—and must be —in the sense that he works with a certain hopeful vision of a "young world," and with certain ideal values upon which the younger men, stained and revolted by war, in all countries are agreeing.

Miro wonders sometimes whether the direction in which he is tending will not bring him around the circle again to a new classicism. The last stage in the history of the man of culture will be that "classic" which he did not understand and which his mind spent its youth in overthrowing. But it will be a classicism far different from that which was so unintelligently handed down to him in the American world. It will be something worked out and lived into. Looking into the future he will have to do what Van Wyck Brooks calls "invent a usable past." Finding little in the American tradition that is not tainted with sweetness and light and burdened with the terrible patronage of bourgeois society, the new classicist will yet rescue Thoreau and Whitman and Mark Twain and try to tap through them a certain eternal human tradition of abounding vitality and moral freedom and so build out the future. If the classic means power with restraint, vitality with harmony, a fusion of intellect and feeling, and a keen sense of the artistic conscience, then the revolutionary world is coming out into the classic. When Miro sees behind the minds of "The Masses" group a desire for form and for expressive beauty, and sees the radicals following Jacques Copeau[3] and reading Checkov, he smiles at the thought of the American critics, young and old, who do not know yet that they are dead.

[3] Copeau, a leading French theatrical producer, was then having a growing influence on American stage design.

Format by Lydia Link
Set in Intertype Baskerville
Composed by York Composition Company
Printed by Murray Printing Company

HARPER & ROW, PUBLISHERS, INCORPORATED

71 72 73   12 11 10 9 8

Revised January, 1970

harper torchbooks

† The New American Nation Series, edited by Henry Steele Commager and Richard B. Morris.
‡ American Perspectives series, edited by Bernard Wishy and William E. Leuchtenburg.
a History of Europe series, edited by J. H. Plumb.
§ The Library of Religion and Culture, edited by Benjamin Nelson.
‖ Researches in the Social, Cultural, and Behavioral Sciences, edited by Benjamin Nelson.
x Harper Modern Science Series, edited by James A. Newman.
° Not for sale in Canada.
+ Documentary History of the United States series, edited by Richard B. Morris.
# Documentary History of Western Civilization series, edited by Eugene C. Black and Leonard W. Levy.
Λ The Economic History of the United States series, edited by Henry David et al.
⁋ European Perspectives series, edited by Eugene C. Black.
** Contemporary Essays series, edited by Leonard W. Levy.
* The Stratum Series, edited by John Hale.

EDMUND S. MORGAN: The Puritan Family: *Religion and Domestic Relations in Seventeenth Century New England*   TB/1227
RICHARD B. MORRIS: Government and Labor in Early America   TB/1244
WALLACE NOTESTEIN: The English People on the Eve of Colonization: 1603-1630. † *Illus.*
                                                     TB/3006
FRANCIS PARKMAN: The Seven Years War: *A Narrative Taken from Montcalm and Wolfe, The Conspiracy of Pontiac, and A Half-Century of Conflict. Edited by John H. McCallum*   TB/3083
LOUIS B. WRIGHT: The Cultural Life of the American Colonies: 1607-1763. † *Illus.*
                                                     TB/3005
YVES F. ZOLTVANY, Ed.: The French Tradition in America +   HR/1425

American Studies: The Revolution to 1860

JOHN R. ALDEN: The American Revolution: 1775-1783. † *Illus.*   TB/3011
MAX BELOFF, Ed.: The Debate on the American Revolution, 1761-1783: *A Sourcebook*
                                                     TB/1225
RAY A. BILLINGTON: The Far Western Frontier: 1830-1860. † *Illus.*   TB/3012
STUART BRUCHEY: The Roots of American Economic Growth, 1607-1861: *An Essay in Social Causation. New Introduction by the Author.*
                                                     TB/1350
WHITNEY R. CROSS: The Burned-Over District: *The Social and Intellectual History of Enthusiastic Religion in Western New York, 1800-1850*   TB/1242
NOBLE E. CUNNINGHAM, JR., Ed.: The Early Republic, 1789-1828 +   HR/1394
GEORGE DANGERFIELD: The Awakening of American Nationalism, 1815-1828. † *Illus.* TB/3061
CLEMENT EATON: The Freedom-of-Thought Struggle in the Old South. *Revised and Enlarged. Illus.*   TB/1150
CLEMENT EATON: The Growth of Southern Civilization, 1790-1860. † *Illus.*   TB/3040
ROBERT H. FERRELL, Ed.: Foundations of American Diplomacy, 1775-1872   HR/1393
LOUIS FILLER: The Crusade against Slavery: 1830-1860. † *Illus.*   TB/3029
DAVID H. FISCHER: The Revolution of American Conservatism: *The Federalist Party in the Era of Jeffersonian Democracy*   TB/1449
WILLIAM W. FREEHLING, Ed.: The Nullification Era: *A Documentary Record* ‡   TB/3079
WILLIM W. FREEHLING: Prelude to Civil War: *The Nullification Controversy in South Carolina, 1816-1836*   TB/1359
PAUL W. GATES: The Farmer's Age: *Agriculture, 1815-1860* Δ   TB/1398
FELIX GILBERT: The Beginnings of American Foreign Policy: *To the Farewell Address*
                                                     TB/1200
ALEXANDER HAMILTON: The Reports of Alexander Hamilton. ‡ *Edited by Jacob E. Cooke*
                                                     TB/3060
THOMAS JEFFERSON: Notes on the State of Virginia. ‡ *Edited by Thomas P. Abernethy*
                                                     TB/3052
FORREST MCDONALD, Ed.: Confederation and Constitution, 1781-1789 +   HR/1396
BERNARD MAYO: Myths and Men: *Patrick Henry, George Washington, Thomas Jefferson*
                                                     TB/1108
JOHN C. MILLER: Alexander Hamilton and the Growth of the New Nation   TB/3057
JOHN C. MILLER: The Federalist Era: 1789-1801. † *Illus.*   TB/3027

RICHARD B. MORRIS, Ed.: Alexander Hamilton and the Founding of the Nation. *New Introduction by the Editor*   TB/1448
RICHARD B. MORRIS: The American Revolution Reconsidered   TB/1363
CURTIS P. NETTELS: The Emergence of a National Economy, 1775-1815 Δ   TB/1438
DOUGLASS C. NORTH & ROBERT PAUL THOMAS, Eds.: *The Growth of the American Economy to 1860* +   HR/1352
R. B. NYE: The Cultural Life of the New Nation: 1776-1830. † *Illus.*   TB/3026
GILBERT OSOFSKY, Ed.: Puttin' On Ole Massa: *The Slave Narratives of Henry Bibb, William Wells Brown, and Solomon Northup* ‡
                                                     TB/1432
JAMES PARTON: The Presidency of Andrew Jackson. *From Volume III of the* Life *of Andrew Jackson. Ed. with Intro. by Robert V. Remini*   TB/3080
FRANCIS S. PHILBRICK: The Rise of the West, 1754-1830. † *Illus.*   TB/3067
MARSHALL SMELSER: The Democratic Republic, 1801-1815 †   TB/1406
TIMOTHY L. SMITH: Revivalism and Social Reform: *American Protestantism on the Eve of the Civil War*   TB/1229
JACK M. SOSIN, Ed.: The Opening of the West +   HR/1424
GEORGE ROGERS TAYLOR: The Transportation Revolution, 1815-1860 Δ   TB/1347
A. F. TYLER: Freedom's Ferment: *Phases of American Social History from the Revolution to the Outbreak of the Civil War. Illus.*
                                                     TB/1074
GLYNDON G. VAN DEUSEN: The Jacksonian Era: 1828-1848. † *Illus.*   TB/3028
LOUIS B. WRIGHT: Culture on the Moving Frontier   TB/1053

American Studies: The Civil War to 1900

W. R. BROCK: An American Crisis: *Congress and Reconstruction, 1865-67* °   TB/1283
T. C. COCHRAN & WILLIAM MILLER: The Age of Enterprise: *A Social History of Industrial America*   TB/1054
W. A. DUNNING: Reconstruction, Political and Economic: 1865-1877   TB/1073
HAROLD U. FAULKNER: Politics, Reform and Expansion: 1890-1900. † *Illus.*   TB/3020
GEORGE M. FREDRICKSON: The Inner Civil War: *Northern Intellectuals and the Crisis of the Union*   TB/1358
JOHN A. GARRATY: The New Commonwealth, 1877-1890 †   TB/1410
JOHN A. GARRATY, Ed.: The Transformation of American Society, 1870-1890 +   HR/1395
HELEN HUNT JACKSON: A Century of Dishonor: *The Early Crusade for Indian Reform.* ‡ *Edited by Andrew F. Rolle*   TB/3063
ALBERT D. KIRWAN: Revolt of the Rednecks: *Mississippi Politics, 1876-1925*   TB/1199
ARTHUR MANN: Yankee Reforms in the Urban Age: *Social Reform in Boston, 1800-1900*
                                                     TB/1247
ARNOLD M. PAUL: Conservative Crisis and the Rule of Law: *Attitudes of Bar and Bench, 1887-1895. New Introduction by Author*
                                                     TB/1415
JAMES S. PIKE: The Prostrate State: *South Carolina under Negro Government.* ‡ *Intro. by Robert F. Durden*   TB/3085
WHITELAW REID: After the War: *A Tour of the Southern States, 1865-1866.* ‡ *Edited by C. Vann Woodward*   TB/3066
FRED A. SHANNON: The Farmer's Last Frontier: *Agriculture, 1860-1897*   TB/1348

VERNON LANE WHARTON: The Negro in Mississippi, 1865-1890   TB/1178

American Studies: The Twentieth Century

RICHARD M. ABRAMS, Ed.: The Issues of the Populist and Progressive Eras, 1892-1912 +   HR/1428
RAY STANNARD BAKER: Following the Color Line: American Negro Citizenship in Progressive Era. ‡ Edited by Dewey W. Grantham, Jr. Illus.   TB/3053
RANDOLPH S. BOURNE: War and the Intellectuals: Collected Essays, 1915-1919. ‡ Edited by Carl Resek   TB/3043
A. RUSSELL BUCHANAN: The United States and World War II. † Illus.
        Vol. I TB/3044; Vol. II TB/3045
THOMAS C. COCHRAN: The American Business System: A Historical Perspective, 1900-1955   TB/1080
FOSTER RHEA DULLES: America's Rise to World Power: 1898-1954. † Illus.   TB/3021
JEAN-BAPTISTE DUROSELLE: From Wilson to Roosevelt: Foreign Policy of the United States, 1913-1945. Trans. by Nancy Lyman Roelker   TB/1370
HAROLD U. FAULKNER: The Decline of Laissez Faire, 1897-1917   TB/1397
JOHN D. HICKS: Republican Ascendancy: 1921-1933. † Illus.   TB/3041
ROBERT HUNTER: Poverty: Social Conscience in the Progressive Era. ‡ Edited by Peter d'A. Jones   TB/3065
WILLIAM E. LEUCHTENBURG: Franklin D. Roosevelt and the New Deal: 1932-1940. † Illus.   TB/3025
WILLIAM E. LEUCHTENBURG, Ed.: The New Deal: A Documentary History +   HR/1354
ARTHUR S. LINK: Woodrow Wilson and the Progressive Era: 1910-1917. † Illus.   TB/3023
BROADUS MITCHELL: Depression Decade: From New Era through New Deal, 1929-1941 ∆   TB/1439
GEORGE E. MOWRY: The Era of Theodore Roosevelt and the Birth of Modern America: 1900-1912. † Illus.   TB/3022
WILLIAM PRESTON, JR.: Aliens and Dissenters: Federal Suppression of Radicals, 1903-1933   TB/1287
WALTER RAUSCHENBUSCH: Christianity and the Social Crisis. ‡ Edited by Robert D. Cross   TB/3059
GEORGE SOULE: Prosperity Decade: From War to Depression, 1917-1929 ∆   TB/1349
GEORGE B. TINDALL, Ed.: A Populist Reader: Selections from the Works of American Populist Leaders   TB/3069
TWELVE SOUTHERNERS: I'll Take My Stand: The South and the Agrarian Tradition. Intro. by Louis D. Rubin, Jr.; Biographical Essays by Virginia Rock   TB/1072

Art, Art History, Aesthetics

CREIGHTON GILBERT, Ed.: Renaissance Art ** Illus.   TB/1465
EMILE MALE: The Gothic Image: Religious Art in France of the Thirteenth Century. § 190 illus.   TB/344
MILLARD MEISS: Painting in Florence and Siena After the Black Death: The Arts, Religion and Society in the Mid-Fourteenth Century. 169 illus.   TB/1148
ERWIN PANOFSKY: Renaissance and Renascences in Western Art. Illus.   TB/1447
ERWIN PANOFSKY: Studies in Iconology: Humanistic Themes in the Art of the Renaissance. 180 illus.   TB/1077

JEAN SEZNEC: The Survival of the Pagan Gods: The Mythological Tradition and Its Place in Renaissance Humanism and Art. 108 illus.   TB/2004
OTTO VON SIMSON: The Gothic Cathedral: Origins of Gothic Architecture and the Medieval Concept of Order. 58 illus.   TB/2018
HEINRICH ZIMMER: Myths and Symbols in Indian Art and Civilization. 70 illus.   TB/2005

Asian Studies

WOLFGANG FRANKE: China and the West: The Cultural Encounter, 13th to 20th Centuries. Trans. by R. A. Wilson   TB/1326
L. CARRINGTON GOODRICH: A Short History of the Chinese People. Illus.   TB/3015
DAN N. JACOBS, Ed.: The New Communist Manifesto and Related Documents. 3rd revised edn.   TB/1078
DAN N. JACOBS & HANS H. BAERWALD, Eds.: Chinese Communism: Selected Documents   TB/3031
BENJAMIN I. SCHWARTZ: Chinese Communism and the Rise of Mao   TB/1308
BENJAMIN I. SCHWARTZ: In Search of Wealth and Power: Yen Fu and the West   TB/1422

Economics & Economic History

C. E. BLACK: The Dynamics of Modernization: A Study in Comparative History   TB/1321
STUART BRUCHEY: The Roots of American Economic Growth, 1607-1861: An Essay in Social Causation. New Introduction by the Author.   TB/1350
GILBERT BURCK & EDITORS OF Fortune: The Computer Age: And its Potential for Management   TB/1179
JOHN ELLIOTT CAIRNES: The Slave Power. ‡ Edited with Introduction by Harold D. Woodman   TB/1433
SHEPARD B. CLOUGH, THOMAS MOODIE & CAROL MOODIE, Eds.: Economic History of Europe: Twentieth Century #   HR/1388
THOMAS C. COCHRAN: The American Business System: A Historical Perspective, 1900-1955   TB/1180
ROBERT A. DAHL & CHARLES E. LINDBLOM: Politics, Economics, and Welfare: Planning and Politico-Economic Systems Resolved into Basic Social Processes   TB/3037
PETER F. DRUCKER: The New Society: The Anatomy of Industrial Order   TB/1082
HAROLD U. FAULKNER: The Decline of Laissez Faire, 1897-1917 ∆   TB/1397
PAUL W. GATES: The Farmer's Age: Agriculture, 1815-1860 ∆   TB/1398
WILLIAM GREENLEAF, Ed.: American Economic Development Since 1860 +   HR/1353
J. L. & BARBARA HAMMOND: The Rise of Modern Industry. || Introduction by R. M. Hartwell   TB/1417
ROBERT L. HEILBRONER: The Future as History: The Historic Currents of Our Time and the Direction in Which They Are Taking America   TB/1386
ROBERT L. HEILBRONER: The Great Ascent: The Struggle for Economic Development in Our Time   TB/3030
FRANK H. KNIGHT: The Economic Organization   TB/1214
DAVID S. LANDES: Bankers and Pashas: International Finance and Economic Imperialism in Egypt. New Preface by the Author   TB/1412
ROBERT LATOUCHE: The Birth of Western Economy: Economic Aspects of the Dark Ages   TB/1290

4

6

ERNST CASSIRER: Rousseau, Kant and Goethe. *Intro. by Peter Gay* TB/1092
FREDERICK COPLESTON, S. J.: Medieval Philosophy TB/376
F. M. CORNFORD: From Religion to Philosophy: *A Study in the Origins of Western Speculation §* TB/20
WILFRID DESAN: The Tragic Finale: *An Essay on the Philosophy of Jean-Paul Sartre* TB/1030
MARVIN FARBER: The Aims of Phenomenology: *The Motives, Methods, and Impact of Husserl's Thought* TB/1291
MARVIN FARBER: Basic Issues of Philosophy: *Experience, Reality, and Human Values* TB/1344
MARVIN FARBERS: Phenomenology and Existence: *Towards a Philosophy within Nature* TB/1295
PAUL FRIEDLANDER: 'Plato: *An Introduction* TB/2017
MICHAEL GELVEN: A Commentary on Heidegger's "Being and Time" TB/1464
J. GLENN GRAY: Hegel and Greek Thought TB/1409
W. K. C. GUTHRIE: The Greek Philosophers: *From Thales to Aristotle* ° TB/1008
G. W. F. HEGEL: On Art, Religion Philosophy: *Introductory Lectures to the Realm of Absolute Spirit. || Edited with an Introduction by J. Glenn Gray* TB/1463
G. W. F. HEGEL: Phenomenology of Mind. ° || *Introduction by George Lichtheim* TB/1303
MARTIN HEIDEGGER: Discourse on Thinking. *Translated with a Preface by John M. Anderson and E. Hans Freund. Introduction by John M. Anderson* TB/1459
F. H. HEINEMANN: Existentialism and the Modern Predicament TB/28
WERER HEISENBERG: Physics and Philosophy: *The Revolution in Modern Science. Intro. by F. S. C. Northrop* TB/549
EDMUND HUSSERL: Phenomenology and the Crisis of Philosophy. *§ Translated with an Introduction by Quentin Lauer* TB/1170
IMMANUEL KANT: Groundwork of the Metaphysic of Morals. *Translated and Analyzed by H. J. Paton* TB/1159
IMMANUEL KANT: Lectures on Ethics. *§ Introduction by Lewis White Beck* TB/105
WALTER KAUFMANN, Ed.: Religion From Tolstoy to Camus: *Basic Writings on Religious Truth and Morals* TB/123
QUENTIN LAUER: Phenomenology: *Its Genesis and Prospect. Preface by Aron Gurwitsch* TB/1169
MAURICE MANDELBAUM: The Problem of Historical Knowledge: *An Answer to Relativism* TB/1198
H. J. PATON: The Categorical Imperative: *A Study in Kant's Moral Philosophy* TB/1325
MICHAEL POLANYI: Personal Knowledge: *Towards a Post-Critical Philosophy* TB/1158
KARL R. POPPER: Conjectures and Refutations: *The Growth of Scientific Knowledge* TB/1376
WILLARD VAN ORMAN QUINE: Elementary Logic *Revised Edition* TB/577
WILLARD VAN ORMAN QUINE: From a Logical Point of View: *Logico-Philosophical Essays* TB/566
JOHN E. SMITH: Themes in American Philosophy: *Purpose, Experience and Community* TB/1466
MORTON WHITE: Foundations of Historical Knowledge TB/1440
WILHELM WINDELBAND: A History of Philosophy *Vol. I: Greek, Roman, Medieval* TB/38
Vol. II: Renaissance, Enlightenment, Modern TB/39

LUDWIG WITTGENSTEIN: The Blue and Brown Books ° TB/1211
LUDWIG WITTGENSTEIN: Notebooks, 1914-1916 TB/1441

Political Science & Government

C. E. BLACK: The Dynamics of Modernization: *A Study in Comparative History* TB/1321
DENIS W. BROGAN: Politics in America. *New Introduction by the Author* TB/1469
CRANE BRINTON: English Political Thought in the Nineteenth Century TB/1071
ROBERT CONQUEST: Power and Policy in the USSR: *The Study of Soviet Dynastics* ° TB/1307
ROBERT A. DAHL & CHARLES E. LINDBLOM: Politics, Economics, and Welfare: *Planning and Politico-Economic Systems Resolved into Basic Social Processes* TB/1277
HANS KOHN: Political Ideologies of the 20th Century TB/1277
ROY C. MACRIDIS, Ed.: Political Parties: *Contemporary Trends and Ideas* ** TB/1322
ROBERT GREEN MC CLOSKEY: American Conservatism in the Age of Enterprise, 1865-1910 TB/1137
MARSILIUS OF PADUA: The Defender of Peace. *The Defensor Pacis. Translated with an Introduction by Alan Gewirth* TB/1310
KINGSLEY MARTIN: French Liberal Thought in the Eighteenth Century: *A Study of Political Ideas from Bayle to Condorcet* TB/1114
BARRINGTON MOORE, JR.: Political Power and Social Theory: *Seven Studies* || TB/1221
BARRINGTON MOORE, JR.: Soviet Politics—The Dilemma of Power: *The Role of Ideas in Social Change* || TB/1222
BARRINGTON MOORE, JR.: Terror and Progress—USSR: *Some Sources of Change and Stability* TB/1266
JOHN B. MORRALL: Political Thought in Medieval Times TB/1076
KARL R. POPPER: The Open Society and Its Enemies *Vol. I: The Spell of Plato* TB/1101
Vol. II: The High Tide of Prophecy: Hegel, Marx, and the Aftermath TB/1102
CONYERS READ, Ed.: The Constitution Reconsidered. *Revised Edition, Preface by Richard B. Morris* TB/1384
JOHN P. ROCHE, Ed.: Origins of American Political Thought: *Selected Readings* TB/1301
JOHN P. ROCHE, Ed.: American Political Thought: *From Jefferson to Progressivism* TB/1332
HENRI DE SAINT-SIMON: Social Organization, The Science of Man, and Other Writings. || *Edited and Translated with an Introduction by Felix Markham* TB/1152
CHARLES SCHOTTLAND, Ed.: The Welfare State ** TB/1323
JOSEPH A. SCHUMPETER: Capitalism, Socialism and Democracy TB/3008

Psychology

ALFRED ADLER: The Individual Psychology of Alfred Adler: *A Systematic Presentation in Selections from His Writings. Edited by Heinz L. & Rowena R. Ansbacher* TB/1154
LUDWIG BINSWANGER: Being-in-the-World: *Selected Papers. || Trans. with Intro. by Jacob Needleman* TB/1365
HADLEY CANTRIL: The Invasion from Mars: *A Study in the Psychology of Panic* || TB/1282
MIRCEA ELIADE: Cosmos and History: *The Myth of the Eternal Return §* TB/2050
MIRCEA ELIADE: Myth and Reality TB/1369

MIRCEA ELIADE: Myths, Dreams and Mysteries: *The Encounter Between Contemporary Faiths and Archaic Realities* § TB/1320
MIRCEA ELIADE: Rites and Symbols of Initiation: *The Mysteries of Birth and Rebirth* § TB/1236
HERBERT FINGARETTE: The Self in Transformation: *Psychoanalysis, Philosophy and the Life of the Spirit* || TB/1177
SIGMUND FREUD: On Creativity and the Unconscious: *Papers on the Psychology of Art, Literature, Love, Religion.* § Intro. by Benjamin Nelson TB/45
J. GLENN GRAY: The Warriors: *Reflections on Men in Battle. Introduction by Hannah Arendt* TB/1294
WILLIAM JAMES: Psychology: *The Briefer Course. Edited with an Intro. by Gordon Allport* TB/1034
C. G. JUNG: Psychological Reflections. *Ed. by J. Jacobi* TB/2001
KARL MENNINGER, M.D.: Theory of Psychoanalytic Technique TB/1144
JOHN H. SCHAAR: Escape from Authority: *The Perspectives of Erich Fromm* TB/1155
MUZAFER SHERIF: The Psychology of Social Norms. *Introduction by Gardner Murphy* TB/3072
HELLMUT WILHELM: Change: *Eight Lectures on the I Ching* TB/2019

Religion: Ancient and Classical, Biblical and Judaic Traditions

W. F. ALBRIGHT: The Biblical Period from Abraham to Ezra TB/102
SALO W. BARON: Modern Nationalism and Religion TB/818
C. K. BARRETT, Ed.: The New Testament Background: *Selected Documents* TB/86
MARTIN BUBER: Eclipse of God: *Studies in the Relation Between Religion and Philosophy* TB/12
MARTIN BUBER: Hasidism and Modern Man. *Edited and Translated by Maurice Friedman* TB/839
MARTIN BUBER: The Knowledge of Man. *Edited with an Introduction by Maurice Friedman. Translated by Maurice Friedman and Ronald Gregor Smith* TB/135
MARTIN BUBER: Moses. *The Revelation and the Covenant* TB/837
MARTIN BUBER: The Origin and Meaning of Hasidism. *Edited and Translated by Maurice Friedman* TB/835
MARTIN BUBER: The Prophetic Faith TB/73
MARTIN BUBER: Two Types of Faith: *Interpenetration of Judaism and Christianity* ° TB/75
MALCOLM L. DIAMOND: Martin Buber: *Jewish Existentialist* TB/840
M. S. ENSLIN: Christian Beginnings TB/5
M. S. ENSLIN: The Literature of the Christian Movement TB/6
ERNST LUDWIG EHRLICH: A Concise History of Israel: *From the Earliest Times to the Destruction of the Temple in A.D. 70* ° TB/128
HENRI FRANKFORT: Ancient Egyptian Religion: *An Interpretation* TB/77
ABRAHAM HESCHEL: The Earth Is the Lord's & The Sabbath. *Two Essays* TB/828
ABRAHAM HESCHEL: God in Search of Man: *A Philosophy of Judaism* TB/807
ABRAHAM HESCHEL: Man Is not Alone: *A Philosophy of Religion* TB/838
ABRAHAM HESCHEL: The Prophets: *An Introduction* TB/1421

T. J. MEEK: Hebrew Origins TB/69
JAMES MUILENBURG: The Way of Israel: *Biblical Faith and Ethics* TB/133
H. J. ROSE: Religion in Greece and Rome TB/55
H. H. ROWLEY: The Growth of the Old Testament TB/107
D. WINTON THOMAS, Ed.: Documents from Old Testament Times TB/85

Religion: General Christianity

ROLAND H. BAINTON: Christendom: *A Short History of Christianity and Its Impact on Western Civilization. Illus.*
Vol. I TB/131; Vol. II TB/132
JOHN T. MCNEILL: Modern Christian Movements. *Revised Edition* TB/1402
ERNST TROELTSCH: The Social Teaching of the Christian Churches. *Intro. by H. Richard Niebuhr* Vol. I TB/71; Vol. II TB/72

Religion: Early Christianity Through Reformation

ANSELM OF CANTERBURY: Truth, Freedom, and Evil: *Three Philosophical Dialogues. Edited and Translated by Jasper Hopkins and Herbert Richardson* TB/317
MARSHALL W. BALDWIN, Ed.: Christianity through the 13th Century # HR/1468
W. D. DAVIES: Paul and Rabbinic Judaism: *Some Rabbinic Elements in Pauline Theology. Revised Edition* ° TB/146
ADOLF DEISSMANN: Paul: *A Study in Social and Religious History* TB/15
JOHANNES ECKHART: Meister Eckhart: *A Modern Translation by R. Blakney* TB/8
EDGAR J. GOODSPEED: A Life of Jesus TB/1
ROBERT M. GRANT: Gnosticism and Early Christianity TB/136
WILLIAM HALLER: The Rise of Puritanism TB/22
GERHART B. LADNER: The Idea of Reform: *Its Impact on the Christian Thought and Action in the Age of the Fathers* TB/149
ARTHUR DARBY NOCK: Early Gentile Christianity and Its Hellenistic Background TB/111
ARTHUR DARBY NOCK: St. Paul ° TB/104
GORDON RUPP: Luther's Progress to the Diet of Worms ° TB/120

Religion: The Protestant Tradition

KARL BARTH: Church Dogmatics: *A Selection. Intro. by H. Gollwitzer. Ed. by G. W. Bromiley* TB/95
KARL BARTH: Dogmatics in Outline TB/56
KARL BARTH: The Word of God and the Word of Man TB/13
HERBERT BRAUN, et al.: God and Christ: *Existence and Province. Volume 5 of Journal for Theology and the Church, edited by Robert W. Funk and Gerhard Ebeling* TB/255
WHITNEY R. CROSS: The Burned-Over District: *The Social and Intellectual History of Enthusiastic Religion in Western New York, 1800-1850* TB/1242
NELS F. S. FERRE: Swedish Contributions to Modern Theology. *New Chapter by William A. Johnson* TB/147
WILLIAM R. HUTCHISON, Ed.: American Protestant Thought: *The Liberal Era* ‡ TB/1385
ERNST KASEMANN, et al.: Distinctive Protestant and Catholic Themes Reconsidered. *Volume 3 of Journal for Theology and the Church,*

8

edited by Robert W. Funk and Gerhard Ebeling TB/253

SOREN KIERKEGAARD: On Authority and Revelation: *The Book on Adler, or a Cycle of Ethico-Religious Essays. Introduction by F. Sontag* TB/139

SOREN KIERKEGAARD: Crisis in the Life of an Actress, *and Other Essays on Drama. Translated with an Introduction by Stephen Crites* TB/145

SOREN KIERKEGAARD: Edifying Discourses. *Edited with an Intro. by Paul Holmer* TB/32

SOREN KIERKEGAARD: The Journals of Kierkegaard. ° *Edited with an Intro. by Alexander Dru* TB/52

SOREN KIERKEGAARD: The Point of View for My Work as an Author: *A Report to History.* § *Preface by Benjamin Nelson* TB/88

SOREN KIERKEGAARD: The Present Age. § *Translated and edited by Alexander Dru. Introduction by Walter Kaufmann* TB/94

SOREN KIERKEGAARD: Purity of Heart. *Trans. by Douglas Steere* TB/4

SOREN KIERKEGAARD: Repetition: *An Essay in Experimental Psychology* § TB/117

SOREN KIERKEGAARD: Works of Love: *Some Christian Reflections in the Form of Discourses* TB/122

WILLIAM G. MCLOUGHLIN, Ed.: The American Evangelicals: 1800-1900: *An Anthology* TB/1382

WOLFHART PANNENBERG, et al.: History and Hermeneutic. *Volume 4 of Journal for Theology and the Church, edited by Robert W. Funk and Gerhard Ebeling* TB/254

JAMES M. ROBINSON, et al.: The Bultmann School of Biblical Interpretation: New Directions? *Volume 1 of Journal for Theology and the Church, edited by Robert W. Funk and Gerhard Ebeling* TB/251

F. SCHLEIERMACHER: The Christian Faith. *Introduction by Richard R. Niebuhr.*
Vol. I TB/108; Vol. II TB/109

F. SCHLEIERMACHER: On Religion: *Speeches to Its Cultured Despisers. Intro. by Rudolf Otto* TB/36

TIMOTHY L. SMITH: Revivalism and Social Reform: *American Protestantism on the Eve of the Civil War* TB/1229

PAUL TILLICH: Dynamics of Faith TB/42

PAUL TILLICH: Morality and Beyond TB/142

EVELYN UNDERHILL: Worship TB/10

Religion: The Roman & Eastern Christian Traditions

A. ROBERT CAPONIGRI, Ed.: Modern Catholic Thinkers II: *The Church and the Political Order* TB/307

G. P. FEDOTOV: The Russian Religious Mind: *Kievan Christianity, the tenth to the thirteenth Centuries* TB/370

GABRIEL MARCEL: Being and Having: *An Existential Diary. Introduction by James Collins* TB/310

GABRIEL MARCEL: Homo Viator: *Introduction to a Metaphysic of Hope* TB/397

Religion: Oriental Religions

TOR ANDRAE: Mohammed: *The Man and His Faith* § TB/62

EDWARD CONZE: Buddhism: *Its Essence and Development.* ° *Foreword by Arthur Waley* TB/58

EDWARD CONZE: Buddhist Meditation TB/1442

EDWARD CONZE et al, Editors: Buddhist Texts through the Ages TB/113

ANANDA COOMARASWAMY: Buddha and the Gospel of Buddhism TB/119

H. G. CREEL: Confucius and the Chinese Way TB/63

FRANKLIN EDGERTON, Trans. & Ed.: The Bhagavad Gita TB/115

SWAMI NIKHILANANDA, Trans. & Ed.: The Upanishads TB/114

D. T. SUZUKI: On Indian Mahayana Buddhism. ° *Ed. with Intro. by Edward Conze.* TB/1403

Religion: Philosophy, Culture, and Society

NICOLAS BERDYAEV: The Destiny of Man TB/61

RUDOLF BULTMANN: History and Eschatology: *The Presence of Eternity* ° TB/91

RUDOLF BULTMANN AND FIVE CRITICS: Kerygma and Myth: *A Theological Debate* TB/80

RUDOLF BULTMANN and KARL KUNDSIN: Form Criticism: *Two Essays on New Testament Research. Trans. by F. C. Grant* TB/96

WILLIAM A. CLEBSCH & CHARLES R. JAEKLE: Pastoral Care in Historical Perspective: *An Essay with Exhibits* TB/148

FREDERICK FERRE: Language, Logic and God. *New Preface by the Author* TB/1407

LUDWIG FEUERBACH: The Essence of Christianity. § *Introduction by Karl Barth. Foreword by H. Richard Niebuhr* TB/11

ADOLF HARNACK: What Is Christianity? § *Introduction by Rudolf Bultmann* TB/17

KYLE HASELDEN: The Racial Problem in Christian Perspective TB/116

MARTIN HEIDEGGER: Discourse on Thinking. *Translated with a Preface by John M. Anderson and E. Hans Freund. Introduction by John M. Anderson* TB/1459

IMMANUEL KANT: Religion Within the Limits of Reason Alone. § *Introduction by Theodore M. Greene and John Silber* TB/FG

WALTER KAUFMANN, Ed.: Religion from Tolstoy to Camus: *Basic Writings on Religious Truth and Morals. Enlarged Edition* TB/123

H. RICHARD NIERUHR: Christ and Culture TB/3

H. RICHARD NIEBUHR: The Kingdom of God in America TB/49

ANDERS NYGREN: Agape and Eros. *Translated by Philip S. Watson* ° TB/1430

JOHN H. RANDALL, JR.: The Meaning of Religion for Man. *Revised with New Intro. by the Author* TB/1379

WALTER RAUSCHENBUSCHS Christianity and the Social Crisis. ‡ *Edited by Robert D. Cross* TB/3059

Science and Mathematics

JOHN TYLER BONNER: The Ideas of Biology. Σ *Illus.* TB/570

W. E. LE GROS CLARK: The Antecedents of Man: *An Introduction to the Evolution of the Primates.* ° *Illus.* TB/559

ROBERT E. COKER: Streams, Lakes, Ponds. *Illus.* TB/586

ROBERT E. COKER: This Great and Wide Sea: *An Introduction to Oceanography and Marine Biology. Illus.* TB/551

W. H. DOWDESWELL: Animal Ecology. *61 illus.* TB/543